The
Un-Canadians

The
Un-Canadians

True Stories
of the Blacklist Era

Len Scher

LESTER PUBLISHING LIMITED

Canadian Cataloguing in Publication Data
Scher, Len, 1948-
The un-Canadians
ISBN 1-8955555-18-3

1. Canada – Politics and government – 1948-1957.*
2. Anti-communist movements – Canada – History –
20th century.   3. Internal security – Canada –
History – 20th century.   4. Blacklisting of
entertainers – Canada.   5. Blacklisting, Labor –
Canada.   I. Title.

FC610.S34 1992   971.063'3   C92-093039 -5
F1034.2.S34 1992

"Old Man Atom," written by Vern Partlow, copyright © 1950 by Polygram International Publishing, Inc. Copyright renewed. Used by permission of Polygram/Island Music Publishing Group.

Lester Publishing Limited
56 The Esplanade
Toronto, Ontario
M5E 1A7

Printed and bound in Canada.

92 93 94 95 5 4 3 2 1

This book is to dedicated to the memory of my father Morris (Moisze) Leib Scher—one of the blacklisted.

CONTENTS

ACKNOWLEDGEMENTS

My sincerest thanks go to the sixty-nine participants in *The Un-Canadians* who allowed me to tell their stories, even if it meant digging deep into memories which were sometimes painful. They welcomed me graciously into their homes, spoke with me for lengthy periods by phone, and allowed me to ask as many questions as necessary to record their accounts properly. In many cases, I selfishly went back to them with transcripts, which meant yet a few more hours of their time devoted to my project.

I am grateful to former CBC Radio colleagues such as producer Doug McDonald, who introduced me to Oscar Brand, and Harry Boyle. Gethin James, a true independent, was a fine scout and recommended some of the interviewees. Jim Littleton, the producer of "Commentary" on CBC Radio and the author of *Target Nation: Canada and the Western Intelligence Network*, gave me advice on how to locate some individuals who were essential to this oral history.

I am grateful for the financial support of the Canada Council's Explorations program. The kind efforts of Lynn Schellenberg, Doug Gibson, Ted Mann, and Diane Chaperon-Lor helped me obtain the above grant. Leuten Rojas of the Canada Council was always available to render advice. Thanks also to Alex Gropper for his letter of recommendation.

Pat Stegenga and her staff at the Dufferin-Clark Library in the city of Vaughan, particularly Glenn Pearson, helped me locate books which were vital to the research.

My thanks to Beverley Slopen for pointing me in Malcolm Lester's direction. My publisher, Malcolm Lester, served as the book's first editor and contributed excellent advice, and Janice Weaver of Lester

Publishing edited the book with extraordinary care.

On a very personal note, I'd like to thank my sister, Ruth Scher, for supporting this effort. She shared my belief that this hidden side of Canadian history should come to the surface. A natural researcher (who is, in fact, a researcher working in the labour movement), Ruth advanced the book by tapping into her network of acquaintances and coming through with the appropriate name or two or three.

My mother, Erna, and late father, Morris, stimulated my interest in history and current events. Our home was always filled with newspapers, books, conversation, and hope for a better world. It is their positive outlook and philosophy which have guided me.

My daughters, Rebecca and Julie, were wonderful throughout the time I was putting this book together. They had to endure this project for three long years. I hope the result answers all the questions they had about blacklisting and McCarthyism.

I would not have completed this undertaking without the encouragement and love of my wife, Christiane Trudeau-Scher. Christiane read every transcript, made valuable suggestions, and spurred me on when all I saw in front of me were piles and piles of audiocassettes. Her sixth sense and support never waned.

INTRODUCTION

"Happy the people whose annals are blank in history-books!"
  —*Thomas Carlyle*
"Blacklist: A list of suspected persons or those to be punished, refused employment, etc."
  —Webster's New World Dictionary *(1957 edition)*

It was the summer of 1967 and Canada was celebrating its hundredth birthday. My father was about to fly from Montreal to Israel via New York. It was to be Morris Scher's first trip abroad to visit his relatives since coming to this country and he had saved the money for the ticket over a period of years. My mother, my nine-year-old sister, Ruth, and I went to see him off. I was a university student working at Expo '67 that summer and had been able to leave work early to drive the family to the airport. My father's luggage departed, but he didn't get out of Montreal that day. Since the plane was stopping over in New York City, a US immigration guard had to check Dad's passport. After he examined the name and consulted a thick book, the US customs official refused to allow my father through the gate to join the other passengers. This was an event we did not anticipate.

Father's face turned ashen and his hands shook when he was told he couldn't board the flight, but he composed himself and politely asked why he was being singled out. The stony-faced US customs man offered no explanation and certainly no apology, but it might have been of some small consolation to my father had he known that the book also contained such names as Farley Mowat, Graham Greene, Charlie Chaplin, and Gabriel Garcia Marquez. I have no doubt my father suffered from the embarrassment. A year later he was dead from cancer at age fifty-one.

This wasn't the first time this type of thing had occurred. I was eight years old when my father was first blacklisted. Actually, I didn't even know what the word "blacklist" meant at the time, but it's an accurate way of describing what was happening to our family. Today, as I look back at the details of our family's story, I can only conclude that both the RCMP and the FBI were involved.

My father, Morris (Moisze) Scher, worked as a tailor in a downtown Montreal factory that manufactured men's coats. He had arrived after the Second World War and, like many working-class European Jews who immigrated to Canada, was passionate about politics. It was a legacy from his formative years in Poland when young Jewish tradesmen broke away from religious orthodoxy and aligned themselves with political forces that promised a better life. There were a number of ideologies, ranging from Zionism to communism, and my father explored a few.

In 1939, when Hitler invaded Poland, Morris Scher enlisted in the Polish Army to resist the Nazis. He was captured in the Russian zone, so he was able to join up with the Free Polish Army under General Wladyslaw Anders. He fought in the Italian campaign in which the Free Polish Army distinguished itself. In Palestine he transferred to the British Army's Jewish Brigade, with whom he also saw action.

At war's end, Morris met twenty-four-year-old Erna Kirchenbaum in a Displaced Persons camp located just inside the American zone of divided Germany. She had survived the war with her family by escaping from Poland just as the Germans entered her village. The Soviets moved them to an area close to Siberia. Life was a struggle there, and Erna had to walk twenty kilometres daily in deep snow and sub-zero weather to procure some food for her family's table. Most days, the only staple available was a solitary potato. Her father died of hunger.

Morris and Erna fell in love and a civil marriage was performed in Bad Salzchlift, near the city of Fulda, Germany, on June 6, 1947. The couple found refuge in the Netherlands and I was born in Rotterdam on March 11, 1948.

Enticed by the stories of friends who launched successful lives in Canada, Morris Scher applied to immigrate. After a lengthy interview with the RCMP and immigration representatives in Holland, his application was accepted. He left Holland alone in 1951 aboard the ship *Anna Salem*. On August 24, he arrived in Halifax. Within six months, he had earned enough money as a sewing-machine operator in Montreal to send two tickets in our name for a trip across the Atlantic on the S.S. *Volendam*. Our first "residence" was a room we rented from a family on St. Urbain Street.

On Sundays we picnicked and strolled through Fletcher's Field on Mount Royal, which we called "The Mountain." That was where hundreds of newly arrived Jewish immigrants and their families would congregate to greet each other and reflect on their good fortune at having survived the Holocaust.

In Montreal my father met Jewish Communists who worked side by side with him in the factory and he was introduced to a Yiddish-language newspaper called the *Vochenblatt*, which was circulated by a member of the party who delivered his bundle of newspapers around town by bicycle. A lot of people along his route wound up on Mountie lists.

We moved to a better apartment on la rue Jeanne Mance, still only a stone's throw away from the mountain that divides the city. We had to take in a boarder to help pay the rent, which was $55 a month—expensive when you're earning only $30 a week. Our lodger, a Communist, moved into the third bedroom of our apartment. He was an ex-seaman named Andy, a quiet, somewhat solemn young man in his thirties, who couldn't find maritime work because his union, the Canadian Seamen's Union (CSU), had been destroyed by Hal Banks.

Eventually, Andy was forced to move back to his hometown, Cornwall, Ontario, a victim of the DNS list—the infamous "Do Not Ship" headcount that discriminated against left-wingers. Hal Banks compiled the blacklist and ordered that no one on the DNS list be allowed to work on a ship in Canadian waters. This dictum was strictly adhered to and it kept Andy, a Communist, away from the docks.

Andy was but one casualty; the DNS list was estimated to contain more than 6,000 names. The tradition of blacklisting seamen had actually begun with the RCMP in 1950 when it undertook security screenings of seamen who worked on the Great Lakes. There were also others who were collecting private lists, and informers who were "naming names" to the RCMP. One of these names was my father's.

We sometimes visited a small but boisterous summer camp operated by Communists in the Laurentian Mountains. It was located only about fifteen metres away from the noisy highway to Montreal, was not much larger than a suburban backyard, and was intended mostly for children of "comrades." It was at this point that my mother became wary of my father's involvement with communism. Might it not threaten our secure existence in our adopted country? She felt safer when my father lost respect for Soviet-style communism after the truth about Stalin's gulags and anti-Semitism emerged. He decided to turn his attention and energy to a Jewish Zionist labour movement called the Farband. Its members were mainly socialists who, among other things, raised funds for Israeli charities. My father became chairman of a branch named after Leon Blum, the first Jewish and socialist premier of France. Soon, my father's experience with communism was all but forgotten.

But the damage was already done. When he applied for citizenship five years after coming to this country, Morris Scher was flatly refused. His application was rejected by the Department of Citizenship and Immigration.

Recently, I tried to piece together his story and obtained letters about him under the Access to Information Act. One note is dated November 5, 1956, and was sent by the RCMP to officials at the Department of Citizenship and Immigration in Ottawa. It reveals that the RCMP was busy looking into my father's activities ("Field enquiries are being conducted . . ."). I can only deduce that the RCMP note influenced the decision to deprive him of citizenship.

It was a source of pain for me as I watched other schoolmates, whose parents were also immigrants but who arrived after us, tell me about the excitement of taking the oath of citizenship and becoming "respectable" Canadians. It was a mark of shame for my parents that we were denied naturalization. They had escaped the Holocaust and desperately wanted to become citizens of their new country. Again, their lives were filled with insecurities and questions: How would this effect my father's employment? How long could we remain in Canada without citizenship? The full rewards that Canada had to offer weren't yet ours. We were still outsiders, not even second-class citizens.

I recall, as a nine-year-old, being told for the first time about my "statelessness." Even though I was born in Holland, Dutch law specified that I couldn't be a citizen unless my parents were. So here I was, officially a "stateless person."

Dad tried writing to the registrar of Canadian citizenship: "Although I understand that you are overburdened with administrative work, I am sure you will be equally sympathetic to my desire for citizenship as early as possible." A letter came back from J.E. Duggan, the registrar. The curt reply didn't offer much: "Your application for citizenship has been rejected by the minister as of December 26, 1957." By law, no further explanation was necessary.

My father reapplied for citizenship as soon as he was eligible to do so—two years later (November 18, 1959). Another terse reply arrived from Ottawa to our home. Again, it simply said "rejected." The official in Ottawa also sent a copy of the rejection to the RCMP. This meant they were still keeping tabs on my father.

Another decade rolled along—the '60s, supposedly a gentler era —but my father still wasn't granted his citizenship papers. My parents were allowed by law to resubmit their application for citizenship two years after the earlier rejection. They applied but heard nothing for months. My mother thought it was time to enlist the services of someone who could unravel the mystery. They paid $500 for the services of a woman who called herself an immigration consultant and claimed to be familiar with these "types of cases."

The RCMP conducted more field enquiries, but my father must have been considered clean by then. He was finally granted Canadian citizenship a few years later, on October 16, 1963. But it wasn't over yet. There was new harassment to come as his name travelled to the FBI's files—a gift from the Mounties—and this resulted in the final episode of blacklisting that took place at the airport in Montreal.

Now it's the '90s. The Soviet Union is no more and communism has perished. But what first attracted my father to communism and the left forty years ago? At the time, the dark side of Stalin was still hidden and the Soviet Union had proved itself a valiant ally during the Second World War. "I joined the left because they were the only group in Canada that were fighting to help the unemployed," said a prominent poet, Dorothy Livesay, in the book *In Their Words: Interviews with Fourteen Canadian Writers*. "It was a genuine battle and no other party except the Communist Party was into that."

The Communist Party, a legal political entity, had grown during the hard times of the Depression. Card-carrying membership nearly doubled in just one year (1934-35), going from 5,500 to 9,000. In 1943, to appeal to more voters, the party was reorganized as the Labor Progressive Party (LPP). The leader of the LPP in Ontario was a Nova Scotia Scot named Alexander A. MacLeod, who was elected a member of provincial Parliament for the riding of Bellwoods in Toronto. J.B. (Joe) Salsberg held the riding of St. Andrew and was an extremely popular labour organizer among the area's predominately Jewish population. In the legislature, they were responsible for initiating and then repeatedly agitating for a human rights code for Ontario. The idea was eventually adopted and legalized by the provincial government. Later, A.A. (Alex) MacLeod became the editor of the government publication *Human Rights*, and his counsel was trusted by many at the Ontario legislature. Two Tory premiers, Leslie Frost and John Robarts, would sometimes employ MacLeod to write important speeches for them.

Eddie Goodman, who became a powerful back-room boy and adviser to Conservative prime ministers, went down to crushing defeat when he was a Tory candidate in a Communist-held riding in the 1945 election. "The Russians were our gallant allies," Goodman wrote in his memoirs, *Life of the Party*, "and this greatly lessened the opprobrium of being a Communist." Another loser to Joe Salsberg was a future mayor of Toronto, Nathan Phillips, who was defeated in the 1948 election.

The term "cold war" was first used publicly by Bernard Baruch, a presidential adviser, during a US congressional debate in 1947 in reference to the growing polarity between the West and the Soviet Union. In Canada, the cold war had begun two years earlier.

On a humid night in September 1945, Igor Gouzenko walked into the offices of the *Ottawa Journal* with a multitude of secrets locked away in his mind. Gouzenko appeared to be under a lot of strain and couldn't get the words out to articulate his story of a Canada-USSR spy ring. As a cipher clerk employed by the Soviet military attaché, Gouzenko's job was to translate messages to Moscow into a special numerical code, and thus he claimed intimate knowledge of the espionage network and managed to convince the RCMP that spies were being recruited here. The Mounties decided to take him seriously when they learned Soviet diplomats had broken into his apartment after his defection.

Five months later, empowered by the War Measures Act, Mackenzie King launched a royal commission to investigate the allegations of espionage. He assigned Mr. Justice Robert Taschereau and Mr. Justice R.L. Kellock, both of the Supreme Court, the task of heading up the commission. Gouzenko was called as the first witness.

First, Gouzenko accused member of Parliament for the Labor Progressive Party (LPP) and dedicated Communist Fred Rose of being a key person in the espionage ring. Next, a McGill scientist and explosives expert with the National Research Council, nicknamed "The Professor" by the Soviets, Dr. Raymond Boyer, was singled out. Soon afterwards another LPP official, Sam Carr, was identified by Gouzenko. In all, the RCMP had thirteen names.

In the early morning of February 15 the surprised targets were arrested. Allowed no visitors, not even their closest relatives, the prisoners were kept in the RCMP barracks in Rockcliffe, a suburb of Ottawa. The captives were denied a proper defence, since a government order-in-council "empowered the Royal Commissioners to force witnesses to give evidence." A.L. Smith, a Conservative MP, was later prompted to lament that "the people of this country will always regret and will never live down the fact that we threw aside and abrogated the rights and liberties of our citizens."

The results of the Gouzenko revelations are still mired in controversy because of the way the trials were conducted. To quote historian J.L. Granatstein: "It was quite extraordinary that the Royal Commission's report, with its clear presumption of guilt, was released before they were tried in court. I think one could argue that it was almost impossible for these suspected spies to have a fair trial after the Royal Commission report." John Diefenbaker felt the way the people were treated justified the need for a Bill of Rights. In all, twenty-one people were charged and eleven were convicted. Ten people were acquitted.

As for Gouzenko, he would find fame on shows such as "Front Page Challenge," never appearing without his trademark protective mask. Gouzenko presumed the government also owed him a living for his actions and claimed so to Michael Starr, the federal minister of labour. Starr believed Gouzenko had invested unwisely and squandered his royalties from his best seller, *Fall of a Titan*, but, with Diefenbaker's approval, Starr settled on a pension of $500 a month for the defector.

AFTER GOUZENKO

The fact that a member of Parliament would work on behalf of a foreign government, and the fear of "an enemy within" made up of Communists and sympathizers, allowed the cabinet to authorize an increase in the RCMP's security activities. A year after the spy trials, in 1947, the RCMP's Special Branch was handed far-ranging responsibilities, including the gathering of intelligence and surveillance. Eventually, keeping track of domestic dissidents and harassing labour unions and peace activists replaced an unsuccessful quest for more spy rings.

Communism was influential in certain parts of the labour movement, and consequently the Mounties increased their surveillance on left-wing unions. Communists had organized unions throughout Canada, fought bitter strikes, and were intensely dedicated to workers. Bill Walsh, a long-time union activist and Communist, told me he believed the real reason for the red-hunting during the cold war wasn't ideological but practical. "There was concern largely because business felt threatened by the ability of Communists to get better wages for their workers," says Walsh. "In the postwar period the establishment talked of their belief in God, that Communists were atheists, didn't believe in private property. They were using the fear of what would happen to our grandchildren if the Communists took over, but primarily we hurt them in the pocket book." Prime Minister Mackenzie King saw labour as a threat, claiming they held mostly "to Marxian doctrines."

The RCMP expanded its investigations into union activity and, within five years, had purged the Communist-influenced unions. One of the tactics was to have companies who worked under contract for the government send lists of their employees to the RCMP as part of a "screening" process. The RCMP filtered the names and sent back reports. Aircraft manufacturers, defence contractors, and even the RCAF discharged workers for no apparent reason. The fact that one "might be or might become" a security risk actually made you one. In a nine-month period alone, October 1950 to June 1951, the red-hunting Mounties processed around 54,000 enquiries in the screening of civil servants and private-sector workers.

By the early '50s, left-wing unions were vulnerable. Some were expelled from the large labour bodies or congresses, the Canadian Congress of Labour (CLC) and the Trades and Labour Congress (TLC). Political waters became especially rough for the Canadian Seamen's Union (CSU), which was decertified by the Canadian Labour Relations Board over its alleged Communist leadership. Other unions struggled to keep the allegiance of their members against raiding unions.

HARASSMENT IN QUEBEC

In Quebec, Premier Maurice Duplessis made the left public enemy number one and warned about the great Communist menace. Even the CCF (Co-operative Commonwealth Federation, the forerunner of the NDP) was a "disguised ante-chamber of communism," according to the premier. He even blamed the collapse of a poorly constructed bridge in Trois Rivières on Communist sabotage.

Duplessis employed the "Red Squad," his provincial anti-subversive police force, to raid private homes and offices in search of "revolutionary" material. The Montreal Police had its own Red Squad, manned by such characters as Lieutenant John Boyczum, whose most prominent facial feature earned him the nickname "Scarface." The two squads often worked together as a tag team. In February 1948 Duplessis' police swooped down on the premises of *Le Combat*, a French-language weekly, and seized typewriters, mimeograph machines, and the subscription list. Then a padlock was placed on the door, in accordance with a Quebec law allowing the shutting down of premises related to communism. Also padlocked was the Jewish Cultural Centre. In one month in 1949 there were raids on the Association of United Ukrainian Canadians, the offices of the *Canadian Tribune* and the National Federation of Labour Youth, and numerous private dwellings.

Duplessis was the scourge of the labour unions in Quebec. In an off-handed attempt at censorship, Le Chef cautioned the press of Quebec not to report labour news: "It is dangerous to give publicity to disorderly strikes, radical people, and Communists." Seamen, textile workers, and members of other trade unions felt his wrath. Duplessis pronounced a strike by Montreal Catholic teachers illegal and lifted their certification rights. Similar action was taken against some two hundred and fifty other unions. Duplessis blamed labour strife on Communists and claimed that "it [was] the duty of the attorney general to see they [were] arrested." Duplessis was also the provincial attorney general.

THE BLACK BOOK

The blacklist at the Canada-US border was another way of harassing the left. The RCMP handed their lists of suspected Communists to the Americans. Under the McCarran Internal Security Act of 1950 and the McCarran-Walter Immigration and Nationality Act of 1952, any person could be restricted from entering the United States for being a Communist and for other political reasons. These names were entered in the "lookout book" or "watch list" at customs points.

Pierre Trudeau found out he was in the "lookout book" in 1954 when he was turned back at the border while driving to New York. Trudeau's trips to China and Moscow may have been the reason his name came to the attention of the US Immigration and Naturalization Service (INS).

Hundreds of Canadian labour leaders were barred entry to the United States and thus were unable to consult with their union executives or attend meetings at international headquarters, usually located in an American city. It was a roadblock, both figuratively and literally.

A NOTE ABOUT APPROACH

Why did I choose oral history as the medium? There already exist a number of important academic and historical books that have examined the cold war. These are crucial to our study of those years, but letting the victims speak for themselves lends an emotional quality to our picture of those times and brings the experience closer to the reader. What did it feel like to live through this period? If you were harassed by the Security Service you were fired from your job and prevented from landing a new one. Some people lost social standing or were abandoned by friends and family.

I've invited many different participants to tell me their memories of the cold-war era. Most, but not all, were victims. Some stories are included to round out the picture of the times. Wherever possible, my questions have been removed during the editing in order to make the stories flow without interruption.

Oral history is a powerful medium. Consider Canada during the Depression as depicted by Barry Broadfoot's *Ten Lost Years*, or Studs Terkel's *Hard Times* about the same period in the United States. These two oral historians led the way and I have emulated their approach.

It wasn't easy to persuade people who were blacklisted or otherwise victimized to tell me their stories. On occasion, I was perceived as an intruder rooting out a painful family secret which had long remained closeted. Some of those I interviewed preferred to remain anonymous, as they are still afraid. They don't want their children to be marked for the political "sins" of their parents.

It took a lot of courage on the part of those who let me use their names. They had to go public with their lives and hope no one would tamper with the careers of their children. As distant as that thought appears at present, the victims of McCarthyism know only too well that political fashions can change.

While I was interested in blacklisting because of my family's story, the impetus for this book came from a CBC Radio program I produced in 1979 called "McCarthyism and the Arts." This was a two-hour special about the events in the United States, where witch-hunts were common in the movie, television, and radio industries. Freelance writer Nat Shuster collected some touching interviews, and the program went on to become a finalist in the competition for that year's ACTRA awards and also won a Columbia University–sponsored Armstrong Award.

A few days after the broadcast, I spoke with another journalist friend who was convinced that "those kind of things didn't happen in Canada." In fact, that's something of a myth. We can be proud of many things as Canadians, but we *can't* say we were innocent during the so-called McCarthy era. Canada didn't have a gavel-banging House on Un-American Activities charade or a spectacle like the Hollywood Ten in which noted writers, directors, and actors actually went to jail. Yet, what most Canadians don't know is that the National Film Board also succumbed to pressure from cold-warrior politicians. A number of employees were forced out of the NFB. Others fled, afraid the axe would fall on them next.

One former NFB manager, James Beveridge, feels remorse about the firings to this day. In an emotional moment, he confided to me that "every fibre in his body" regrets not standing up and fighting for those who were fired at the film board. But the overall political climate suppressed acts of individual heroism.

The people we meet in this oral history are among Canada's most respected citizens. They were politicians, university teachers, labour leaders, writers, musicians, producers, and directors. If the US Congress was searching for "Un-Americans," then these were our "Un-Canadians."

I have included a chapter about Canadians who lived through the

McCarthy period in the United States—people like folk-singer Oscar Brand, whose income went from thousands of dollars a week to zero when he was blacklisted off network radio. Overnight. The memories of those times remained with Brand after he survived the blacklisting and was invited back to Canada to start up a folk music series for CTV called "Let's Sing Out." As part of his agreement to emcee the show, Brand insisted there be no blacklisting imposed on any talent.

Lastly, this book doesn't deal with many of the people named by Gouzenko in the espionage case and later convicted—people like Fred Rose, Sam Carr, Dr. Raymond Boyer, and Emma Woikin. Their stories have been documented in two excellent books (Merrily Weisbord's *The Strangest Dream* and June Callwood's biography of Woikin, *Emma: The True Story of Canada's Unlikely Spy*). "Lottie," a pseudonym for a woman named by Gouzenko, begins this oral history because all charges against her were withdrawn by the government and because she has never told her story before.

PROLOGUE

GOUZENKO AFTERMATH:
LOTTIE'S STORY

HELD FOR THREE MONTHS

"Lottie" lives in a downtown apartment in a working-class area of Montreal. In 1945, after the Gouzenko revelations, she was accused of being part of a spy ring. She fled Montreal, went into hiding in the United States, and lived through some harrowing incidents. Eventually, she was cleared of any wrongdoing. Now retired, she lives peacefully under a different name and wants to go on with her life—"I don't want my name to be used, but getting a chance to talk about my experiences has made me feel good."

It was just at the war's end. I was in Reno getting a divorce. I had to be there for six weeks, so I decided to work for a gambling casino as a change girl. I wanted to be a dealer, but I had to start as a change girl. Stupid me didn't realize that you had to be fingerprinted to get the job. When I got to the police station I couldn't back out, so I had myself fingerprinted. That's where I got caught. I guess the RCMP and the FBI worked together. You could say they "fingered" me. The FBI came knocking at the place where I was staying and I was picked up.

I had my baby with me. They took me by train to San Francisco. They questioned me and questioned me. I was taken to the immigration detention quarters in San Francisco. I was supposed to be sent back to Canada immediately because I had waived extradition. I was going to come back to Canada and face the music here. But they kept me and they kept me and kept me. We spent three and a half months there. Every day the director of this detention centre would call me down to his office to ask me if I had anything to tell him. When I said no, I went back up again. This same routine went on day

17

after day. One day I took my daughter down with me and she peed on his carpet. I was so happy because he was mad as hell!

There was a young Russian couple there. There were lots of Chinese, too. As a matter of fact, it was the little Chinese children who got my daughter up on her feet for the first time. Because we moved around from place to place, she'd never gotten up on her feet. Anyway, these little Chinese girls were fascinated with her. She was a little over a year old at the time. One day I had gone down to talk with the Chinese women, and at the end of the long hall the kids starting shouting and shouting. There was my daughter up on her feet and running! Oh my God, it was such an exciting moment.

I had written a long letter to the Canadian consul in San Francisco complaining about the fact that my child was eating bologna day after day. I mean, she was only a year old. I had no milk for her and I wasn't able to take her out. I still have the letter.

After I sent my letter to the Canadian consulate in San Francisco, they called me and I was taken to the office of the director of the immigration centre. There I was handed the phone to talk to someone at the Canadian consulate. At a certain point in the conversation the director grabbed the phone out of my hand and hung up the receiver. He was concerned that I was giving information about my treatment there. It was pretty awful.

Anyway, I got in touch with the Canadian embassy. Lester Pearson was in Washington at the time. They got in touch with the Canadian consul in San Francisco. That's when things started getting better. The American Civil Liberties Union got in on it, too.

Things changed, and before I knew it I was able to take the child out to the park with a matron. Every day, I was able to take her out, and her diet improved. Then they took me before the grand jury and this was where the fun started. I wasn't permitted to have an attorney with me. There was a US attorney who asked questions. I still remember his name, but I won't mention it.

Do you know what a grand jury is like? Before a trial they will call a grand jury to see if there is enough cause to hold a trial. There were between thirty and forty ordinary US citizens who listened to evidence taken by the attorney. Some were black and there were women too. They were to decide whether they were going to let me go back home or keep me there. Before it started this attorney swore me into not revealing anything of what went on because nothing is supposed to be revealed of what goes on in a grand jury. So I asked him, "Will you be making a statement to the newspapers?" He said no, so I said fine and agreed.

The grand jury decided there was no evidence to keep me in the States. It was a nightmare for me because my daughter was in the arms of a matron. I could hear her howling, and I would go out during the lunch hour to hold her and comfort her. When I had to leave her again she'd be frightened.

When it was all over they sent me to New York with an escort, but the plane had to stop on the way. I was told there were a lot of news-papermen and that they were saving me from the reporters. They put me in the VIP lounge with the child. That was fine. Then we embarked again. I never saw the newspapermen. When I got to New York there was an immigration officer waiting for me and he said, "Oh, you're lucky. There were a lot of newspapermen, but they got tired of waiting for you." Then I saw the headline in the newspaper. This attorney claimed that I had made all kinds of revelations to the grand jury and that I had named names. I was so furious. There wasn't a word of truth in it. I had no names to name anyway.

I was so furious that I handed the baby over and ran around the station, looking for a newspaperman so I could deny this statement and really blast off at the attorney. He had stated categorically that he would not be permitted to reveal any facts, yet he had portrayed me as an informer. Unfortunately, I couldn't find a reporter.

We were put on a train to Montreal. I had no escort. We were in a sleeper—my daughter was above me and I was on the berth below. Suddenly, I was awakened. Something had banged my head; the train had gone off the track. At Vermont there had been a flood, and the train went off the rail and was lying on its side. All the crew ran to get help; not one of them stayed behind to help the passengers. Fortu-nately, some other passengers helped. I couldn't walk. There was something pushing me back. I had the child in my arms. The air con-ditioning broke and a vacuum was created and I couldn't breathe.

When they banged on the door I cried out, "Take the baby, take the baby!" They managed to open the door and it was easier to move.

We were all sent to a hotel to spend the night. There was a young reporter in this town, and he came over to me and said, "I know who you are. If you will give me a statement, I promise you I won't print it until you leave town." He helped me considerably by getting a room and I was very grateful to him. I still don't know if he published the story or not, but I vehemently denied the charges of the attorney. Then we took another train to Montreal, but when I got in there were no newspapermen because we were delayed. My sister said, "Oh you're so lucky, the reporters were cramming this place and now they're all gone." I was gritting my teeth in anger.

Then, don't forget, I had to go through a trial here. It took just one morning and the case was dismissed. They had no evidence against me.

A lot of people don't like talking about religion and politics. I love talking about them because I love getting other people's ideas and comparing them with mine. After all, you don't go through life with one set of ideas, you're changing them all the time. How do you do that? By listening to the views of others.

I remember how I became interested in the Communist Party. I was sixteen at the time. I had a friend who was seventeen, this was at the time of the Spanish Civil War, and she was talking to me about Spain, Japan, and China. I thought, "How does she get to have all this information?" I had just left high school and I didn't know any of these things because I wasn't reading the newspapers. Anyway, I was intrigued, so she took me down to a [Communist Party] meeting. I found them all so intellectual. It was a real eye-opener for me and I wanted to know more. I don't regret anything that's happened to me because it was all an experience. There haven't been too many people, especially women, who have been through what I have been through and survived.

The Atmosphere of Cold War

The Privileged Few: A Reporter's Cold War

Jack McAndrew is a bearded legend among Canadian broadcasters. He has had a distinguished career with the CBC. He was the head of CBC Television Variety and worked as an on-air broadcaster. Now he lives in Charlottetown where he operates his own video production company and also travels throughout the country, training journalists and producers for the CBC. In the 1980s he played a major role in Joe Ghiz's successful campaign to become premier of Prince Edward Island.

I was working as an outside broadcast commentator for the CBC in Halifax in the '50s. I was also an anti–nuclear arms advocate and was secretary of the local association. One day a group of broadcasters was assembled for a special briefing by the director of radio, a man who was a retired brigadier-general. He told us that we had been specially selected to carry on as broadcasters if and when "the balloon went up." He said we would have about twenty minutes' notice to drop everything, including our families, and race to the Halifax airport. An aircraft would be waiting there to fly us to Debert, about fifty miles away. There we would go underground into a deep bunker and transmit to those wandering about in the nuclear fallout, including the families we had abandoned.

He was perfectly serious about this mad scheme. It had all been worked out and carefully planned. He could see nothing ludicrous about it. Unfortunately I could, so I asked the director of radio, with a straight face, how long the airplane would wait for stragglers. I suggested that there would be some, since the entire population of

Halifax would likely be trying to squeeze through the Armdale Rotary, a notorious traffic tie-up. I can't remember his answers, but I kept pressing with questions like, "What about a blizzard?" He became more and more discomfited. The meeting turned into a bit of a shambles.

A couple of days later I learned that I was off the list of the privileged few. I was to be incinerated along with my wife and kids, like the rest of the population. That suited me just fine. It was clear that anyone who asked obvious questions wasn't to be trusted.

A SCHOOL'S COLD WAR

Lolly Golt lives in Montreal, where she was born and educated. She has worked as a teacher, publicist, freelance writer, and broadcaster.

When I was twelve my father bought a big estate in the country around a lake in Quebec's Laurentian Mountains. My father's home was filled with my uncles, aunts, and cousins. There was always a lot of joking, laughing, and music. The women mostly sat and knitted or crocheted beautiful items and talked recipes while the men talked business. There were numerous other houses nearby.

Just within walking distance there was a small house that Max Bailey rented with his wife, Anne, and his daughter Phyllis, who was about two years younger than I was. Max Bailey was very active in the Labor Progressive Party, so going up to my friend Phyllis' house was a lot more interesting than my home. It was heady stuff.

I learned songs like "You Can't Scare Me, I'm Stickin' to the Union" and I was given all kinds of material. They didn't proselytize, they just talked about the issues. It was such an idealistic time; everyone believed the world could change and would change. There was optimism and an openness; Russia was still looked to as a guiding light. There were a lot of books about communism for a new age and I would bring these books home to our country house. Even in the fall I would continue looking around in bookstores and wherever I could find them. An older cousin called me "red" and some people looked askance at me. Remember, this was all from the time I was twelve until I was sixteen.

One day, I brought home *Das Kapital* to read. I read every word and really identified with it. Today, as an adult, I think I probably didn't understand anything. It sounded like solutions, but I really was very young. Anyway, my mother burst into tears and said, "Why are you always reading those books? We're going to have the door padlocked."

That was the first time I realized something was wrong. But I guess those ideas went into the underground river that flowed in my subconscious because I didn't talk about it, even though I had a lot of close girlfriends and became active in high school politics.

I was president every year and by 1950, in grade ten, I was elected to serve as head prefect the following year. I had my socialist tendencies and was interested in things that went on. I was very active in the peace movement and was raising money for the Red Cross. Here I was: sixteen years old, finishing grade ten, elected as head prefect, and editor of the high school paper. One day we were given an assignment to write a composition on some aspect of government. What came out of me spontaneously were the words, "I call my neighbour 'comrade'." I fantasized that I had friends who believed, as I did, that there was going to be a better world.

I wrote the composition and did a lot of research as to how the Russians supposedly lived and how they cooperated. For instance, their education policies included "responsibility." We went to school and we were responsible for ourselves, but in Russia people were trained to use the "buddy" system, like the one we used in camp at swimming. You were responsible for your friend and if he was late you were held accountable. If he was mischievous, then you were accountable. That kind of thing went into the composition, but it just came out of my creative pool without any thought.

I handed it in and about a week later I forgot about it. Nobody had their compositions back yet when I was called to the principal's office. I wasn't worried because that was a frequent occurrence for me since I was president of the class, head prefect, and editor of the newspaper. There were always discussions like "Shall we plan a dance?" or "What do we do about this?" or "How is the discipline in the school?"

Such an emotional thing happened next. The principal was a career teacher and she had never married. She was a very beautiful, very dignified woman and I really got along well with her. She was always very understanding. She picked up my composition from the desk and asked, "Did you write this?"

I looked at her and knew something horrendous was to come, but I didn't know what it would be. And then she said very quietly, "Do you really believe this?"

I said, "Yes I do, actually. I think it's an ideal. I don't think it's realized, but I think it can be realized and I think in the Soviet Union they are struggling to realize it and eventually it will spread."

She spoke to me very quietly in a way she had never spoken to me. I guess she was afraid of losing control and this was a way of trying to stay in control. She said, "Do you talk to other people about it?" That's when the floodgates just opened and I began to get the full meaning of what was happening and I said no. And I didn't.

I was hearing the news about McCarthy and about the Un-American Activities Committee, but as a sixteen-year-old it had very little to do with me anymore because by then I had changed and I was into other kinds of politics. But she had a tiger by the tail. She had somebody who was editor of the paper, and they called the head prefect the "first girl" in the school. There was a lot of power that went with that position. It was an old-fashioned kind of school with no democracy, very authoritarian, and as head prefect I wielded that authority. I had to usher assemblies in and out and I had to make sure girls didn't go into the boys' side of the school. I had to rubber-stamp every project that was going on in the school, including all the clubs.

I had been elected prefect by the girls and the teachers. The head prefect was then elected by the other prefects and rubber-stamped by the principal. It was the first time a Jewish girl was head prefect. Oh, it was a tremendous honour. The rabbi had my parents to dinner. For me it was just something I had drifted into without necessarily choosing it. People just appointed me. It was fun and I liked being busy. Anyway, she had asked if I talked to people about this. I said no, but I could see she wasn't sure. She asked if I had spoken to any girls about this when I was conducting meetings. I said no.

I felt it was unjust and it was so unfair and so contrary to what it really was—just a creative composition. The questioning went on for almost an hour. "Have you spoken to the grade niners? Do you talk to girls in your own class? Do you talk to your close friends?"

Indeed, I never brought it up with close friends. The girls and I talked about boys. We talked about how we had to get rid of pimples and that kind of thing. But the questioning was a harrowing experience. A friend—a very wise friend, very cynical—was waiting outside when I came out. I tried to hold back my tears, but I burst out crying. It was so emotional. I wasn't a crier in those days, but I guess I felt unjustly accused of something to even be suspected of fomenting revolutionary ideas.

"DON'T BE NAÏVE"

Al Purdy is a poet and winner of many writing prizes, including the Governor-General's Award for Poetry. He served with the RCAF during the Second World War. He is the most famous son of Ameliasburg, Ontario.

When I think of fear and the cold war in Canada I think of Cuba and my trip there in 1964. A well-known photographer was going to take pictures and I was going to write a book and we were going to have a great time in Cuba. At the last minute he got kind of scared and backed out because he claimed, "I'd be blacklisted around Toronto."

That's kind of strange if you think of it—a Canadian would be blacklisted in Canada for going to Cuba? We headed to Mexico first and then to Cuba because you couldn't go straight to Cuba then. Anyway, he was worried that he'd get blacklisted when he went back to Canada. Of course, for all I know he might have been. My point of view was that it was a great thing to do to go to Cuba. You couldn't have kept me away from the place at all. The trip itself was wonderful and I would have loved to have written that book.

Pierre Trudeau was on that particular trip and *he* didn't care about getting blacklisted. Trudeau and I seemed to get along all right. Once we left a ballet performance and walked all over Havana, drinking apple cider, which, by the way, he bought. Then later we visited a schoolhouse in southern Cuba. I was sitting in one of those uncomfortable tiny chairs as a Communist organizer or somebody was telling us how things worked in his country and explaining how decisions are arrived at. Trudeau was behind me and I said, "Do you arrive at decisions by majority vote?" I heard this little voice behind me and the voice said, "Al, don't be naïve." I shrank down to about two feet tall. Trudeau never did go easy on fools, and I was a fool and I've always been apolitical.

But Cuba was a real eye-opener to me and I saw how other people regarded the US. In Havana there was an American warship just outside the twelve-mile limit. All the Cubans were mad as hell because that warship was spying on Havana. Anti-aircraft guns were rumbling through the mountains, everything was so strange. Here I come from a rather peaceful town in Ontario, Ameliasburg, and I was talking to red Chinese sailors in a nightclub and there were anti-aircraft guns mounted on the waterfront. So strange. It's strange when you see what the US has done to Latin American and middle American countries all through the years. You can't dislike certain things about the US, but that is when I dislike the US very strongly. Cuba was Communist, and they were exporting their revolution. They're just as bad in their own way, except they are not as powerful. Two hundred and forty million people can do a lot more than ten million.

PART ONE

ARTS BACKWARDS

CHAPTER ONE

PLAY NO EVIL: *THE SYMPHONY SIX*

NOTES OF A BLACKLISTED BASSIST

Ruth Budd *was a bassist with the Toronto Symphony Orchestra and one of the so-called Symphony Six. Her contract was terminated when she and five other members of the TSO were denied entry into the United States. Today, she is still a very active musician and performs in many parts of Canada, including the Arctic.*

The Symphony Six were Dirk Keetbaas, who played the flute; Abe Manheim, Bill Kuinka, and myself, who were all bass players; Steve Staryk, violin; and Johnny Moskalyk (who has since died), violin. It was 1951 and we were going to Detroit for one concert. For whatever reason, we couldn't get across the border. No one ever gave us any reason.

We had absolutely no idea we wouldn't get across. We hadn't done anything to deserve that sort of treatment. I had been a member of a left-wing youth group and I suppose that was the reason for me, but I was very much involved with music to the point where I had no time to do anything else. I was also married and had a household to look after. Dirk said he had never been connected with any organization whatsoever.

It got ridiculous. I remember coming to work one day and passing the women's dressing-room and hearing somebody say, "Well, she must be a Communist, she reads a lot!" The following year our contracts were not renewed. We no longer had jobs.

We raised the issue with the press and with various friends. We became a group, although we were not even close friends and we

29

were not connected socially in any way. We worked together and that was as far as our association went; however, we were thrown together because we were victims of the same situation.

We did some investigative work and found out the reason we lost our jobs was because we weren't allowed across the border to Detroit. Naturally, I was dismayed. It seemed to me that getting across the border to do one concert in the United States had nothing to do with my job in my own country. Then I found out there were five others in the same situation. Together, we decided to write to our union and, if necessary, to go back to the press and our friends. But we had no support whatsoever from our local union. I don't know why. I suspect fear is the basis for things like this. I don't know why we couldn't have been left at home for that concert in the first place. Or the orchestra could have put in substitute players, as it has subsequently done.

I found that people with whom I had worked for the past five years were really nervous about talking to me. I noticed my colleagues would cross the street when they saw me coming in order to avoid being seen with me. I had thought we were quite good friends. Obviously, there were some people in the orchestra who felt very upset at the situation and were very supportive. Those people are still my close friends and I knew who they were. But when the news broke in the press, people who were formerly supporters of the Toronto Symphony started writing letters saying they would no longer be subscribers. Some people on the board resigned in protest and many people wrote letters to us individually.

Many supporters said, "This is our country, our orchestra, our city. What can we do?" A committee was formed by very good people from all walks of life, including insurance industry people, poets, and housewives. People really rallied around us. When we felt that kind of support we decided to further investigate the situation and try to remedy it. There was a major campaign. The results were not immediate but it did become a public issue.

Up until that point, my whole life had been spent in learning to be a symphony musician and now I had to change my way of living. I never overcame it psychologically—I was deeply affected by it.

It took me some time to pull myself together and stop licking my wounds. I still had to make a living and I still wanted to play. I'm the kind of person who says, "Let's get on with life," and I did just that by joining a folk-singing group. I also got a different kind of job playing at the Royal Alex every night. Of course, I was profoundly affected because my training had been to play in a symphony orchestra and I could no longer do that in *the* major orchestra in this country.

Sir Ernest MacMillan was the conductor [of the Toronto Symphony]. I believe he should really have stood up for the musicians in his orchestra. The same kind of thing actually happened to the Dutch orchestra, the Concertgebouw. Two of its musicians were denied visas to the US but the conductor said, "The whole orchestra goes or we don't go at all." And that was precisely what happened— the orchestra did not play there at that time. It seems to me that should have happened here.

I never had any self-doubt, but I really had serious doubts about my own country as it succumbed to pressure from a foreign power. That another nation should have an effect on my making a living in my own country I found quite unacceptable, shocking, and devastating.

The Irony of It All

Steven Staryk is a leading violinist, a teacher, and one of the Symphony Six. He was blacklisted and fired by the TSO after he was refused a visa by the US government to perform at a concert in 1951. By the age of thirty-five, he had already been concert-master of three of the world's major orchestras—an unprecedented achievement. He lives in Seattle, Washington, where he is head of the string division at the School of Music, University of Washington.

I was nineteen and the youngest member of the Toronto Symphony Orchestra when, during my second season, the symphony decided to go on a "tour" to Ann Arbor, Michigan. I, like the other members of the orchestra, was required to get a visa from the US consulate. I was shocked that I wasn't issued a visa.

I was advised to get "cleared." In order to do that, I was told, one had to go to the RCMP. I went to the RCMP but was told they couldn't help me. The officer said, "It's very difficult to just clear you. If we let you through and refused clearance to anyone else it would imply that only you were OK but everyone else was a Communist or 'fellow traveller'."

The TSO found it appropriate to fire the six of us who were refused visas to the US. Neither the manager of the orchestra, Jack Elton, nor the conductor, Ernest MacMillan, ever confronted me face to face. I was informed mainly by the media and probably by correspondence from the TSO or the Toronto Musicians' Association or both.

The situation was extremely frustrating and ironic because I was studying violin in the States at this time with Oscar Shumsky, and was constantly travelling back and forth between New York and Toronto. What saved me economcally was primarily the CBC. I managed to make a living freelancing (for the CBC Symphony, CBC musical and dramatic programs, etc.) and doing some "outside" work, which could include virtually anything from weddings to wakes.

Since I couldn't go south to the United States, I went to Europe four years later. Soon after my arrival, Sir Thomas Beecham offered me the position of concert-master of the Royal Philharmonic Orchestra of London. This most certainly assured me of artistic growth, as well as recognition and prestige to boot!

Do you know what got you into trouble with US immigration? Was there a hall, theatre, or organization in which you performed that was considered a security risk or "communistic"?

I performed everywhere. I was a youngster with some talent, which comes complete with a necessary desire to perform, and therefore played whenever I got the opportunity. I performed for a lot of ethnic and religious groups—Ukrainian, Polish, Jewish, Macedonian, etc., in halls, in churches, and for any organization where music was supposedly appreciated, including the Red Cross.

At times there was a modest fee (much needed), but mostly it was the experience I sought. To this day I couldn't tell you whether the Red Cross or any other organization was especially musical. I was seeking stage experience, and opportunities to perform new repertoire as is only natural in the performing arts, and it appears to have been beneficial in my career.

Around the same time that the Toronto Symphony incident occurred, a world famous orchestra, the Concertgebouw of Amsterdam, encountered similar difficulties. However, the members of that orchestra who were not admitted into the United States were not dismissed from the Concertgebouw—they simply stayed home and were replaced by other musicians for that particular tour. Ironically, again, I later became the first concert-master of this orchestra and with them did a coast-to-coast tour of the US. We covered fifty-five cities and I was allowed in on a temporary permit.

By 1963 I was recommended by Szell, Martinson, and Szeryng [of the Chicago Symphony] and invited to become the concert-master. I took up the position with a temporary visa and was "cleared" two years later by this orchestra. There obviously wasn't that much to clear; however, in getting documentation together for the alien residence card, it was necessary to get police clearance from all the countries in which one had resided. Ironically, I also got approval from the RCMP, who could not do this twelve years earlier. The hypocrisy of persecution in my own country and clearance by an American orchestra was quite extraordinary!

After other positions in the US (where my daughter was born) and in Canada, everything came full circle when, in 1982, I became concert-master of the Toronto Symphony Orchestra. Fortunately, by this time it was an entirely different organization, from management to board to conductor. The tour during this period was also a little more significant. Instead of Ann Arbor there was London, Paris, Amsterdam, Prague, etc., the music capitals of Europe.

During the 1986-87 season it became obvious, for various reasons, that I would be more involved with the teaching rather than the playing aspect of my career. The lack of comparable major teaching positions in Canada led me south to the States once again. On this occasion it was only necessary to provide qualifications, or more accurately over-qualifications, to prove I was not displacing a competing US citizen. I believe this to be fair game, having encountered the process in all other countries (including Canada) where I permanently resided and worked.

A Critic Fights Back

Langford Dixon *is a former music reviewer for the* Globe and Mail *and is now a poet who has written six books. He publicly defended the Symphony Six.*

I supported the musicians who were fired because I believed in freedom of speech. When society doesn't like what somebody thinks, it says, "You're out." I hated that. I was a loyal subject of Her Majesty's and I was a Conservative, as I am to this very day, but I defended them because it was corrupt the way these people were hounded. They had a right to keep their jobs. For example, Ruth Budd was one of the finest double-bass players you could ever come across. She's terrific and to boot her out of the orchestra was like destroying a jolly good part of it.

The rest of the [non-blacklisted] musicians in the orchestra were unable to act boldly in opposition to their persecutors because they needed their jobs. They were afraid they were going to be treated like the Symphony Six. There were some, and I promised never to mention their names, who donated money to help out. They asked me not to say who they were because they feared trouble too, you see.

A group known as the Assembly for Canadian Arts got involved in the controversy too. This was a group who got together to fight the corruption, in defence of the Symphony Six. When the pressure was on they held a meeting. The *Toronto Telegram* had an unbelievable headline about it. It was about three inches thick and talked about this "Communist meeting."

At this gathering there was a chairman who was going to do the speaking. When he got ready to talk he saw two Mounties sitting there right in the front row. They weren't undercover either, they were in uniform . . . they were taking notes. When the fellow who was to be chairman saw the Mounties he refused to get up on the platform. He told me, "Look, *you* go up and speak."

So I became the chairman just like that and then I gave a talk. One of the Mounties, a very nice chap by the way, came up to me when I finished and I told him I believed every word I said. He just said, "Oh yes, I know." I believe I suffered because of that. I was fired from my job—I was the music critic for the *Globe and Mail*—I was just told my services were no longer required. I'm sure it stemmed from the fact that I defended the Symphony Six. It put me out of a very respectable position.

It reminds me of my start in writing. During the Second World War, I studied in England at the London School of Engineering and Technology. The school had a top course in modern journalism. I went through the course by correspondence because I was an engineer in the navy and I was aboard ship. Periodically, we'd get into town and I'd attend a lecture. I wrote the journalism exam and I knew I'd done well. When I came back a few months later to get my papers, the professor took me into his office. He said to me, "Writing *is* your vocation, but don't try to be a journalist."

I didn't appreciate what he said then, but I do now. He told me I had to believe everything I wrote, meaning that as a journalist you couldn't do that. I think he's quite right, but to this day I speak my mind on things. I was opposed to the treatment of the Symphony Six but I paid for it, let me tell you. A clique was running things, and anyone who opposed them was out.

But those people in the Symphony Six were banged around. They were accused of being Communists and couldn't cross over to the United States with the orchestra. Yet, at the same time they were being accused of being Communists by the head of the musicians' union, two of the Symphony Six were *already* in the States studying.

The people who were involved with the Symphony Six outvoted Walter Murdoch, head of the musicians' union at the time. In those days, if there was an election in that union there was an open list—it would say who you were supporting. When Murdoch saw that he was being outvoted someone handling the election added eighteen names to the list of people who would support Murdoch and that's how the leadership of the musicians' union stayed in. Certainly Murdoch wanted to get rid of the Symphony Six because they had tried to put him out, and he had enough pull with the board at the TSO to keep them out. It was definitely a conspiracy. This whole idea of the union being overrun by Communists was absolutely made up. Only a couple had left-wing leanings.

Did you reflect on the cold war era in your poetry?

[Reads from his poem "As the World Goes"]

Tis the sensitive ones
get clawed
in a world ruled
by leaders riding tigers so ferocious
they dare not
dismount,

In a world ruled
by power
where man's potential as a being
is being
denied
its finest hour,

In a time
when Time itself is awed,
tis the sensitive
ones get clawed,

Aye, in a world ruled
by tigers
riding
lust and bent on debasing a world
so ruled. . . .

Til men
in Time's revealing light
get tumbled
from their fraud and in the light
of Time as well
get clawed,

Tis in their fright
that humbled
men
know of the light
of God.

Reprinted by kind permission of the author.

A MUSICIAN GIVES IN

Harry Freedman *is a respected composer, musician, and art lover.*
During the Symphony Six episode in 1951, he served on the executive
of the musicians' union.

I was elected to the executive board of the musicians' union and I was
playing in the Toronto Symphony as well. We were going on a trip to
Detroit, Ann Arbor, and so on. We went on this trip every year.
Then we were suddenly told that six people in the orchestra hadn't
been granted visas. The six were not allowed into the States and then
they were let go.

I contended that the orchestra should put in six subs for the tour
and the [original] six should be back in the orchestra when we
returned to Canada. I tried to point out that being a Canadian in an
orchestra now meant you had to fulfil some conditions which were
laid down by foreign governments. Well, the head of the musicians'
union wouldn't have any of it. Everybody was so afraid of standing
up because they thought they'd be smeared with the same brush.

I was so sick of the whole thing and was so disgusted with Sir

Ernest MacMillan, the conductor, for not standing up for the members of the orchestra. He could have been a real national hero at the time if he'd have simply said, "If these people are not allowed to go into the States then the orchestra is not going. Period."

What was needed was people of that stature making a statement. Few did. One of the few was Walt Kelly, whose comic strip "Pogo" was one of the first to lambaste McCarthy. But, apart from that, it was like the Salem witch-hunts.

Steve Staryk was one of the of the Symphony Six who couldn't get a visa to go the States. He went over to Holland and became concert-master of the Concertgebouw, one of the great orchestras of the world. He also became Sir Thomas Beecham's concert-master. He was good enough for them but he wasn't good enough for the Toronto Symphony. It was such a slap in the face.

Did any of the Symphony Six ever actively promote the cause of communism to other musicians in the TSO?

Not that I know of. One of them, I believe, was involved with a Jewish Folk Choir in a sort of left-wing labour organization. One of the things they did was sponsor music there. In those days, anyone involved with music was looking for places to perform and the RCMP must simply have assumed that because someone was performing in this organization he was automatically a Communist.

I remember the union meeting about the Symphony Six at which I finally gave in to the pressure. They wanted it to be a unanimous decision to let the six people go from the orchestra. I was the only one who was holding out. I'm sorry to this day that I didn't stick it out and not vote with the rest of the board of the musicians' union, but there was just too much pressure. I was getting phone calls from members of the orchestra, asking me things like, "Why are you protecting these Commies?" Finally, I gave in. We all have things in our lives that we regret. It's one of my great regrets that I gave in. There was pressure from every angle.

CHAPTER TWO

BROADCAST NO EVIL:
THE CBC AND THE BLACKLIST

LEAVING THE COUNTRY

Ted Allan is one of Canada's best-known writers. Among his credits are the screenplays for the films Lies My Father Told Me *(nominated for an Academy Award in 1975 for best original screenplay and winner of a Golden Globe for best foreign film),* Love Streams *(which won the Berlin Golden Bear Award for best picture of 1985), and* Bethune—The Making of a Hero *(1989). He was a member of the International Brigade during the Spanish Civil War. Today, he spends his winters in Los Angeles and the rest of the year in Toronto.*

My experiences fell into categories. One was the attempted blacklisting by the RCMP during early '50s. Fanatical right-wing members of the RCMP thought it was their job to hound left-wingers and suspected Communists, and they did it very diligently. I was working for the Canadian Broadcasting Corporation as a disc jockey—playing music and talking on the air—and was on the payroll of the CBC. Some RCMP zealots went to the CBC brass and said I was a Communist. I had never tried to hide my activities in Spain nor my earlier activities as a member of the Young Communist League. Neither do I hide it now, as I'm rather proud of those activities in those years. It was a time to be an activist and a left-winger.

However, they [the RCMP] went to the CBC, and Harry Boyle, who was my immediate boss, called me and said, "The RCMP have been here and told us you were a Communist and it would be too embarrassing for us if you remained on the staff of the CBC. So, henceforth, you're getting a week's notice and you are no longer on the staff."

What happened next could only happen in Canada. Boyle then said, "Now that you're not on staff, how would you like to do a free-lance program for the CBC?" I was fired and rehired by Harry Boyle, who was a unique man, and who didn't allow himself to be intimidated. So the blacklisting story isn't all black. There were men like Harry Boyle and [producer] Andrew Allan who didn't give a shit about all of this.

Once I was visited by the RCMP, who were accompanied by a man from the FBI. They went through all the formalities: the RCMP introduced the guy as "an officer of the Federal Bureau of Investigation, and you do not have to speak to him if you don't want to, but they would like to question you."

The FBI man was trying to connect me with someone they were after in the States whom I did not know. I found it rather interesting, this marvellous cooperation between the FBI and the RCMP. In Canada one can understand them going after people who were alleged to have given secrets to Russia, but when they go after writers, actors, artists, you begin to realize the RCMP were devout McCarthyites. It was their religion at the time.

The most insidious form of McCarthyism came about as a result of an advertising agency which was representing a company who were then sponsoring a drama series on the CBC. This was on television. It must be made clear that *never* was anything of mine ever censored on radio. But in 1954 I had adapted for television *Legend of Pepito*, a play of mine that had been done on the "CBC Stage" series. David Greene was the director, and most of the well-known actors of Toronto were in it. They had the sets and had started rehearsals; I had been paid for it. Then it was pulled because this American-controlled advertising agency said they that did not want to have the play performed because it made fun of American mass production. It was an innocent comedy that had already been done on Canadian radio. They were probably worried about my left-wing reputation at the time and so this was their way of not blacklisting me.

The title was later changed to *Legend of Paradiso* and it was produced by Joan Littlewood at Theatre Workshop and eventually by the Berliner Ensemble in East Berlin on East Berlin Television. When I realized that a play of mine could be pulled on the second day of rehearsals by the mere nod and demand of an advertising agency I went home and told my wife to pack. That's why I left Canada for England.

I knew from that moment on that if the blacklist had come to Canada, in any form, I didn't want to be here. I'm a writer and if you take my play off during rehearsal then you're telling me to get out. I got out. It was the best thing that ever happened to me. As it happened, the BBC and ITV, between them, bought twelve of my original television plays the same month I arrived. I never had a problem in London.

In London I wrote for radio, television, and the theatre. I had a rather successful career and I had a great time there. It was the '50s and the '60s. We had quite a contingent of Canadians by then. In television you had Sydney Newman, Ted Kotcheff, Silvio Narrizano, and Alvin Rakoff. I was writing for Hannah Weinstein, who was the producer of the "Robin Hood" and the "Four Just Men" television series. Ring Lardner Jr. and another blacklisted writer from the States were the story editors for both those series. Of course, I wrote under a pseudonym. We all worked under pseudonyms because the shows were being presented in the United States. Not because of England but because of the US market.

It was a time when Joseph McCarthy controlled the US and no one dared to take him on until later. There was a hysteria, a terrible fear—they had created a terrible bogey called "communism." Anybody suspected of any left-wing affiliation of any kind was immediately a "witch." Some of it was frightening, some of it was farcical. In those days, if anyone ever asked me, "Are you or are you not a Communist?" I'd always reply, deadpan, "We're not allowed to tell."

BOYLE'S IRREGULARS

Harry J. Boyle was an author and broadcaster with the CBC who later became chairman of the CRTC. During his time as a producer and

executive, he hired a lot of talented people for CBC Radio. Boyle's team at
the CBC was known affectionately by some as "Boyle's Irregulars."

I have always thought that the red scares in the past fifty years were silly, often vindictive, and usually self-serving. Alistair Cooke tells the story of an author of penny dreadfuls in England who actually got a petition before cabinet about the great number of German "spies" in England when war broke out in 1914. As a result, fourteen thousand were rounded up but only two were charged. One of these was acquitted. But the interesting fact is that the cabinet committee set up to handle the affair kept on and became MI5!

I had a few brushes with "security spooks" when I was at the CBC. Most of the time, the matters turned out to be silly. They sometimes came from civilians at the urging of the security people.

I remember scheduling a recital on Christmas Day by Paul Robeson, the magnificent basso profundo. The Roman Catholic bishop of Sault Ste. Marie protested to the CBC brass. There were some others who also claimed we shouldn't schedule Robeson, a Communist, on CBC, and particularly not on Christmas Day. Some mysterious guy called saying he was a security agent and I would do myself career damage if I kept Robeson on. That really set my teeth on edge.

I told my superiors the program was made up of spirituals and choral works and contained no political references by the singer. I noted the program had been carried by the BBC without a complaint and, what was more, Robeson, who had been hounded from America, was living in London and was a vestryman at St. Paul's Cathedral.

The fuss died down. The program was deeply appreciated by our listeners. We had a few letters of protest from the States, all identical and saying we were Communists for helping Robeson. Years later, I had a correspondent interview the singer who had returned to the US. He praised the BBC and CBC for keeping his career alive when he was blacklisted in his own country.

No doubt Robeson was an idealist about Russia who, like so many, became disillusioned, but I could never understand why people were so anxious to send him and other outspoken advocates of change to Coventry. As someone said, you can't sing "Old Man River" in a Communist way.

There were a lot of artists banned in the States. Some were officially banned, others were shunned at the direction of anti-red groups. We used to carry Pete Seeger, for instance, on the CBC when he was shut out of all American broadcasting. I scheduled him because he was an outstanding folk-singer, not because of any political opinions he had. We invariably got some hate mail from Americans.

FIDEL CASTRO ON THE CBC

In 1958 I was fascinated by the revolt in Cuba by Fidel Castro, against the dictator Batista. I hired a Hungarian cameraman-writer to accompany two *Time* magazine people into the Castro headquarters in the mountains. He took a tape recorder to try and get a taped interview.

The correspondent brought the tape back to me in New York. Before I left I was told that the American spooks were after it. They had already persuaded *Time* not to carry a story on Castro. Even then there was the story going around that he was a Communist.

The tapes were only so so. Castro had made him hide the recorder, and part of the interview was Fidel teaching his troops to read and write. But the program was fleshed out with material on Cuba. It was scheduled in a series of radio programs called *Venture*. We got it on the air before the protests could start pouring in because all of a sudden there seemed to be an orchestrated campaign against Castro, suggesting he was a red. He certainly didn't come across that way on the program: he appeared to be a crusader liberating his country from a corrupt dictator and an economy dominated by the American mafia, at least in so far as Havana was concerned.

After the program there was hell to pay. The program was to be repeated in six days. The Cuban ambassador threatened to boot Air Canada, the Bank of Commerce, and I don't know who all if the program was repeated. There was a new board at the CBC. This was their first crisis and they chickened out. In a rather futile gesture, I refused to actually cancel the program. I said further that Castro would be in Havana within a week and we would look silly. It was sheer bravado. The CBC gave the Cuban ambassador a period on TV on a Sunday night to rebut the radio program, and during the following week Fidel Castro took over Havana and ultimately the country. I was vindicated!

On our program Castro didn't advocate communism. I think, as I remember it, he wanted help from North and South America rather than Russia. He may well have harboured anger at the way his country had been handled by the Americans. Yet friends who knew the Cuban situation told me later that the Americans blew it because they wanted to protect the companies and the groups that had literally ravaged Cuba over the years.

RADICALS

I often wondered where the allegations of people being subversive actually came from. I remember Ted Allan, who was a friend of Dr. Norman Bethune, being called a radical and an agitator. For some reason he was dropped from the CBC staff. I hired him as a writer-producer. I don't know if he was ever a Communist. I hired him because he was a good writer and not as a political commentator.

I knew a lot of talented people who had great difficulty in getting established after the Depression. They weren't for the most part twisted, corrupt, deviant, or even revolutionary. They had simply watched the misery and hardships of ordinary people during the Depression and felt it shouldn't be allowed to happen again. Most were willing to work hard to accomplish better things. Some fell for a Communist dream that was overly simplistic and often substituted a new tyranny for an old one. A lot of good people fell through the cracks and some were hounded for reasons that today seem like lunacy.

What about the RCMP?

They periodically came to check on someone. I think some of them were embarrassed by it all. I remember when I was a young lad bumming in the Depression and some outfit with "Labour and Democracy" in its title would hold meetings and give out food. You could tell the RCMP in plain clothes because they were the well-fed–looking ones.

I asked one of the officers who came to my office if he knew what was in the dossier I assumed they had on me. He said he couldn't reveal it but later on he admitted it had some stuff in it, mostly about [a program I worked on called] "Farm Radio Forum" and the use of such radicals as Father Tompkins and Father Coady of the St. Francis Xavier Co-op movement. Even he admitted it was silly.

It struck me then how stupid the government policy was in isolating people with progressive thoughts or radical ideas, and how much more sensible Father Jimmy Tompkins was when he hired the so-called Communist organizer to work for the co-ops. The man became a brilliant convert to the philosophy of co-operation and spent a lifetime at the work.

There were some rumblings within the CBC but I can't remember extreme witch-hunts or the noxious atmosphere created by the House Un-American Activities Committee.

I have often been asked how I managed to survive at the CBC. The answer lies in the fact that the creative forces in those days wielded power in the CBC, and they would go to bat when you were targeted by the right and the champions of the status quo. Reactionary forces, I found, were always a bit reluctant to take on creative people directly.

There was also an atmosphere of intellectual freedom in the CBC when A. Davidson Dunton was chairman. Everyone knew it and ultra-conservative executives were not inclined to tackle him. That was how producers such as Andrew Allan could create such lively and controversial drama on the *Stage* series.

I remember being in Andrew's office when Dunton called him to say he wondered how it was he hadn't been called on to defend the series for some time to answer politician's complaints. It was this attitude that nurtured intellectual freedom in the CBC and it survived for some time after Dunton left. It's what helped to make it a truly Golden Age for the corporation.

TAKEN OFF THE AIR

Susan Fletcher *is an actress and a writer-producer who has worked in Montreal, Vancouver, Los Angeles, and Toronto for the CBC. She currently resides in Toronto, where she coaches actors and business people in speech and performance.*

I had a radio program which ran in the 1940s on the Dominion radio network of the CBC. It was run by a former announcer who had risen to "great heights" to become head of the second network of CBC Radio. I had already been working in Vancouver and had a local program from CJOR with the awful title of "Flicks and Flash."

Then I asked the CBC in Toronto if they would like a Hollywood show on the network because, even in those days, there were a number of Canadians who were down in that part of the world. The show would be about Canadian music, art, artists, and actors. So they said, "Fine, go ahead."

I earned about thirty-five dollars a program, out of which I paid my own fares up and down to Los Angeles and paid for a lot of wax discs for a half-hour program, which I brought back with me and which was put on the air in CBC Vancouver and relayed to the rest of the Dominion network.

The people were very nice in Hollywood, although I was surprised that there were severe regulations about having "stars" appear on anything that had commercials. But as my program was non-commercial I was greeted as a representative of Canada and I got people like Bob Hope and Bing Crosby even though they couldn't appear on other programs in the States.

Once, Jane Wyman couldn't make it to the little studio where we did these recordings. When Jane couldn't come she said, "Well you must interview my husband who loves talking about things to do with economics and history, and he wants to be president of the Screen Actors Guild one day."

I asked, "Who is he and what pictures has he done?"

"His name is Ronald Reagan and he'll be there," said Ms. Wyman. So he showed up and we talked about politics and economics instead of *Bedtime for Bonzo* or whatever his current terrible picture was.

At this time in Hollywood there was the most ridiculous sense of terror around the studios and among the people I interviewed. Some of them had been friends of mine in my Broadway days when I was in the theatre. During a get together with actor-friends Arthur "Oakie" O'Connell, Fred Clark, and Henry Brandon, we realized how silly it was to have [Chairman of the House Un-American Activities Committee] J. Parnell Thomas still carrying on. I thought it would be fun to do a little spoof, so I wrote a tiny sketch for insert into the program about a cowboy and his agent and a very irate female journalist who could have been Hedda Hopper or Louella Parsons. They were having a big discussion about how wrong it was to have the cowboy ride off into a "red" sunset. We had a lot of fun with it and laughed a lot when we put it together.

The actors did it for nothing and got permission from the union to do it free for Canada. They felt that Parnell Thomas was out to lunch and the world was going crazy. The Un-American Activities Committee had divided people sharply. When I went to a cocktail party at Warner Brothers I noticed that there was a division because several people were under indictment then and some people didn't talk with other people.

Fred Clark, at the time, was finding it difficult to get jobs and because of their problems I thought it was a tremendous thing for them to come on and do this. And it was fun because they were all comedians and they loved to do something that was lively and a bit different. So we put on this fifteen-minute skit. When I performed the voice of the Hollywood lady it broke up Henry Brandon and we had to make another cut. Fred Clark, the great character actor, played the big "heavy" who was the head of the production studio. We finished it and we sent it up to Canada and it was broadcast.

Nobody said anything until I got a wire from the head of the CBC's Dominion network in Toronto which said, "There have been complaints about your work. Your show is cancelled."

I couldn't understand what this was about, so I wired back, "Cannot close show without difficulties for corporation because have booked Igor Stravinsky for next show."

An answer wire came back: "Who is Stravinsky? Come home. Show cancelled and end of this series." Maybe he thought Stravinsky was a dangerous Russian. I lost thirty-five dollars a week.

There was an organization in Hollywood that had written the CBC complaining about my show. Apparently, as a CBC broadcaster I was not supposed to have any opinions on my own show. Years later, Elwy Yost used to talk to me about "The Susan Fletcher Show," which he remembered listening to. So did other Canadians like Clyde Gilmour and Gerald Pratley.

The head of the network didn't support me, unlike Harry Boyle, a CBC executive producer, who was a maverick and who was truly involved with doing good radio. I worked with Harry Boyle on *Project* in '59, '60, and '61, and it was the greatest time of my life and when I was happiest. He cared about quality and didn't give one damn about anybody's politics. But the management were after him all the time in case he should put on something that was "offensive."

The CBC was then beginning to be polarized into the bureaucracy versus the creators. Boyle was a creative man who got people with ability together—even those who rubbed each other the wrong way because there were a lot of disagreements among his people, who I called "Boyle's Irregulars." The name stuck. Boyle made me a supervising producer and I asked, "What do you want me to do?" He said, "Just go ahead and do it. If it's wrong, I'll let you know immediately." I used to work forty-eight hours at a time when I was working with Harry and I would do it all over again.

A CHILD OF THE BLACKLIST

Trudy Ship is a film editor. Among her credits are the critically acclaimed movies House of Games *and* Things Change *(directed by David Mamet), and she was an assistant film editor on* Sleeper *(directed by Woody Allen). Currently, she's finishing off a film called* The Man in the Moon, *directed by Robert Mulligan and starring Sam Waterston. Her father was Montreal-born writer Reuben Ship, a comic genius within the Hollywood writing community who co-scripted the very popular radio*

series "The Life of Riley" for eight years. When the blacklist hit the enter-
tainment industry in Hollywood, Ship was called to testify in front of the
House Un-American Activities Committee and was deported to Canada
in September 1953. Back in Canada, Reuben Ship helped break the black-
list with his satirical radio play The Investigator, *which aired on CBC*
Radio. But CBC Television was cruel to Reuben Ship and his blacklist days
continued in Canada.

I certainly feel like a child of the blacklist and it sets me apart from almost everybody I know. It is something very few of my friends share with me. They can sympathize with me but it is hard for them to know what it felt like. But I'm very proud of it—for many years I wore it as a badge. I sort of dropped it now that I'm grown up but, in my twenties, I would always introduce myself as Trudy Ship, the daughter of Reuben Ship the blacklisted writer. I would sell myself through him and I was proud of him, but somehow Trudy got lost. Reuben Ship and his story was the star of the family and I used it.

Why was it painful for me? Hollywood, 1953, and I was nine years old when it happened. I had no idea what was going on. At the time, I was attending a progressive school called Westland in Los Angeles. It was one of the first progressive schools and all the left-wingers sent their kids there. In my class were Danny Kaye's daughter, Adrian Scott's child, Alvah Bessie's daughter Eva, Cy Endfield's children, and Jack Berry's kids. Name the Hollywood Ten and their children were there. We were all very close and I'm still in touch with many of those kids.

All of a sudden, I am listening to "Wild Bill Hickock" on the radio in my room and they interrupt the program to bring a special bulletin on the latest news from the hearings of the House on Un-American Activities Committee. They mentioned my father's name on the air. I didn't know what the word "contempt" meant, but that word was used. I just remember getting very excited and running downstairs. The only person home was our housekeeper, Helen.

I said, " Daddy's name is on the radio!"
She said, "That's nice."
Then there's a big jump cut in my memory to a time when the

house is filled with weeping friends. My mother's there and she's saying, "Who wants the couch? Who wants the books? Who wants the dogs, the fish?" She was giving away everything we owned. Then I have this memory of furniture disappearing and Daddy going away. What had happened was that he was being deported out of the US to Windsor, Ontario. We didn't know where he was being taken and were not told. We figured he'd probably go to Canada because it was the cheapest place for them to send him.

He was first sent to Detroit but there were problems for him there. He was on crutches when he was deported—he had osteomyelitis of the leg, which he had developed as a teenager in a hockey accident in school. In those days there was no penicillin and no cure. His leg was really a mess and it suffered infection from years and years of chronic illness. In fact, he told a story once of a cure which they tried. It was almost medieval. They put live maggots on the bone of his leg with the theory that the maggots would eat away the infected tissue. Well, needless to say, the maggots also ate away the good stuff. It was a real nightmare for him as a teenager because it cut down all his activities. As an adult he was always in pain and in and out of hospital after operations. The right kind of antibiotics eventually came along and he was cured, but when he left Hollywood he was draining and he was on crutches.

In Detroit he had another bout and he was on crutches and was handcuffed in this hospital, and he kept saying to this nurse, "You can uncuff me. I'm just being escorted out of the country." The nurse treated him like a crazy patient and said, "There, there, Mr. Ship."

Anyway, he finally ends up in Windsor and phones my mother and tells her that he's in Canada. She was also Canadian. The next day, she received a letter from the immigration authorities, asking her to come down for an interview. She wrote "FUCK YOU" on the letter, mailed it back, and we got out of the country. With us were my two baby sisters—I was nine and the girls, who were twins, were three.

So we joined my father in Montreal and immediately went to live in the Laurentian Mountains. I just remember not wanting to be there. I didn't even have a chance to say goodbye to my friends in Los Angeles. Although I do remember some teachers coming over to me in school and saying, "Tell your father we're very proud of him."

It all seemed to happen so suddenly and it was the most wrenching thing that had ever happened to me. Even the death of my parents, years later, was easier to live with than being pulled out of Los Angeles at that age and under those circumstances. I've never really recovered. Now that I can go back to L.A. whenever I want (and I do for business), I'm healing a lot of painful stuff for myself. I had a golden, sunshiny childhood, and suddenly I'm in Canada and it's snowing. I had never seen snow before. You can't imagine how exciting that is to a kid who grew up in California. To this day I skate and I do have Canada to thank for that.

My aunt owned a hotel in Ivry near Ste. Agathe and we were there a good six or seven months. I'm in a French-Canadian school and don't understand the language. I had been singing Russian revolutionary songs in the progressive school in L.A., making Chinese gongs, planting cactus, and making tortillas, and now I'm in this rigid French-Canadian school run by Catholics.

I had to wear a school uniform. My dogs and animals were gone, my friends were gone, and I didn't know what hit me. I think Father remained defiant and his attitude to the US authorities was "fuck 'em." I remember we left Ivry to go to Toronto and we lived in Willowdale when there was nothing but a few houses and dead-end streets—not even sidewalks yet. He wrote *The Investigator* and I remember we had the recording but I don't remember all the hoopla about it.

I liked the school in Toronto better and finally made some good friends and was beginning to feel a bit more comfortable. To this day I hate Montreal. I don't blame the city, but it just represents so much pain for me that I can't go there without having tremendous feelings of sadness. I thought if I kept going back I'd get rid of those cobwebs, but every time I return I start crying. I get off the airplane and I weep. Being there does that to me.

My father left my mother shortly after that. By the time I was twelve they were separated. Daddy went to England in 1955. He must have been lured there by other writers who said it was great. He knew Donald Ogden Stewart, the guy who wrote *The Philadelphia Story*, and

Ted Allan, whom he had known since childhood, who were both living in London. England was civilized and opened its arms to liberals.

My mother wanted to stay in Canada with me and the girls, but he convinced her to come over to England because it would be easier to give her alimony and child support if she and he were living in the same country. I also suspect that she thought there might be a reconciliation between them. They divorced anyway.

He remarried, a woman named Elaine Grand, who was well known as an interviewer on the CBC-TV show "Tabloid." My mother, the girls, and I lived in England all those years. And my father lived with Elaine and he continued writing situation comedies for British television. They were not great and I don't think his writing was ever that funny again.

My mother died in 1965. My sisters lived with Reuben and Elaine from the age of fourteen on and I returned to the United States in 1965 when I was twenty-two. But I didn't speak with an English accent because I wanted so much to stay in California right through our time in Canada and England that I fought to hold on to this little piece of America that I owned, and that was my accent. I thought, "They can't take that away from me." I kept it to be different.

THE REUBEN SHIP STORY IN CANADA

John Aylesworth has lived in Palm Springs, California, for six years, still writing and always "trying to get something going since the demise of variety" on TV. He was born in Toronto and worked on several of the early CBC-TV variety shows. He and partner Frank Peppiatt wrote many programs for CBC during the '50s, including "After Hours," "Cross Canada Hit Parade," and "Front Page Challenge." Peppiatt and Aylesworth moved to the States and created "Hee-Haw," a syndicated hit featuring Gordie Tapp and Don Harron. They also won an Emmy for "Frank Sinatra—A Man and His Music." During his early years at CBC-TV, a co-writer on a show called "On Stage" was Reuben Ship, who was blacklisted in the States and then on Canadian TV.

Frank Peppiatt and I started in CBC Television when a producer we knew told us the CBC was looking for comedians. He knew us from McLaren Advertising where we were working as copywriters, but our ambition was to be comedians. At that time, there weren't too many comedians in Canada: there was Alan Young, and then Bernie Braden did sort of a funny show after Alan left for the States. Wayne and Shuster became big on radio, but they didn't want to try television yet.

This producer we knew was stuck when he was told to do a comedy show. So he said, "Gee, I knew a couple of guys who were real funny around the office and at parties at the agency."

He called us and asked if we would like to do a show. Naturally we did, and there was an audition set for us at six in the morning on the following day. We stayed up all night and wrote some funny stuff. We got Jill Foster, an actress friend, to come in. She was going out with Bernie Slade whom she eventually married (and they're still living in L.A.). Anyway, Jill came in and at six a.m. we did a twenty-minute audition tape, a bunch of crazy stuff, and the following week we were on the air with an hour every week. That was in January in 1953 and continued right on to June.

The following year we got a bigger show. We went on to "The Big Review," where we were the featured comedians. We did sketches and production numbers there. That show continued for thirty-nine weeks. It was our third year when we got our own show, a half-hour show called "On Stage," produced and directed by Norman Jewison.

Now not only were there no comedians in Canada but, outside of Wayne and Shuster and us, there were also no comedy writers. So we had to do all that ourselves and we were going nuts. We were writing all night, rehearsing all day, and taping the shows. It was just crazy but we couldn't find any help.

Finally, we heard that Reuben Ship had returned to Canada. We thought, "Wow! A real comedy writer." He had written some of the top shows south of the border like "Life of Riley" and "The Gleason Show," and was a top-notch radio and TV comedy writer. It was a sad time for him because he was thrown out of the States and named as a Communist. He was a very literate man and a very funny writer. He was worth his weight in gold for us.

But there were problems over credits on the show. We were told that the "Kremlin," which housed the offices of CBC managers in Toronto, felt that Reuben shouldn't get a credit. Nobody knew who was behind it. The powers that be, so-called. He was disappointed about it but, Christ, he had to make a living. We were just so bloody glad to have help that we grabbed him.

I don't know what they were paying him, but it was great and we had a wonderful year. He was liberal but he certainly wasn't a Communist. Our office was in an apartment away from the CBC and that's where we created the script. Then we would take it in and go through it with Norman. It was a quiet blacklist—nobody really knew who was behind it.

THE BLACKLISTING OF NATHAN COHEN

Cliff Solway is a former CBC-TV producer. He is a dynamic whirlwind of a man who guided, directed, and produced the popular "Fighting Words," a program hosted by Nathan Cohen, a respected arts critic. During the run of the show, Nathan Cohen believed he was being forced off the air because he had once been involved in the Communist Party. Solway, who was a friend as well as the producer, helped break the blacklist against Cohen.

I was one of the first wave of producers in television in this country. My first job in the public affairs department of the CBC was to produce a daily show from the United Nations. Nobody watched it, including my mother. I came back to Toronto and the chief producer, Mavor Moore, asked me to take over a show which had just started, called "Fighting Words." The format was his and the idea was his. Some of the trimming came from Harvey Hart who was the first producer, but they both had things to do and they asked me to take it over.

In 1955 I came back from the United Nations in New York and took over "Fighting Words" from Harvey Hart. I led, directed, and produced it for the rest of its life in the '50s. Nathan Cohen was the moderator and things were going well. There was no suggestion of a problem of any kind. Nathan Cohen was an emotional intellectual, a contradiction in terms, who bathed and drenched himself in his emotions and displayed them willingly. When you got to know him you got hooked on him, like opium. Just like the public did. He was direct and frank.

The CBC bosses all loved "Fighting Words." It had pretty fair ratings, although it was hard to tell in those days because there were so few television sets. The network consisted of three cities: Ottawa, Montreal, and Toronto. There was no national network yet, but the people who saw it loved it. As prizes we gave away encyclopedias to people who sent in quotations whose source was to be guessed. We were bombarded by letters.

Then it all seemed to creep up on us. Nathan himself said he would be pulled off the air. I said to him that it was more rumour than fact, but he insisted that he had good reliable information and wasn't just being paranoid. He feared something was going on, but the problem was we couldn't put our finger on it. Who was the source of it? None of our superiors at the CBC admitted to anything even remotely suggesting blacklisting. It came right out of the blue. But Nathan felt it, so he did a very smart thing: he went to a very bright lawyer who happened to be a frequent guest on "Fighting Words." A nice guy, his name was Ted Jolliffe and he was one of the early heads of the CCF in Ontario. Jolliffe was a good man and an interested man, who would take up the cudgels on behalf of another person. Nathan went to him and it took God knows how long to find out but, indeed, Nathan was being blacklisted.

Nathan once had a link to the Communist Party and had written for them and, I think, worked for the party for a very short period. He had long since given up ties with the party.

As a result, Nathan was afraid, scared stiff of crossing the border. Some of our plans, which included producing "Fighting Words" out of New York, had to be deferred and even cancelled. It was almost like recently, when Farley Mowat wasn't allowed to enter the States where his books sell very widely. It was revealed that Mowat was on a blacklist of people who could not, or should not, be accepted at entry into the United States. Nathan was on the same list. A secret list.

Nathan was offered jobs in New York that he couldn't be sure if he could accept. And he had shows to do for me in New York, specials with people like Norman Mailer and the English theatre critic Kenneth Tynan. We had these hour-long specials arranged and we had to postpone them because he couldn't get across the border. It was all heightened by the recent binge of McCarthyism, which was still a news item then. It was not many years since Senator Joe McCarthy had gone after Communists in the State Department. But, apparently, Ted Jolliffe pursued the American government long enough and with enough pressure to have them remove Nathan's name from the list.

Nathan's career in Canada was also affected by the limitations of his activities in the States. What happened in Canada was a rebound of what was happening in the United States. The election of Diefenbaker in the Conservative landslide of the '50s gave confidence to the people who ran the security services to interfere with the CBC and other Crown corporations.

So Nathan was asked to leave "Fighting Words" by a CBC manager who said, "It's been decided that we would have guest moderators." Nathan asked why and the answer was that they wanted to "spread the job" and make the position available to other talented people who could act as moderator. A list of these guest moderators was drawn up accordingly.

I was shocked. Nathan was stunned. Don't forget, Nathan didn't have any other position besides "Fighting Words," which wasn't paying very much. It was income he sorely needed. He had children, two charming little girls who were going to school. Nathan's income was hammered.

FIGHTING BACK

I decided to act, so I started a letter campaign. I had a million addresses from people who had written to the show with their quotes looking to win sets of the *Encyclopaedia Britannica*. I compiled these and sent out a letter to the public that Nathan was being taken off the show and we weren't sure why. I made no imputation of any kind but just said that. And the viewers inundated the network, by phone and by letter. I was elated. Nathan was bucked up and the people who were putting pressure on the CBC to remove him must have been stunned and surprised. Their target was Nathan and they didn't think he had such a following. It would be something like taking Peter Gzowski off the air today.

This campaign took six months. I also did something else. I sabotaged the other guys who were guest hosts. I misdirected them intentionally and gave them no cues. I did everything I could to louse up their act. But it took about six months to bring Nathan back. To use a cliché, cooler heads prevailed. Or should I say "larger heads" prevailed. People who were close to him at the CBC, like Sydney Newman, went to bat for him.

FIGHTING WITH WORDS

*On the walls of **Gloria Cohen's** mid-Toronto home are photographs and memorabilia about her late husband, Nathan Cohen, a respected critic and television personality who was blacklisted at the CBC.*

My mother resides in a home for the elderly and I met a man who lives there who had a career as a lawyer and is now eighty-five years old. Once, he and I were chatting about many things and he talked about his life. Then he asked me about my husband. During the course of our conversation I mentioned that my husband, Nat, had been blacklisted by the CBC. This man said, "Oh, that's impossible. This is Canada and it doesn't happen here." I assured him it did. This man, who had been a lawyer, was absolutely shocked.

Nat had been a member of the Communist Party, which was always a source of tension for him at the CBC. It was never overt, but was always very, very subtle until Nat was blacklisted. We heard about [the blacklisting] when one of the regular panel members on "Fighting Words" phoned Nathan. This panel member told Nathan that he had been invited to chair "Fighting Words."

Nathan hadn't known anything about it and was very shocked. He phoned around to various people and discovered it was true and his contract would likely not be renewed. The atmosphere was very cool and the excuse given to him was that he'd had a long shot at hosting and it was time for someone else to have a shot. You know, the old excuse.

Cliff Solway, the producer-director of "Fighting Words," also phoned around. And Cliff talked to a critic at the *Toronto Telegram* who had appeared fairly regularly on "Fighting Words" and very much a supporter of the show—not because he was on it that often but because he really seemed to like it. Cliff found other people who were supporters of the program and sent out a whole series of letters asking these people to support Nathan.

But, in the meantime, Nat did lose his job and he couldn't find any work anywhere in Canada. Of course, Nat had been working on a yearly or monthly contract and had never been given a staff job on the CBC. He tried many, many places, but there were doors slammed in his face and he didn't know why. He assumed it was due to his membership in the Communist Party.

He had once been a young and rising theoretician and a writer who had written many articles for [the Canadian Jewish weekly] the *Vochenblatt*. He had worked for the *Glace Bay Gazette*, which was a left-leaning paper in Cape Breton, a union paper. I later met some of the people who had worked with him on the *Glace Bay Gazette* and considered him the best editor they had ever had. I'm sure that reputation followed him across Canada.

I later discovered from a neighbour that there had been an RCMP investigation going on. It was probably related to the fact that Nat had been a member of the Communist Party and that some of the shows he worked on had been very close to the kind of thing which was considered treasonous. Like a show he did with Gordon Sinclair, which discussed the pros and cons of substituting a Canadian-designed flag for the Union Jack, for instance, or the show about Pierre Trudeau and René Lévesque.

My neighbours were very nice people and, believe me, not socialists in any way. One of my neighbours, whose husband was an architect, was the first to tell me about people who came to interview her.

She and I assumed they were RCMP. Nobody showed up in a uniform but you could tell from the questions. We lived in a very short block and there were just three houses on the block. The neighbour on the other side was a gambler, and his wife also came over and told me the same thing. That was very sweet, since these people had no reason to tell me anything at all. It sort of renewed your faith in people because those I had depended upon didn't write or call or anything.

There was never an official blacklist but there were people who had to go overseas to work: Reuben Ship went overseas, Ted Allan went overseas, Syd Gordon was already in London at the time. There were many, many people who had to find jobs elsewhere. I gave Nathan all the money we had saved for him to go to London. It was obvious that he wasn't going to get a job here, so we took whatever money we had saved and I gave it to Nat and he went to London to look for openings there.

Meanwhile, Cliff was working very hard here to get Nathan reinstated on "Fighting Words." In London Nat lived with actor Lou Jacobi and stayed there six months. I was left here with my children and was living with my mother and dad and that sort of cocooned me from what I considered this "catastrophe." I have Nathan's letters from England downstairs and I've always felt it too painful to read them through again.

My parents, and especially my mother, were very supportive at the time. My mother was supportive because her mother had once been a member of a Communist cell in Russia. In fact, it was from her place that the printing of various pamphlets and papers was done. My mother remembered this because when she was a young girl, around eight years old, her family had been raided by the Cossacks and she was the one selected by my grandmother to take out the printing press and hide it. She hid it in the farm animal manure so that the Cossacks wouldn't go looking for it. So she had had experience with this type of thing before and never said a word about my husband's problems.

I wasn't able to get work either. Nat and I used to run a little magazine called *The Critic*. I had been a writer-editor for a couple of small magazines, *Magazine Digest* and *Canadian Woman*. I wrote

some lousy articles and was general factotum for the whole operation—you know, chief cook and bottle washer. I was, quite literally, a
bottle washer because the woman I worked for had several children.
I did some babysitting too. But now I found it difficult to get work. I
had the children and I didn't have enough money to pay for nursery
school or to hire anybody to look after them since my mother and
father were working in their store. Nobody from the CBC called,
except for Cliff Solway. I didn't hear anything from anybody. It was
almost like living in a totally sealed-off room.

Nat came back to Canada when Cliff's campaign worked. Cliff
wrote to tell Nat that he was reinstated. I felt immense relief and
thought, "Well, at least it's over." But although he got his job back,
he never really felt secure. It wasn't until 1959 that he was offered a
position as a critic for the *Toronto Daily Star*.

I didn't realize that for years after that the matter would come up
again and again in relationship to Nat's working elsewhere, particularly with his work in the United States. We even had to get clearance
for Nat to go across the border. He could've gone across quietly and
nobody would have said anything, but Nat wanted to be sure that
everything was above-board. So he got a lawyer, Ted Jolliffe, to see
what his status was in the States. It took years before Nat was cleared
and could go across the border freely. He didn't want to get jobs
there—he just wanted to see plays, that's all. It took maybe four years
or longer before he could get permission to see plays in New York.

Once, we were told that Nat was on a short list of five or six people
who were being considered for the position of drama critic for the
New York Times. Brooks Atkinson was leaving. Nat had been invited
several times to write articles for the paper and then we were told he
was on the short list for drama critic. Nat came home all excited
when he heard and he felt honoured. It was more than a rumour
because he got the information from a good source, but then he was
told that he wasn't selected and that it was because of his background
as a member of the Communist Party.

In the States they were really frightened. People were getting
blacklisted all over the place, like the Hollywood Ten and Dalton
Trumbo. It really did hurt Nat at the time. This took an awful lot

out of him and he died very young. He was devastated by a lot of what happened.

[Nathan Cohen died in Toronto on March 26, 1971.]

LOYALTY CHECKS

Frank Peers *was a former CBC manager in Toronto. He joined the CBC in 1947 as a producer and became supervisor of a department called Talks and Public Affairs. Peers fought ardently to keep freedom of thought and diversity of opinion alive on CBC broadcasts.*

The first time I can remember being aware that the CBC was concerned about the political affiliation of its employees, and political stands of its writers and speakers, was a year or two after I joined the corporation. The CBC management asked its staff to fill out employment records as part of the federal government's security clearances and checks on government and Crown corporation employees. This loyalty check included details about age, employment background, education, and so on. On the surface, these seemed to be routine personnel forms. Of course, we knew these forms were related to security. There were two questions on the form that I refused to answer because I thought it was none of my employer's business. One of the questions asked for a list of all my immediate relatives. In my case, that meant five brothers, one sister, and a father and mother who were all living in Alberta. The second question had to do with what associations I had belonged to and to which I continued to belong. I thought these questions smacked of guilt by association. My understanding was that our performance would be judged by the programs we produced. The essential thing was the program we put on the air. I refused to fill out the information requested in these two questions, as did some others. I sent along a written response about why I refused to answer those questions.

The result was that I was called down to the office of the personnel department. Not only was I quizzed by the head of the local personnel office, but also by the person in charge of that department at the head office in Ottawa, Colonel R.P. Landry. He took a rather belligerent attitude towards me and cast doubts on my loyalty to the CBC and so forth. I rebutted these heatedly since I was unwilling to accept any slurs or innuendoes about my loyalty to the corporation. Others in my department were interrogated as well. One of the concerns expressed to me was whether I, as assistant supervisor, was leading a kind of concerted protest roused against CBC management. With a written explanation of my stand, the matter seemed to drop. We assumed that copies of the forms were sent to the RCMP and used in the file they kept on people at the CBC.

Let's look at the circumstances of the time. This was three or four years after the war. Canada and other Allies were joined with the USSR in the wartime effort. During that time, a lot of people were caught up with the emotion of the period and became fervent supporters of the Soviet Union in its brave defence of its homeland. Some of them headed organizations like the Canada-Soviet Friendship Association. Very respected leaders were recruited in this effort. Many people who tended to be leftists in their political opinions joined such associations. There was a certain amount of sympathy for the Soviet Union and its suffering. Undoubtedly, among the intellectuals of the period, there was some compassion for that country and its political isolation. There was a greatly justified feeling that the leadership of the western Allies—in particular, Britain and France—acted pretty shamefully in the way they did not stand up to Hitler in time. The CBC wanted to find out how far the sympathies of their employees went towards the Soviet Union—I suppose they had security concerns about transmitters and those kinds of things. In 1948 the Stalin period was in full swing and, as he became more paranoid, Stalin moved against the democratic leaders of Czechoslovakia and flexed his muscles against Eastern Europe. More and more, the Soviet Union came to be regarded as a threat in the West. This was also around the time of Churchill's famous "Iron Curtain" speech at Fulton, Missouri.

The next incident happened a year or so after the loyalty check. An instruction came down to our department. It was transmitted through the department supervisor, Neil Morrison. He told us he had been instructed by the chairman of the CBC to ensure that Communist speakers were not employed or presented on the air unless there were special reasons, in which case it would involve getting permission from the hierarchy at the CBC. Morrison had told us he fought against this instruction but had been unsuccessful in changing the mind of the chairman of the CBC, A.D. Dunton. Within the department, we took the stand that we were quite prepared to be judged about the kind of balance and variety of expression on controversial issues that we presented on the air, but many subjects might require representatives from different parts of the political spectrum. Some broadcasts on international affairs had to reflect the realities of the world. We would be inhibited if there were such an ironclad rule that no person with a Communist background, or even someone with a Marxist perspective, could be heard on broadcasts we produced.

Several of us drew up a memo of two or three pages asking for a review of this position. We used the argument that if such a directive were implemented all sorts of people who favoured free speech would come down on the CBC like a ton of bricks. We mentioned certain newspapers, journals like *Saturday Night*, and associations such as Adult Education and others, who would have no sympathy with this directive. They would regard it as a serious restriction on the part of the corporation. We did not send our memo through the supervisor of our department because we did not want to make it seem as if he had rallied support for himself against the instructions of management. Instead, we forwarded it directly to the chairman and about ten of us signed individually. The memorandum went to Mr. Dunton, who was, I think, a person of liberal sentiments and opinions. After some time, the word came back that he was withdrawing the instruction to the department but expected us to be careful. In other words, caution was impressed upon us as a necessity of the times.

THE MACKENZIE KING INCIDENT

There was a book about Mackenzie King written by two Canadians living in London: H.S. (Harry) Ferns and Bernard Ostry. Ferns had been a member of Prime Minister Mackenzie King's staff in Ottawa. He didn't have great respect for King as a person or as politician because he felt King refused to take strong stands on international issues. Ferns had been a Marxist during his youth and was thought to be a Marxist throughout the time he was on King's staff. Bernard Ostry was a younger man who had gone from the University of Manitoba to the London School of Economics (LSE). Ferns had an academic appointment with a university outside London and Ostry was a graduate student at the LSE. The two of them joined forces to examine Mackenzie King's early career and their book was published about five or six years after King's death. Also at this time, an official biography was being prepared in Ottawa by a group headed by MacGregor Dawson.

Ferns and Ostry published their book in London and its sale in Canada was to follow a few weeks later. The CBC representative in London at the time, Bernard Trotter, was made aware of the King book and that it was likely to create a certain amount of controversy. He knew it was a new appraisal of King's career by two writers who were not enthralled by his leadership before and during the war. He alerted us, and we thought it was a sufficiently important event in Canadian political life that some attention should be given to the book on radio and television in this country. We wanted a debate of the propositions of the book by knowledgeable people in Canada. There was to be a half-hour discussion on radio and some on TV. We began investigating the best possible speakers for each program but we found a roadblock. People were not interested in giving their opinions on this book.

The next thing we knew was that an enquiry came from the office of the chairman, A.D. Dunton, instructing us to put our plans on hold while this matter was reviewed. I quickly got a copy of the book and read it during the weekend. By this time, I was supervisor of the department and it was my responsibility to explain our actions and defend our plans for broadcasts. Thus, I wrote a memo in which I explained that this book was a fresh examination of the career of an important Canadian prime minister and our intention was to find people of different positions to discuss the arguments put forth in the book. Therefore, we felt we were quite justified in mounting a program about this subject on radio and television. But my arguments were rejected even though I put them as forcibly as I could. We were instructed to cut down the exposure given to this publication. We were to cancel the plans for television and restrict our coverage on radio to what we would normally give to books. A review was broadcast, but we could not have the more elaborate discussion of the book which we had intended.

Later, I was able to go through some of the archives in Ottawa and found that among those who objected to the book was Brooke Claxton, who had been in the government and was a kind of protégé of Mackenzie King's. Claxton had been minister of health and welfare and also minister of national defence. By the time of our broadcast, around 1956, Claxton had left government and had become a chairman or president of the Metropolitan Life Assurance Company in Ottawa. Claxton had written to one of his colleagues that he had objected to Davidson Dunton about the attention given a book by two people who had no reputation as scholars, and one of whom was known to be a Communist or fellow traveller.

THE OUTSIDE FORCES

During this time, we were aware that material was being circulated which criticized speakers and writers on the CBC who were thought to be Communists, fellow travellers, and left-wingers. The organization that probably had the most influence in this respect was the public relations firm Johnson, Everson, and Charlesworth in Toronto. They monitored CBC broadcasts to see whether they could detect the expression of left-wing opinions and they would issue periodic reports, which would go to people in the business community. Members of Parliament would, on occasion, ask for certain broadcasts and we could tell by the nature of the questions put in Parliament, and the content of some speeches, that these MPs were relying on information provided by this PR firm.

A publication called *The Ensign*, which was under the editorship of Robert Keyserlingk of Montreal, also tried to detect evidence of left-wing opinion, if not treason. It was a Catholic weekly that was stirred by any unorthodox opinions. *The Ensign* helped to increase the volume of criticism against the CBC in Parliament. That bothered us because the chairman of the CBC was frequently given a hard time when he appeared in front of a parliamentary committee. Members of Parliament such as Donald Fleming from Toronto, or E.G. Hansell, a Social Credit member from Alberta, or Solon Low, the leader of the Social Credit Party, and a number of others, went after the CBC and our chairman because of certain points of view which were represented in broadcasts. They particularly attacked our foreign correspondents, such as Matthew Halton and Doug Lachance, who they thought were pretty far to the left and in danger of being fellow travellers.

There was also a less reputable publication that went after many of our programs. Printed in Flesherton, Ontario, by a renegade Social Crediter, this publication was really a mimeographed sheet that went to a small subscription list. They saw Communists in every wood pile. The importance of this sheet was that certain MPs, such as John Blackmore who had once been the leader of the Social Credit group in Ottawa, fed on this kind of material. Incidentally, Blackmore became discredited in later years because he was so obviously anti-Semitic.

Overall, at the CBC we did not have the purges they had at the National Film Board. I think that was due to the spirit of some CBC employees and to a very skilful defence of the CBC by A.D. Dunton, who, in the main, was a defender of freedom of speech and not a person who wanted to restrict it.

THE RCMP CLEARS A PRODUCER

"Morris Mann" was a producer-director with CBC Television during the '50s. He had a fine career in TV drama. Recently retired from a teaching position, he is also an accomplished writer and painter. Morris Mann is not his real name.

I didn't go through any security check when I was hired by the CBC.

I was hired with the belief that I would become a director and producer within six months' time. After six months, nothing had happened. I was still a floor director. I was anxious about what was going to happen with me in the future, so I waited a respectable amount of time and then I made some enquiries. At first I thought that there wasn't an opening yet, but about nine months after I'd started to work I had to follow it through.

Somebody suggested, "Why don't you talk with Fergus Mutrie about this? Maybe he knows why you're not being made director or producer." Mutrie was the director of the English television network for Ontario at that time. I made an appointment and went up to see him. He was a very nice man, very good-looking, and he liked to sing. He was interested in opera and music. When I talked to him he seemed to like me and I liked him.

I said, "Someone suggested I come and talk to you about why I'm not being made a producer or director."

"Oh yes, Morris. Won't you sit down?" he said.

About an hour later I got the idea, through his hemming and hawing and other obtuse remarks, that maybe I was a security risk. So I asked why.

"Well, we seem to have some information," he answered, and so on.

I was absolutely astounded. In other words, they had a record of me with the RCMP. All this came out in my talk with Mutrie.

My father was a socialist and my mother was kind of an emotional communist. She never belonged to the party but my father belonged to the Socialist Party. They both subscribed to the left-wing newspapers: my mother to the Communist newspapers and my father to the Socialist newspapers. I myself subscribed to the *Daily Worker* and I had been a member of a Communist group, a cell, as they called them then, which had been organized at the time for the Spanish Civil War.

I had joined it as an act of rebellion against my father who belonged to the CCF, which, as you know, is the NDP now. I was very rebellious at that time—I was eighteen or nineteen—against my father, more so than against society. So I decided to join the Communists and I suppose, emotionally, I was aligning myself with my mother as opposed to my father. It's kind of a rotten pattern that I've finally overcome and that I now see in my boys, for instance.

So it was on the basis of the newspapers that we subscribed to and the organizations that my father and mother belonged to [that I was declared a security risk]. They belonged to the Workmen's Circle organization, which was a conglomerate of people who came from Europe, and they sort of banded together because they came from certain towns. They knew each other and they formed brotherhoods and they all had kind of a socialistic leaning. Actually, in the Workmen's Circle, I think that the majority of the members were really emotional capitalists and I don't think they were really strong for socialism or communism. But the government seemed to think they were, and I guess because of the fact they were Jewish or ethnic, as they say these days, they were suspect. The government at that time was very Anglo-Saxon, very Waspish, very restrictive and Victorian really, and it wasn't until television began to proliferate that a lot of that broke down.

I joined the party in 1940 and I was a member for six months. There was an election going on in Toronto and they wanted to have a liaison between the Socialist parties and the Communist parties and the Trotskyite parties and the people who were running for office. We were indoctrinated at those meetings as to how to go about canvassing, what to say to people when we knocked on doors, and how to tell them we wanted them to vote our way. [The meeting organizers] would give us questions and, willy-nilly, different people would stand up to give the proper answer for that particular question. I remember that all we had to do is say that the Communists are right, the CCF are wishy-washy, and the Trotskyites are way off track. So you had to vote the Communist way. I thought it was so patently stupid and I spoke up a number of times and said, "Who's going to believe this bullshit? Who's going to believe it?" They didn't like me very much because I was not saying the right things.

Six months of this and I was so fed up with their approach that I wrote a letter of resignation. The letter was in the form of a poem. I'm certainly not a party member. If anything, it rails against my whole nature to be a member of any group. So I wrote this frivolous verse. I forget how it went now, but it was obviously a piece of froth which said that I resigned and it was all in metre and rhyme.

So I resigned from the Communist Party. I had a card—I was a card-carrying member—but I tore it up. The whole thing lasted six months. Then, I think, I joined the Socialist Party of the time, the CCF, and there was a youth branch that was being formed at the Workmen's Circle. This is all in 1940-41. I joined them and stayed with them for only three months. I couldn't stand them. I said, "You're as bad as the Communists. I don't need either of you." That was the extent of my left-wing affiliation. But, apparently, it was enough for the RCMP to have a record of me.

So the RCMP had begun an investigation. What did you do then? How did you eventually become a TV director?

What happened was I asked, "Well, how can I become a director if you've got this against me?"

The manager at CBC Television said, "The only thing I can suggest, Morris, is that you go to the RCMP and make a clean breast of it. They have you on record. If you went down and talked to them and convinced them that you're no longer a Communist, or that you don't have that kind of affiliation, they will exonerate you. And if they do, we will."

I called, and made my way down to the RCMP. I said, "I'm working at the CBC and I understand you've got something on record about me? It's keeping me from becoming a producer and director and I'd like to know what I can do about this." So they got the files and we sat down and we talked. They wanted to know what I had done, why I had done it, and all the rest of it. I was there about three or four hours, interrogated by two different Mounties.

"Well now, you subscribe to the *Daily Worker*, don't you?" I was asked.

And I said, "I don't subscribe anymore."

They countered with, "But you did between the years of so-and-so and so-and-so when you were living at such-and-such an address." They had information like that.

"Your father subscribes to the *Forward*. What is that?"

"It's a Jewish newspaper from New York and they like the romances," I answered.

Anyway, through the course of the questioning, I found out all the things I mentioned earlier were already on the record. The organizations I belonged to, the subscriptions we had, all of it was on the record. They asked me a number of questions about why I'd gotten involved, but it was quite loose and easy. I think I quoted Bernard Shaw and said something about, "Any man who is not a socialist at a young age is an idiot and any man who is a socialist at the age of forty is a fool." Something like that.

Then I said that I'd been going through a period of rebellion in my life and that it was natural, that I was intelligent and anybody with any intelligence had those feelings. We had just come through the Depression, and justice and equality for people were burning issues in everybody's mind.

I guess through it all they got the feeling I wasn't really a dangerous Communist anymore. They must have written a favourable report because shortly thereafter I became a producer at the CBC.

I suppose the blackballing that went on here is a pale reflection of what went on in the States. Here it went on quietly, *sub rosa*, behind the scenes. It was as though we were above those silly ass Americans: we don't do things that way.

I would add that the story lies more in Canada than in McCarthy. I think that our hypocrisy here is probably the most outstanding feature of our culture. It's all under the surface here. There is the same undercurrent of anti-communism, anti-liberalism, anti–ethnic groups in Canada. I think, you know, we tolerate them. To tolerate means to put up with. It also means to sort of live with, to sort of understand and go along with. But what it really means in Canada is: let's not make a fuss about it. And I think that's our kind of tolerance here.

EARLY TELEVISION

Bob Mutrie *was a student at Queen's University during the height of*

McCarthyism. Today, he's an architect and a partner in a firm in down-
town Toronto, and has also worked in organizing political campaigns for
the former mayor of Toronto, John Sewell. His father, Fergus Mutrie,
was head of CBC Television during the early '50s.

My father had been hired by the CBC in 1940 as the farm commentator in Vancouver. The family had had a ranch in the Okanagan
since 1908, but with the war the apple business went down the spout
and we yanked out all the old orchards. So my father decided on this
adventure with the CBC. He went to Toronto in '44. By 1948 about
six CBC people started studying television. They went off to
London, Paris, and New York, which I guess were the only centres
which were broadcasting TV at that time. Al Ouimet was leading the
group, and TV was new and exciting.

I remember watching my first television broadcast in Ernie Bushnell's living-room. We watched a little eight-inch-diameter GE set. I
was sure impressed as we watched Ed Sullivan's "Toast of the Town."
But these six people only had about three years to get the whole damn
network on the air in Canada. There were all sorts of people who
were interested in this new medium, so they didn't have any trouble
attracting people to hire. The TV station went on the air in 1952.

There was this new thing in our culture called "espionage." Nobody
had thought in these terms in this country because North Americans
thought they were immune to espionage. It was foreign somehow.
Canadians didn't even give it a thought until Gouzenko and the
Rosenbergs. Then the authorities became concerned about the power
of mass communications like television and the movies. Police always
seem to have the view that they have to protect us from ourselves.
Only *they* are aware of the gritty underbelly of society and the rest of us
are wet behind the ears and wouldn't know when to come in out of the
rain. So they have to protect us and they probably looked at the CBC.

Did the RCMP visit your father at the CBC?

I seem to recall it happened frequently. The one that I remember,
because it was such a shock to my father, had to do with Stu Griffiths.

It was the early days of television. He had a visit from this man who identified himself as an RCMP officer and who beat around the bush a bit. He finally said television was very important and they were obviously concerned about it. He said it might be better if Stu Griffiths didn't work there. I don't know exactly what happened, but I do know Griffiths stayed.

I think this incident caused my father to do a lot of soul searching. I mean, how could this happen? Our society thought those sorts of things didn't happen to people. Canada was a pretty naïve country before the war. Having even the necessity for political police was anathema to Canadians as a whole, particularly my father, and to see the silly grounds on which judgements were applied to people really bothered him.

My father was wrestling with a whole bunch of new experiences—after all, he was a farm boy. Now there were all these pressures, like the pressure of the press. The newspapers were worried about the power of television to attract advertising revenue. I can remember when a reporter from a large city newspaper came down to the CBC to do a story and he was squired around by the PR man. He got the tour of the studios and saw everything. At that end of the week, when he was about to head back to his city, they were having a drink at the airport. Then this reporter told the CBC man, "You've been very open and honest with me. You've really shown me everything, but I have to tell you that I have to go back and write a whole series of articles that are anti-CBC. On a personal basis I have to apologize, but my newspaper has a policy now that three times a week there's going to be something anti-CBC in the newspaper. It may be an editorial cartoon, a front-page story, an editorial, or whatever. There will be something to discredit the CBC."

There were other pressures, like dealing with the burgeoning staff. During the time my father was there they went from a staff of one (him) to over a thousand, if you include performers. There were only two stations back then.

When I look back at the period now, I think what a conservative, stodgy time it was. We sort of ended up after the war with everybody feeling that they had won the opportunity to build a new world. Very quickly, selfish motives took over. People had been through the Depression, then the war, and they figured that we would build this new world. But they quickly went from altruistic motives to their personal needs. People came back from the war, which had put their personal lives on hold, and they came home, got married, had kids. That nest building resulted in conservatism.

LENIN AND THE QUEBEC SEPARATISTS

Noel Moore is an award-winning writer and director of television documentaries. He lives in Greenbush, Ontario, which is located midway between Ottawa and Kingston. He calls his converted Victorian farmhouse "an electronic cottage." His current project is working in the computer-related interactive network field. The long arm of the anti-Communist fearmongers extended to 1971 when a film he wrote and directed for CBC Television was suddenly taken off the air.

Bill Harcourt, who was in charge of a CBC network public affairs program called "Tuesday Night" which was very popular at the time, approached me and asked me if I'd do an hour-long film to mark the 100th anniversary of Lenin's birth. It so happened that Prime Minister Pierre Elliott Trudeau was scheduled to go to the Soviet Union, so I guessed that it might be a topical item. But I was bored to tears with the Russian thing, having earlier done a series called *Revolution Plus 50*. Moses Znaimer had acted as the producer and it had been very well received by everybody, including the Russians. Nathan Cohen wrote that it was the first time television had ever demonstrated its true capability or something like that. Anyway, Bill approached me to do this film on Lenin and I said, "I'm bored to tears with it."

I forgot about it and went off on a holiday in Ireland. When I came back he rang me up and said the program was scheduled for October. Gordon Donaldson was to be the producer; they had already made it public. I was a freelancer and did it to keep my credibility high and to keep from letting Harcourt down. That's how I got into it. Then I thought, "What the hell can I say about Lenin that's interesting and new?" I racked my brains about it. I didn't want to do a pro-Lenin documentary which would get me labelled a Communist, and I didn't want it to be an anti-Lenin film which would get me labelled a Fascist. So I had to tread that medium ground between the two extremes and try and report about a unique individual and a very dramatic event.

From documentation supplied by Novosti press agency, I learned that the only publication that Lenin took on all his journeys while in exile was not *Das Kapital* by Karl Marx, but Goethe's *Faust*. He read it every night. So I decided to read Goethe's *Faust*, and while reading it I began to realize that the entire plot for the revolution had been written by Goethe for the stage manager character. He said, "Give them a theatrical event, have lots of noise and excitement." He was talking about how to take over and create an historical drama spectacle, a costume epic as Hollywood calls it. Revolution as a theatrical art form.

My wife, Bernice, said, "That's the way to do it." So I wrote it from that position and the more I interpreted it from that perspective the more sense it made. Everything Lenin did had been a calculated theatrical event, including the critique of the tzar's court. Lenin was the writer and producer, Trotsky was the stage manager. Then I showed how Sergei Eisenstein, the Russian film director, had created the cinematic or media version of the Russian Revolution, which was accepted around the world. He directed films such as *October* [*Ten Days that Shook the World*], in which you saw the Red Guards storming the winter palace and being mowed down by the tzarist imperial troops and finally climbing the gates and hoisting the flag of revolution. It was very exciting stuff, great footage!

I'd always accepted this as the real version of the Russian Revolution until I read the actual figures which came out of Moscow. During the battle for the winter palace, six Red Guards were killed. Only six. More people have been killed in a bus crash. Yet Eisenstein made it look like it was one of the great battles and turning-points of history. I began to realize that, while it was presented as documentary fact by Eisenstein and the Soviets, it was, in actual fact, total bullshit! As a documentary film-maker and journalist, I was outraged.

I was living on a farm outside Ottawa and had to come up to Toronto where the film was produced. It was to be an hour-long documentary and Gordon Donaldson was the producer. At the time the film was produced, there was a major student movement going on in Germany and in Paris. Do you remember Red Rudi, one of the leaders? The people in the movement called themselves the "Situationist International" and they said you have to create a counter-spectacle to overthrow the state. As a matter of fact, there was a Jean-Luc Godard film at the time called *La Chinoise* about these students in Paris who wanted to burn the university. Godard's film showed that they saw life and reality as an ongoing film drama. This was the first generation that had grown up with television and film. Their whole idea of politics had been transformed: they saw the political process as theatrical or dramatic spectacle.

I had directed two ninety-minute films previously for Cameron Graham of the CBC. One was *Hail and Farewell*, on Diefenbaker and the emergence of Stanfield in the 1967 convention. The next year I did *The Style Is the Man Himself* about the emergence of Pierre Elliott Trudeau. And that too was all pure theatre! It started with Dalton Camp at the Conservative convention when they tried to get rid of old John Diefenbaker. In order to do this, they created a palace revolt and made it happen on television. In actual fact, the caucus did not have the authority to remove John Diefenbaker.

Both films won the Wilderness Award as the best documentaries made in Canada that year. The Trudeau film showed how Trudeau-mania was generated deliberately. Another theatrical event. Trudeau came in, like [Jean-Paul] Belmondo, swinging his arms like a simian and said, "Take my hand and we will venture together." The *nouvelle vague* had come up against Victorian melodrama. I became convinced that television was changing politics and that something dangerous was happening to democracy. By the time I came to write the Lenin film I had evolved my theory of film, television, *and* revolution as an art form.

When the film was due to be shown on CBC Television some reactionary guy on the back benches of the Conservative Party queried it. He stood up in the House and asked if it was true that a document of revolution was going to be shown tomorrow night? So the CBC cancelled my film in 1971 and showed two other films—one was about the life of Hitler and the other was a skiing film which showed you how to set off dynamite to blow up avalanches and in the process they showed in infinite detail how a bomb was made. And at the same time, my harmless little film essay was denounced. That was when the whole October Crisis blew up.

Trudeau cancelled his trip to Russia and I always suspected, though I could never prove it, that the entire Canadian October Crisis spectacle was contrived. Let's go back to the election of Pierre Elliott Trudeau in June 1968. He was the first politician to be able to get under the 24-hour ban on pre-election broadcasts. He did that by going to Montreal and confronting all those nasty separatists at the Place D'Armes. Remember the balcony scene, which was shown the night before the election? He attended the St. Jean Baptiste Day parade and the election was the following morning. For the first time in history, the St. Jean Baptiste Day parade was carried on the network right across Canada. All the cameras had shots of Trudeau shouting down the separatists. What they didn't tell you was that there were more cops than separatists in the square. I always felt that too was a contrived political spectacle.

The CBC pulled my film on the weakest of excuses. They claimed it was because of this Conservative backbencher, but the phone call came from the Prime Minister's Office—the PMO. I know that for a fact. We know about this because of a screening of the film in Toronto attended by the English television network executives. They looked at the film and they said, "It's a good film and we'll let it go on." The next day they made a decision to can it. The producer, Gordon Donaldson, had heard that a call had come in from the PMO. The PMO denied it. The National Television Producers' Association got really angry over the whole thing and said, "The PMO called and it was cowardly self-censorship by management because they're allowing the CBC to be censored by the government."

The CBC took all the flak over it, but I got all the damned publicity out of that thing. It made the international headlines. In Moscow they said, "McCarthyism Arrives in Canada." It made headlines in Paris and in the United States. I was blackballed by the CBC after this film. I never did another job for them even though I had won national and international awards. I'm not the most diplomatic of people and the CBC president at the time was a dreadful little bureaucrat and I described him as a "spineless twit," or something like that, and the newspapers quoted me on it. It was McCarthyism.

Ironically, the CBC had just shown an American documentary about the Hollywood Ten and said, "Look how normal we are in Canada. These kinds of things can't happen here." It was happening in Canada and it was cold-war hysteria. Anyway, my film about Lenin did go on the air eventually. It was aired about six months later. The CBC couldn't afford *not* to show it this time, there was too much at stake.

CHAPTER THREE

Making Short Waves:
The CBC's International Service

Transferred

John "Mac" Reynolds is a sculptor and painter. A former employee of the CBC, he was "transferred" out of the International Service in Montreal to CBC Television in Toronto. His studio in his central Toronto home is adorned with busts and large sculptures.

I joined the CBC in 1942 as a PR person in Toronto. The war was still on and I had been in the merchant navy. There weren't many people around who could take a job doing PR at the CBC. I had going for me the fact that my father owned an advertising agency, which I had worked in quite a bit. I then applied for the opportunity to become a radio producer and was given that chance, largely by Charlie Jennings. I became a radio producer and worked with Andrew Allan and J. Frank Willis.

My best friend at the CBC, who I knew before I joined the corporation, was a chap named Stuart Griffiths. He was an interesting character within the CBC—he was a doer. Griffiths had moved down to the International Service of the CBC in Montreal which was, in effect, the voice of the Department of External Affairs, and the CBC didn't govern the program content—that really was suggested or dictated by Ottawa.

So I, too, moved to Montreal. It was an interesting experience for me on a personal level and at the CBC I met a well-known poet of the time named Gilles Hénault. Gilles and I shared a "garçonnière" [bachelor apartment] on Sherbrooke Street and a whole new scene opened up to me. I knew people in the arts who had declared themselves to be Communists and so on. I was never a card-carrying Communist but I knew a great many of them and I liked a lot of them. I met French Canadians who are now prominent and were, in fact, card-carrying members in Montreal. I had the feeling that Communism was anti-religious and that people would join the Communist Party so they could say nasty things about the pope.

The practical matters at the International Service were handled by Stuart Griffiths and my major task was to publish a schedule of broadcasts, which would then be mailed each month to Europe. It expanded until each of the language areas had a section, and it ended up having seventeen languages and about forty pages and it became very popular. I did an interesting issue on Canadian painting and I managed to get a four-colour cover on it.

A man named Jean Désy was the Canadian ambassador in Italy who managed to get himself extracted from the embassy and brought back to Montreal. I always felt he was a rather sinister character with unpleasant personal qualities. He had been promised the French embassy but Georges Vanier was there and Vanier enjoyed being there. Since Vanier was in his way they had to do something with Désy, so they appointed him the director of the International Service, while still retaining the title of ambassador.

Désy was connected to a man named Keyserlingk, who published a Catholic newspaper in Montreal [*The Ensign*]. It was a very right-wing organ. The CBC soon became a dangerous place for me because I never hesitated to express views from the left. Nor did Stuart Griffiths who, at one time, had been with the extreme left before he joined the CBC. Somebody knew of that.

Keyserlingk and Désy thought this was a wonderful opportunity for Désy to become the saviour of our nation's institutions by finding Communists in the CBC. At that point, Désy became a very dangerous man to have around the International Service—dangerous, that is, to anyone who ever had left-wing thoughts.

Soon after Désy arrived, Griffiths was brought to Toronto to start the programs on television. That left me naked, in a sense. Gossip is like a brush fire when it starts. Someone thought Griffiths would suit Keyserlingk and Désy's purposes very well, but he was removed.

What was left was Griffith's best friend, who was me, and I had a loose tongue and there was a fair amount of evidence of where I stood politically. So I put in three of the worst months I ever had in my life.

I got memos questioning [my competence]. There was a personnel man there who was very embarrassed about having to put pressure on me to resign. All they needed was for me to quit and I would have been declared a Communist and would have had no defence. That was the atmosphere at the time—as McCarthy had been doing in the States, you just had to call a person a Communist.

I had to do something to save myself. I had two bosses. There was a chap in Toronto who was the head of PR at the CBC and I came under him in a way—but I was working in the International Service and so I was also under another man there. Neither of these two would tell me anything and nobody wanted to talk. I went over the memos I had written to my Toronto boss—every month I had written to tell him what difficulties I was having in Montreal getting the attention of the executive head of the International Service. I assembled all these memos, which made a good defence of the work I was there to do. Nobody had said anything against the job I was doing and, in fact, there was good comment about the magazine I was publishing. And people I knew in Ottawa agreed there was substance to what I believed about attacks on me being the result of McCarthyism.

I talked to Alphonse Ouimet, who I think at the time was assistant general manager of the CBC. He had two offices, one in Toronto and one in Ottawa. He was a fairly agreeable guy and was approachable. I buttonholed him and he said, "Well, the general manager is going to be in his office in Montreal tomorrow and you should decide what you want to do."

So I took my batch of memos and went to Ottawa and went into the ante-room of Donald Manson's office—he was the general manager. He wasn't going to see me but I just sat there. He went out to lunch and I was still there. Finally, Al Ouimet went into Manson's office, then came out and shook my hand. I thought that was a good sign. It was about one o'clock.

Manson eventually agreed to see me and I started to read him this memo in my own defence. He kept asking me questions like, "Have you always lived in Montreal?" I said no. Then he asked if I was married. I said, "Yes, I have two children."

Then he asked me to tell him something more about myself. I said, "Well, you know my father."

"Is your father Eddie Reynolds?" he wanted to know. I said yes and he said, "Why didn't you tell me?" Then he didn't want me to read anymore. He told me to come back around three, so I walked around Ottawa for a while. I went back and it had been arranged that I would be transferred to Toronto. I was back in Toronto in 1952.

"A Gentlemanly McCarthyism"

Eric Koch retired from the CBC after a successful career, first with the International Service in Montreal, then as a program organizer in public affairs, an area head in arts and science, and a regional director in Montreal. He's the author of a number of books, including Deemed Suspect (1980) *and* Inside 7 Days—The Show That Shook the Nation (1986). *"We were much less democratic in Canada than they were in the States. After all, McCarthy did it in public. He lied, but at least it was open. Why did this gentlemanly McCarthyism happen here? Because however much we deny it, Canadian culture is very close to American culture. Nothing happens down there that doesn't sooner or later come through here. The forms are different but the essence is very much the same."*

Let me get the atmosphere straight first. We were in the International Service, which came about because of the war. People like myself—there were two or three of us in the German section—were refugees. We were anti-Nazis who'd been interned in England and shipped to camps in Canada. We were the original team, later others were added. Together with members of other sections, such as the Czechs, the Dutch, and the Danish, we formed a little enclave of "interesting" Europeans who were assembled by the CBC to broadcast on short wave to Europe and Latin America. The authorities must have thought of us as a bunch of wild foreigners. I wouldn't be surprised if some of them were a little afraid of us.

When I look back at the years I worked at the International Service, I find my first decade at the CBC was very good. There were nine years altogether—from '44 to '53. I cannot claim that any unpleasant stories affected my sleep or mood or good feeling about the CBC in those years. We thought we were doing important work. During the last year of the war we were part of the psychological warfare and later, during the Nuremberg trials, we were involved in the re-education process. We felt we were making a contribution together with our colleagues at the Voice of America and the BBC. We were all broadcasting into Germany. We made broadcasts for the German schools, etc. All of this was undisturbed by ideological difficulties. The Gouzenko affair didn't affect us at all, it was just an Ottawa story. I don't remember any visitations from the RCMP, but I knew about people in the film board who were having trouble.

This kind of changed after the cold war, which started in '48 with the Berlin Blockade. The CBC took care of the International Service in trust for external affairs. So we had two masters. External affairs was responsible for policy matters and matters of security, I guess, together with the CBC. In '49 external affairs sent a man to Montreal to study us, to do a little enquiry. He interviewed us all. It was very civilized, nothing hostile, nothing ungentlemanly. I didn't feel threatened.

Our director was Ira Dilworth. He was a former school principal, an expert in Victorian poetry. To put it mildly, he was a little out of his depth. Dilworth was like a mother hen and wanted to protect us against evil people, but they were asking questions which he didn't understand—about Stalin and all this. Dilworth had never been outside Canada, except when he had studied at Harvard for a graduate degree in Victorian literature. While at the CBC, I think, he had once gone abroad to a UNESCO meeting. But he was not very well equipped to handle the politics of an institution like the International Service. His field was the Brontës. Since he knew he was out of his depth, he suffered a lot. He was a very decent man.

Then this man from Ottawa wrote his report. It must have been very damaging to us because Dilworth had to leave and Jean Désy was brought in. He had been an ambassador and had some relationship to St. Laurent, who was prime minister at the time. The whole atmosphere changed totally—from this benevolent, Anglo-Saxon Protestant Dilworth to the hard-nosed, violently anti-Soviet, French Catholic Jean Désy. It was a totally different mentality with none of the previous concern about individual freedom.

A man named Keyserlingk was the editor of *The Ensign* [in Montreal], which I always assumed had something to do with the Roman Catholic Church. He was a member of the Keyserlingk family which was a distinguished East Prussian dynasty. His uncle or great uncle was a famous philosopher, Count von Keyserlingk. I know Keyserlingk was in Berlin in the '30s and had several interviews with Goering. I think he was there for United Press and wrote for an English paper. I'm sure he wasn't a Nazi—he was anti-Communist, anti-Russian. East Prussia is close to the Baltic states and they all hate the Russians. It wasn't unusual to hate the Soviets. It was a perfectly honourable position to take. But it's one thing to have political convictions which are anti-Communist and it's quite another to go out on a witch-hunt. What Keyserlingk was doing with his paper was what McCarthy was doing in the States—he was naming names. And he was going after particular institutions and one of them was the CBC. The International Service was also in Montreal and he singled it out.

We all thought he was a kind of scourge. I don't know if anybody read him, but management at the CBC was sensitive to him. I was, in those years, head of the German section of the International Service. I think I was mentioned a couple of times in the magazine but I don't remember actually seeing it. This was another world from ours—the Keyserlingk world.

I had no trouble, but I knew of two victims. They may have already been named in the earlier report [from Ottawa]. It may have been that Jean Désy had the blacklist as soon as he arrived. The two people who I assume were on it were Stuart Griffiths and Sally Solomon. They were my friends. Sally Solomon was a bright lady who was in charge of policy at our end and in constant touch with external affairs in Ottawa. If she was particularly left-wing, none of us was aware of it. She was thrown out, as was Stuart Griffiths. He came out of CBC publicity—P&I we called it, Press and Information—and worked his way up in program management. I considered it unthinkable at the time that either of them was a security risk. Nothing has happened since that's changed my mind.

Stu Griffiths was rescued by Ernie Bushnell, the program director, and he gave Griffiths CBLT [the CBC's flagship television station in Toronto]. That was in '52. Griffiths and Mavor Moore were responsible for the golden age of TV at the beginning of CBC Television. They hired the producers who made the programs during the great years of CBC Television—Norman Campbell, Harvey Hart, Sydney Newman, Leo Orenstein, Franz Kraemer, and many others. So Griffiths, who was removed from Montreal, was rescued by Bushnell, who was thoroughly unpolitical but who recognized Griffiths' talent. Sally Solomon was not so lucky and I don't think she ever got an important and interesting job again.

CHAPTER FOUR

FILM NO EVIL:
The NFB and the Blacklist

LIVES ON THE CUTTING ROOM FLOOR

Today, **Doris Rands** *lives in Regina. During the height of the Gouzenko hysteria, she lived through the purge and blacklist period of the National Film Board. Her husband, Stan Rands, lost his job with the NFB when he was fired in 1950.*

My husband, Stan, worked in adult education in Manitoba and used the films of the NFB as tools for community organizing, farm organizing, and all kinds of grass-roots work. These programs were discontinued and we moved to Ottawa and a job with the National Film Board. Stan had met John Grierson earlier and was excited about his view of documentary film-making.

I remember people used to stay up all night talking about what could be done around the film board and what good could be done with documentary films. When the purge happened they stopped doing that and the atmosphere around the NFB changed from high creativity and optimism to caution and fear.

The RCMP had Stan on their blacklist because he was trying to make the civil service association into a union with collective bargaining. He was among a group on the executive who wanted to change it into a union with some clout. He was also on a civil liberties committee organized to help the people arrested during the Gouzenko period. We knew several of the people who were accused of being spies and we worked on their behalf with the civil liberties committee. We had a friend named David Shugar who lost his job in Ottawa even though he was acquitted. Grace, his wife, took a hard waitressing job to pay the bills and, as she was pregnant and had a lot of health problems, it was a hard time for them.

We didn't leave Ottawa until the fall of 1950. Stan's immediate bosses were very sad to see him go. Because I was pregnant, they gave us an extension before he was actually fired. The extension was from the spring of '50 to the fall of '50. They told him he could stay until the new baby came. We left when our baby was one month old. It was a really difficult time.

I remember the summer of 1950. My mom was one of those who got forced out during the Winnipeg flood and she came to live with us in Ottawa. It was the worst possible timing because she was very conservative and was totally appalled by what we were going through. We tried to keep it all from her. We would watch for the newsboy and grab the paper before she could read it. It was very nerve-racking. She knew about it though, and was very upset because she didn't believe in getting mixed up in left-wing politics.

I think Stan was more worried about our future than I was because I was preoccupied with the kids and didn't have time to worry too much. We didn't have any other source of income, so Stan started applying for jobs. We bought an old car, a Buick, and, with our three kids in the back, we rattled our way from Ottawa to Regina. A friend who was a film-maker at the NFB, Evelyn Cherry, gave us a car hammock to put the baby in and it kept [the baby] happy. We were on our way, but we didn't know if Stan had a job or not. We worried about that, and about the crazy world scene where the Soviet Union was supposed to be our friend one day and our enemy the next. But I guess my main memory of that trip is of how thankful we were to be safe and together, with our three healthy kids.

We got to Winnipeg and found out Stan had a job with the health department in Regina. But he was still hounded after this. The RCMP came right to the health education office to talk with Stan's immediate boss and check up on him. Even some CCFers were doubtful about whether Stan should have been hired. Notably, one famous politician who is still around wrote to Tommy Douglas saying it was a big mistake to hire Stan Rands. Many years later, Stan found the letter in the archives. Luckily, the minister of health, Tom

Bentley, was a really wonderful guy and very scornful of the investigations of the RCMP. Stan was with health education first and then he moved to psychiatric services and was there when medicare started. Then he took a job organizing community clinics.

On our fortieth wedding anniversary, our daughter made us a wall hanging which described our married life. She depicted a figure in it who was a big capitalist wearing a top hat and big boots and he was kicking us from one province to another. The last scene shows the same figure standing in the way of community clinics.

A COMPOSER'S STORY

Lou Applebaum is a talented composer who wrote the musical scores for hundreds of the early films produced by the National Film Board. He joined the staff of the NFB in 1941 and was hired personally by the board's founder, John Grierson. Now in his seventies, he remains vigorous, still creating music in his downtown Toronto studio.

I started to work for the film board in 1940 as a freelance composer. I had just returned from my studies in New York, where I had become absolutely fascinated by film music. It happened during the World's Fair in New York. There was one pavilion run by the US Department of Agriculture which showed what are now considered two classic documentaries by Pare Lorentz. One was called *The River* and had a score by Aaron Copland, the other was called *The City* and had a score by Virgil Thomson. A friend, Reuven Frank, a Torontonian who later became president of NBC News, was a reporter for the *Newark News* and he had a pass to the fair. We took advantage of that pass and I'm sure I saw those films fifteen or twenty times.

When I came back to Canada, I heard about this brand new thing called the film board. This was in April or May of 1940, and I bumped into a composer on Bloor Street who had just been asked to do a score. I also bumped into another friend of mine, Sydney Newman, who was then working for the National Film Board. He had been a freelance artist and stage designer. A friend of his at the film board asked me to do a score and then Norman McLaren asked me to do a score. I became completely sold.

In 1940 I asked John Grierson if he could use me on a regular basis. I remember the interview with Grierson, who was a little man but all energy. Here I was: twenty-two years old and I say, "I must work for you."

He said, "How much are you earning?"

At that time I was earning around ten dollars a week as a group worker at the YMHA and also giving piano lessons. With a lot of chutzpah and a lot of mathematics, I multiplied what I was really earning. I said eighty dollars.

He said, "I'll give you forty."

"I'll take it," I said.

That's how I got on the staff of the film board and started to write an incredible number of scores—around fifty or sixty a year. It was a marvellous period. Everybody at the film board, with the exception of two Englishmen who Grierson brought over, were Canadians. The Canadians there had had nothing to do with film previously because there wasn't much film-making around. The film board had taken over what was the Canadian Motion Picture Bureau. They had had a cameraman and a couple of producers who had been making travelogues for the CNR: a visit to Banff and aren't these mountains beautiful and look at the rolling wheat and that sort of thing.

Grierson had persuaded the Mackenzie King government that film was *the* powerful communicating medium and we had a selling job to do for the war effort. Grierson started from scratch and had to build up a staff. He just combed the country. There was no real model to work from. When I got there, there were thirty or forty people. The film board was located in this old sawmill [in Ottawa]. Can you imagine a thing as flammable as nitrate film in a sawmill? This was a converted sawmill in one corner of which the Department of Agriculture also had a lab, so we had formaldehyde and guinea pigs to contend with as well. Our main theatre was a little studio with maybe thirty or forty seats and it was also our music recording room, a mixing room, and the storage room for cameras.

Within two or three years, Grierson had a staff of 400 and it was undoubtedly the most exciting place in the world in which to work. It was stimulating. Grierson enlisted people who wanted to change the world: first, to build up the sense of pride in the country which was needed for the war effort, and second, to provide information about the war.

Many countries, and Russia was one of them, took a very keen interest in what was going on at the National Film Board. We used to have many visitors and participants. It was not unusual for us to have the cultural attaché from the Russian embassy at the film board looking at our films.

As far as the government was concerned, the film board was a maverick operation. How could these bearded, check-shirted, undisciplined film-makers fit into a civil service pattern? The two are not reconcilable, so there was a fundamental problem. We were not government types: we didn't work that way and we didn't think that way. We didn't work nine to five. We would work fifteen hours and then spend the next eight hours talking about what we were doing. We were totally absorbed in our life.

The government looked upon us as not only outsiders, but also potential rebels. The word "Communist" was associated with all kinds of people at the film board, almost from day one. I don't remember whether we ever went through an RCMP check to get the job, but Grierson was grabbing people right and left—people who had a social conscience and had the energy to do something about society. Who had time to really penetrate into the backgrounds of these people? Besides, the more activist they were, the better film-makers they were going to be. They were going to generate public involvement in what was going on. It didn't take too long for the film board to be painted, mostly wrongly, as a hotbed of Communists and Socialists.

I'm sure that amongst us at the NFB were right-wingers, left-wingers, maybe some Communists, certainly Socialists, and so on. But we were there to make films and to make Canada better. Then the Gouzenko thing happened. The awful revelation to me was that Grierson's secretary was allegedly involved with Fred Rose in Montreal.

What secrets could she have given to the Soviets?

What secrets did we have? None that I know of. Grierson had always been painted as a kind of socialist type from his Scottish background, his Rockefeller Foundation activities, and his desire to expose the country to itself. If you wanted to hurt the National Film Board— and there were a lot of people who wanted to hurt this upstart agency—you hurt Grierson. A few months after the furore around the Gouzenko revelations, Grierson left the film board. He was forced out and I'm pretty sure life was unbearable for him. He was an embarrassment to the government, and an understanding was made and he left. He went to New York and established a company called The World Today Inc. I also left the film board. I went to work on electronic music and that sort of thing.

BLACKLISTED

I was invited to write the music for a Fred Zinneman film. Zinneman was a great director. The film was being produced by David Loew, the son of the Loew family [of Metro Goldwyn Mayer studios]. It was called *Theresa*, Pier Angeli's first film. I was asked to do the music for this film out of New York and it meant that I had to spend time there. I had done a lot of scoring in New York after I had gone there in 1946 and I had been going back and forth. In fact, I earned most of my income out of New York when I came back to Canada in 1950.

Since I was going to be down there for an extended period of time, I thought I'd better get a visa or something. I almost didn't get across. After weeks of delay, the film company was getting ready to cancel the deal because I wasn't showing up. I managed to find out what the hold-up was. After pressuring them, I got an interview and was asked if I knew Grierson.

I said, "Certainly I know Grierson."

"Did you ever talk politics with Grierson?" was the next question.

I told them, "We'd talk about everything."

That was the issue: I was an associate of Grierson's, therefore

I was tainted, and therefore I was almost not allowed into America. This was 1953.

THE PERVADING FEAR

Marjorie McKay *is a former NFB employee. She spent twenty years at the board and worked in many departments, including production research. She is now retired and living in Victoria, British Columbia.*

There was a pervading sense of fear which permeated the film board right after the war. The fear was worse than the actions taken because a great number of people expected the RCMP to tag them any minute. We were worried when we went down to protest things like the atom bomb. Several people went down with me and we all expected the roof to fall in over that but it never did. When the RCMP was campaigning to dig all the Communists out of the film board, I kept waiting for somebody to tap me on the shoulder. But nobody ever did.

The RCMP sent forms to be filled out and I filled out the same one everybody did. But there were a number of people who were fired. We heard the story of one man who was an NFB employee in Winnipeg. It was suggested to him that he resign because he'd taken part in a public meeting during which two well-known Communists appeared on the platform with him. Arthur Irwin, the film commissioner, was given a list of names by the RCMP and he knows who was let go. It was extremely difficult for anyone fired at that time to get another job. There just weren't jobs going.

The film board was under attack by private film producers who were making their move to try and get permission to approach government departments. All government departments were supposed to have all their films made by the National Film Board. Private film producers wanted to cut in and make films for such departments as health and welfare, national defence, the post office, and justice. There was more money for private producers from government than from anywhere else.

There was a film made by the NFB about China called *The People Between*, which was about Mao's defeat of Chiang Kaishek and the social developments which were going on in China. Grant McLean made the film but external would not allow it to be released. There was pressure like that. Private producers attacked the film board and said their films would be better because the board was communist and couldn't be trusted to make these films.

In my own case, my brother had been a member of the Communist Party. It was widely known in Vancouver that he was a member. He'd been quite open about being a member and had been jailed for taking part in a union strike. He was accused of assaulting an RCMP officer although there was the question of how my brother could assault him when my brother was on foot and the RCMP man was on horseback. Then my brother went over to Spain with the MacKenzie Papineau brigade where he was killed. All of this was well known, but the RCMP at no time ever questioned me. As a matter of fact, I went to some party meetings in Vancouver with friends of my brother's before the end of the war.

The people I knew at the NFB were politically closer to the NDP [or CCF, as it was then] than to any other party. A few were beyond the CCF and were really Communists, but it was all rather a social thing to be NDP or Communist, we were all too busy making films. There were at least two groups within the film board who formed Communist cells. I went to one of these groups quite often. It usually took place at someone's home but nobody of importance from the party ever showed up. The meetings weren't particularly well organized and because we were all too busy making films nobody had time to prepare for them. In fact, we did nothing but get lectured to by one or two of the members. I ceased going because they weren't interesting and you never had the feeling you were accomplishing anything. Our primary work was the National Film Board, yet nothing was ever related to that at these Communist meetings. The emphasis was usually on Canada's foreign policy, but the NFB had nothing to do with Canada's foreign policy and in no way could affect it. I began to feel it was a bloody waste of time. I was disillusioned because I thought I would be involved in a great, interesting, fascinating adventure by attending these meetings. I grew progressively more bored. I became closer to the NDP, which was really much more specific in its aims. We were no great threat to the government or to anybody.

Freda Linton, who was mentioned by Gouzenko as a spy, was what we called an overflow secretary. When Grierson's regular secretary had too much work, then Freda Linton was employed. None of us knew she was a Communist but I don't think she was a threat at all. In fact, hardly anything came over Grierson's desk that was important from a security point of view. Anyway, she was never at any of these meetings. Neither was Grierson. He was left-wing but not that far left. If Grierson had been there maybe these meetings would have been more interesting.

CHAPTER FIVE
LIVELY ARTISTS:
DANCE, THEATRE, AND JOURNALISM

BALLET RUSE

Ray Stevenson worked underground for INCO and was an elected executive board member of the Sudbury local of the Mine, Mill, and Smelter Workers Union. He helped organize an event with the Royal Winnipeg Ballet—an event that never took place. It was his job to assist in reimbursing thousands of ticket holders for this blacklisted event.

We developed a program at the local level to raise the cultural and artistic views of people living in Sudbury, a community which had been dominated for many years by INCO. We invited world-renowned artists to perform, such as Paul Robeson, Pete Seeger, and a whole number of people. Our program was under the general managership of a man named Weir Reid, who worked full time for the local union to develop this type of program.

Reid had made arrangements with the Royal Winnipeg Ballet to come to Sudbury at the end of January in 1954. Of course, this was in the midst of the McCarthyite period, but we never for a moment suspected that there would be any problem with a national ballet company from Winnipeg. We proceeded with our plans and had sold out the Union Hall, which seated around 1,200 people, for two, if not three, concerts.

At the beginning of the week the shows were to take place we were dumbfounded to receive a wired cancellation of the ballet company's plans to come to Sudbury. When we tried to investigate their reasons for it and what was involved, we were told there was some health

94

problem or someone had developed an ingrown toenail or whatever.*
We knew we were being fed pure nonsense and we strongly
suspected other reasons. Investigating the matter, we found that the
Royal Winnipeg Ballet company had planned a tour of the United
States which included a presentation before the president of the
United States, Dwight Eisenhower.

We were even more suspicious that the fine hand of the State
Department was involved in the cancellation because some of the
leading people in our union were barred from going to the United
States. Also, John Foster Dulles, the US secretary of state, was formerly a top-level INCO executive working as a solicitor for
Cromwell and Sullivan. In fact, Dulles had been the secretary of the
INCO executive council and was one of the top managerial people.
He was certainly on their board of directors and we believed the
dance cancellation included intervention by INCO. We assumed,
quite naturally, that they would try to embarrass the union. The ballet
was prevented from appearing on threat of having their tour cancelled or possibly being prevented themselves as individuals from
going to the United States. In the minds of the McCarthyites, by
appearing in the Mine Mill Hall the ballet company was keeping
company with the enemy.

We had quite a time returning the tickets, having sold thousands.
We returned the money with what explanations we could, but we
also raised a public fuss about the thing because we weren't going to
roll over and play dead. To us in Sudbury, it was a direct onslaught on
the rights of the community, as well as on civil and personal rights, to
deprive us of the opportunity of viewing of Canadian artists, or any
artists for that matter. But nobody in government was ever willing to
back us up or raise a finger of protest.

* In his history of the company, *The Royal Winnipeg Ballet*, Max Wyman writes:
"It was announced that the performances would have to be cancelled due to
'24-hour-flu'." The real problem was politics, notes Wyman: "The Mine, Mill,
and Smelter Workers Union had been expelled from the Canadian Congress of
Labour for having Communist leadership."

SETTING THE STAGE FOR MCCARTHYISM

*Toby Gordon Ryan is an actor, director, and drama teacher. She
lives in Toronto where, from the 1930s to the 1950s, she was very much a
part of the cultural scene as a member of a left-wing troupe called Theatre
of Action, as well as The Play Actors.*

The point has to be made that Canada was a forerunner to the
McCarthy period in the United States. It happened here first. I went
down to New York to study and came back to Toronto in 1932.
Toronto was such an oppressive city then. The police were everywhere. Whether you were making a speech or demonstrating at
Queen's Park, the City of Toronto Police Department had its "Red
Squad" in operation at all times. They even came to theatre
rehearsals. Rehearsals of the Workers' Theatre were held in various
labour halls and the Red Squad were present at every one, noting
every person who was there. They took pictures too.

The idea was to frighten, to harass, and, in some cases, the police
actually picked up people. Two of our actors were picked up when we
were about to do a play for May Day called *Unity*. The police picked
them up just before the performance. We had one hell of a time
getting them released. It was just to frighten us but, as they found
out, when young people are harassed they become more radical and
less frightened. Still, it was all very unpleasant to see three beefy
individuals from the Red Squad standing at the back of the rehearsal
hall, heckling and interfering in a rude manner in order to disrupt.

When we played *Eight Men Speak*, the province allowed only one
performance. They did it in a "legal" way by visiting the manager
of the theatre and telling him, "If you allow another performance,
we will revoke your licence." It was a grim time for civil liberties in
this country.

In the '30s, Canada pointed the way for discrimination against
the left. It wasn't so in the States. In New York it was possible
to have huge May Day gatherings without police harassment.
When I came back to Toronto from New York I was shocked at how
much more forbidding it was here compared to the States. So many

organizations were forced to go underground and were outlawed.

In Montreal our theatre was hounded by Duplessis and his Padlock Law. The theatre was producing *Bury the Dead* at the United Jewish Peoples' Order hall. When the company got there with all their sets and were ready to perform, the door was padlocked and the actors couldn't get in! It was a form of McCarthyism carried to extremes. It was meant not only to frighten, but also to stifle protest and anti-establishment thought. It worked in many cases, until theatres found ways to circumvent police tactics.

In the '30s many Canadian theatre companies entered plays in the Dominion Drama Festival, plays like *Waiting for Lefty* by Clifford Odets and *Bury the Dead* by Irwin Shaw—different kind of theatre for those times. We wanted to enter plays that dealt with social issues and had something relevant to say about our times. In Montreal new theatres always had a terrible time trying to enter their plays in the regional festivals. In one case, a production was halted just after it started. The adjudicator and the judge wouldn't let them continue. McCarthyism isn't just a phenomenon of the United States. This country can't claim to be "holier than thou" on the question of McCarthyism.

Audiences were craving our kind of theatre. In British Columbia *Waiting for Lefty* was allowed, and played during an absolutely brutal waterfront strike involving vigilantes and goons. There were more performances of this play in B.C. than any other place in the world— sixty-two of them, all over the province. It played for audiences in many cities across Canada on its way to the Dominion Drama Festival. It was so popular.

SCENES FROM THE COLD WAR

Then the Gouzenko spy trials took place. Just before Gouzenko, Russia had been our gallant ally. Then, almost overnight, there were suddenly spies all over the place. Heaven only knows what these spies discovered in Canada—what secrets did we have?—but it was a terrible period. My husband knew some of the people who were picked up by the RCMP. They were radicals and belonged to various organizations, but they certainly weren't spies for Russia.

I should tell you the story of the first director of our acting company, Theatre of Action, in Toronto. His name was David Pressman, a very creative director. He joined the army and fought in the Second World War. When he came back from the war, he went to New York and directed some plays on Broadway. Then he got into television. He was doing quite well but then McCarthy appeared on the scene. Pressman's name was published in this book called *Red Channels* and suddenly he was out of work. Blacklisted. It happened so fast; he had a family and was quite desperate. He was a radical, but not a danger to his country. He told me it might have had something to do with what he'd done twenty years earlier during the Depression of the '30s. It didn't matter that he had gone to war and been wounded, his loyalty was questionable. Eventually, he got a teaching job at his old alma mater, The Neighborhood Playhouse, who were quite happy to have him on staff.

By 1953 theatre audiences changed. As a result of the cold war, the left-wing movement was devastated to some extent. When your morale is low, you don't respond to things as you should. When we started Theatre of Action in the '30s, we received rave reviews from newspaper critics and audience response was favourable. In the '50s we organized a troupe called The Play Actors, a theatre for its time, and we produced plays that were relevant for that period. We were roundly denounced by newspaper theatre critics. As an example, Toronto critic Herbert Whittaker used his favourite term, agitprop, as a pejorative to describe us.

There weren't many great plays in the '50s, but we did find George Tabori's play *The Emperor's Clothes*, which dealt with guilt by association and also Howard Fast's play *Thirty Pieces of Silver*, which specifically related to McCarthyism. In that period, it was also harder to find patrons and obtain funding. It was difficult because there weren't grants in those days. In the '30s there were people with money and "progressive" ideas who became patrons of the Theatre of Action. There wasn't the fear that there was in the '50s. I still ponder that because people should have been more afraid in the '30s but they weren't worried back then. They reacted to the conditions around them with militant action and went out to march and demonstrate.

THE BLACKLISTED JOURNALIST

Carl Dow is a novelist and former newspaper journalist. He lives in Ottawa where he drives a school bus part time "to help keep the wolf from the door." Two of his novels will be published this year.

I was born in Ottawa, had been well churched and free enterprised by the time I was fifteen. I most sincerely believed that our press told the truth and nothing but the truth. Then, in June 1949, I accidentally discovered, during the heat of the federal election campaign, the *Ottawa Morning Citizen* lying in a front-page banner headline: Communists Pay Children 50 Cents to Distribute Leaflets. Until that point, aside from the conviction that our way was the best of all ways, I had no more interest in hardcore politics than any other boy scout or air cadet (the uniforms of both of which I had been wearing). However, upon reading that headline and the story that supported it, I felt betrayed. My neck, ears, and head burned with shock. The interest in politics which had hitherto lain quiescent in my genes was fired. Trying to find logic midst the ruins, I reasoned: the *Citizen*, my bastion of democracy, was lying about the Communists. If I wanted to learn about the Communists, it was obvious that I would have to go to the Communists to find out what they had to say about themselves. And so I did.

At first, the Ottawa Communist leader was too busy to talk with me. His party was very much involved in the federal election campaign. He gave me Labor Progressive Party [the name the Communists adopted after the Communist Party was banned following the outbreak of the Second World War] election material and some works of Lenin to read. I spent the next year in a fascinating novel world of ideas.

I became an active volunteer in the Communist organization, the National Federation of Labour Youth, which based its action on two themes: peace and putting Canada first. In the NFLY I met persons of the highest integrity, some of whom have remained close friends to this day. Curious, I joined the parent body—the LPP. Altogether, I don't think I paid more than eight months' dues. At the end of a one-week summer party school, when it came to assessment, it was concluded I had either lumpenproletariat or petty bourgeois tendencies. They couldn't decide which. I lost no sleep over the conundrum, but a few months later the Ottawa-Hull district committee of the LPP gave me the boot because they had concluded that I was an individualist.

From time to time, during the handful of years I was active in the Communist youth movement, I would pause in the wonderful excitement of the action and say: "What am I doing with all this? I couldn't handle all this collective stuff. If I lived over there, I'd choke to death or explode." Meanwhile, two of my most reliable sources who had visited the Soviet Union had confirmed that bureaucrats now held control of, and had all but strangled, the world's first experiment in socialism.

Nevertheless, I was in Canada and what happened in the USSR was their problem. As far as I was concerned, a Canadian version of socialism was a good idea for my country. However, by mid 1956 I had come to the conclusion that, as a socialist, I would have to find a better vehicle for my economic and political aspirations for the country. I came to this conclusion not because of what happened in Hungary, but because of what I saw as the Canadian-Communist slavish allegiance to Moscow. This allegiance was forcing it to lose touch with Canadian reality and rendering it politically impotent. I decided, at about age twenty-one, to become a journalist.

Despite the fact that my experience in the Communist movement was limited to my youth, despite the fact I was expelled by the Ottawa-Hull district committee of the LPP, the RCMP Security Service selected me as a target to be run to the ground.

The RCMP Security Service, or SS as I refer to them, harassed me when I was a newspaper boy selling the three Ottawa papers at the old income tax building on Sussex Street. They tried to convince the commissionaires at the two doors inside of which I laid out my papers Monday through Saturday, to put me out in the weather. Veterans all, they refused. However, as the years passed, most employers buckled, especially as the McCarthy hysteria climbed to a shriek.

In February 1957, at the age of twenty-three, I entered the editorial side of the newspaper business. About seven months later I was hired by Ewart Taylor, then suburban editor of the *Globe and Mail*. I was given a beat. Ten days later, Taylor called me at home and said, "The men in the red coats and big black boots have been here asking about you."

"Oh," I said, thinking, there goes the *Globe and Mail*.

But Taylor said, "Don't worry about it. 'Cyclops' says he'll be damned if he'll let the police tell him who he'll hire and fire." ["Cyclops" was the nickname for Oakley Dalgleish, then editor and publisher of the *Globe and Mail*, who wore a patch over one eye.]

During Dalgleish's reign I covered my beat so well that for a time I was averaging a twenty-five dollar bonus cheque every three months, and the *Globe* nominated me for a national newspaper award. In 1960 I resigned from the *Globe* for reasons that had no direct link to the SS.

PROPOSITIONED BY THE RCMP

In 1964, while I was a youth editor and columnist at the *Montreal Star*, one Sergeant Lefevre of the RCMP SS propositioned me. He said the SS wanted me to act as an informer on a Ukrainian organization (my mother is of Ukrainian origin) or on a peace group or on my fellow journalists. I said no.

Lefevre said, "If you don't do at least one, we'll make sure you never hold a full-time job."

I said, "You've been doing a good job of that already. Do what you will; I won't be your stooge."

In 1967, as a staffer, I was holding down the Montreal bureau of the *Toronto Telegram*. In May, the RCMP SS used the fact they were issuing press passes for Expo '67 to bring to *Tely* chairman and publisher John Bassett's attention the lie that I was a Communist. I wasn't a Communist in 1957; I wasn't a Communist in 1967. How unlike Dalgleish's was Bassett's response. I could fill a courtroom with witnesses from the editorial and accounting departments who could testify that Bassett ran around shouting, "I'll be goddamned if I'm going to have a Communist working for me!" He forced the powers that were in his editorial department to fire me on the grounds that I didn't get along with my editors. I was given six weeks' notice.

The Toronto Newspaper Guild gave me an honourable withdrawal card and in the next contract with the *Tely* included a new clause which stated that no one could be dismissed because of their political persuasion. The point was never won: Bassett wrote "30" on the *Tely* and closed it down—for reasons, needless to say, that had nothing to do with me.

PART TWO

WINGING THE LEFT

CHAPTER SIX

SAY NO EVIL: *POLITICIANS, RADICALS, AND THE MOUNTIES*

THE STUDENT RADICAL

Irving Layton is one of Canada's best-known poets. He is in a Toronto studio recording his poetry for a commercial audio tape. In between takes, he pauses to tell his story. At age seventy-seven, he can still vent anger at those who persecuted him for his political beliefs. A left-winger during his student days at MacDonald College near Montreal, he was blacklisted by the RCMP.

At MacDonald College I used to do a lot of speaking and debating. I attracted attention because I criticized the appeasement policy of [Neville] Chamberlain. I was saying that it would lead to war. When the Spanish Civil War broke out I said that it was just the dress rehearsal for the Second World War. Naturally, that didn't make me very popular because many of the students who came to study in Canada at MacDonald College were the black sheep of the English upper classes. They came with all the fixed ideas of the upper-middle-class Englishmen.

A student who had heard me speaking wrote to his father about me. He wrote, "This fellow, Issie Lazarovitch, goes around saying dreadful things about Prime Minister Chamberlain and the appeasement policy." The father, a prominent doctor in London, was a real colonial type. You know the type—the sort who says, "How dare colonials criticize His Majesty's government?" And the idiot also sent a letter to the RCMP attacking me as "Issie Lazarovitch, a subversive who's saying terrible things about our foreign policy and Prime Minister Neville Chamberlain." That put me on the blacklist.

Because of that letter I was prevented for fifteen years from crossing the border from Canada to the USA. That's the way it was.

If you criticized the policy of Great Britain, or if you defended the Spanish loyalists, that made Canadian dullards think you were a Communist or subversive. If you subscribed to some liberal magazine like *The Nation* or *The New Republic* that got you on the blacklist. They exchanged information. Any name listed with the RCMP would be handed to the FBI, or whatever the service is, in the United States.

I began going to the United States because I had several brothers living in New York City. I first went there in the early '30s and I was there during the Depression. But I was on the blacklist and was prevented from crossing to the States for fifteen years. I didn't have a car so I could only get there by train or flight, and they wouldn't let me through. Finally, I got a lawyer to investigate. What was it that was keeping me from going to the United States of America? He came back to me with the news and said, "Why, you're on the blacklist!" I saw the files and I was on the RCMP blacklist as a "dangerous subversive." They had me down as a Communist and a firebrand.

I had to "clear" myself with the help of a lawyer who said, "You better go to Rouses Point, near the border in New York State, and clear your name. Tell them you're not a Communist."

I didn't feel like a prisoner in Rouses Point, but I was definitely being judged. The man asked me a series of questions and I replied to them. On the basis of my replies, they would judge me and decide whether or not to give me permission [to enter the country]. The first two or three times I tried, I didn't get permission. Eventually things eased, and later my fervent anti-Communist stance became evident even to the contingent of idiots in the RCMP and the ban on my going to the United States was lifted. Luckily, the whole process didn't cost me too much because my lawyer was a left-wing sympathizer himself and understood my plight. For some it was expensive, but not for me.

I was never a Communist, but I was sympathetic to the left-wing movement and to left-wing causes. I was also sympathetic to the Soviet Union then and thought they were trying to do something worthwhile. However, I didn't agree with their methods. I simply don't like to be a member of any group. I don't like to march with others.

The authorities can be incredibly stupid. Recently, it came out that they had files on June Callwood and in the files were listed columns she had written for the newspapers. Even that was considered subversive, and the fellows who were on her tail had written "confidential" on these articles and put them in the file even though they had already appeared in newspapers.

Of course, at MacDonald College, I had distinguished myself as being a radical. At that time, I was a lot more favourable to the Soviet Union than I became later on when disillusionment set in. But even if you weren't a member of the Communist Party, the very fact that you were well disposed towards the Soviet Union was enough to get you on the blacklist as a dangerous subversive or a Communist.

Even if you attended certain meetings [you could end up on a blacklist]. For example, Frank Scott and I were supposed to address a meeting at the McGill Students Union on Sherbrooke Street in Montreal. When we arrived, we found the door padlocked. Just because they didn't like our views they had padlocked the door. So much for democracy! So much for freedom in Canada!

Undoubtedly, the fact that I was prevented from going to the States harmed my career. I could have gone down earlier and made friends and contacts. To that degree, it affected me, but now I wear the event as a medal or a badge of honour. I'm very glad I'm in the RCMP files; I have nothing but contempt for them.

Excitement at Queen's Park

Alex Barris is a freelance writer and broadcaster. In the '40s and '50s he worked at the Globe and Mail *and also at the CBC. He was the host of a TV show called "The Barris Beat" and wrote shows such as "Front Page Challenge."*

I worked as a reporter at the *Globe and Mail* in the late '40s and early '50s. I covered Queen's Park [the Ontario legislature] for a couple of years. There's no doubt in my mind, and I'm not alone in believing this, that Joe Salsberg and Alex (A.A.) MacLeod, the two Communist Party members, were frequently the liveliest and most cogent debaters in the legislature at Queen's Park. They could speak on a wide range of issues and were both excellent orators in their individual ways. MacLeod was rather laid back and formal, a little bit like Leslie Frost, the premier, used to be—but obviously they had different views. On the other hand, Joe Salsberg was like a volcano and he would shout, rant, and rave, but quite articulately.

Between the two of them, they sparked some of the liveliest and most interesting debates in the provincial House at that time. They didn't frequently win their points, but they sure made other politicians aware that there were issues to be discussed. And even though the Liberals and Tories may have tried to ignore them and laugh them off because they were this little island of Communists, they were damn good politicians who added a lot to the debate of public issues in the province of Ontario.

Despite the swell of anti-communism on the continent at that time, these two guys kept getting re-elected and obviously had the confidence of their constituents in the Spadina riding and the other riding they represented.

A COMMUNIST IN THE PROVINCIAL LEGISLATURE

J.B. "Joe" Salsberg is a Toronto resident and former politician who was elected to Toronto's city council and to the Ontario legislature. He is now in his late eighties and is still very active as a columnist for the Canadian Jewish News.

Since I was associated with the left-wing movement for years, discrimination and opposition were as natural as breathing. You knew you were going to get it. For instance, I was a member of the city council in Toronto but was still very active publicly in the left movement: Communists, trade unions. Once, city council sent a municipal delegation to Ottawa to meet with certain ministries. I was the one who kicked up a row about coal. There was a shortage of coal and I found out that there were carloads of it on the railway tracks north of Toronto. There was a big fuss about it and so we sent a delegation to Ottawa.

Bob Saunders, who was later mayor of Toronto, was a member of the delegation. Saunders and I were walking up the streets in Ottawa to the Parliament Buildings and he said, "Joe, watch out, there's an RCMP officer behind you." He said it jokingly. And I replied, "Bob, don't worry. I'm keeping my eye on the officer that's ahead of me." That was an awareness that people were being watched and followed. It was nothing new. You took it for granted.

Also, a known Communist had no chance of getting a government job. That was discrimination too, of course, but there was a discrimination of another type which was worse—and it was very prevalent—and that was "industrial espionage." For instance, in the city of Sudbury the dominant industrial force was International Nickel, INCO. It was a company which dominated the community, so much so that when I came to Sudbury to speak, which was at least two or three times a year, there was a routine I followed. I would leave Toronto on the usual eleven o'clock train and arrive in Sudbury in the morning around eight o'clock, but I wouldn't get off the train at the station in Sudbury because there were always two kinds of police—the CPR and the INCO police—waiting for me. At that time, the engines were all steam driven. Before entering Sudbury station there was a water tower and the train would stop there. The engineer and the firemen of the train would get out and turn the tower outlet right into the engine to fill it up with water so the train would run. Well, that was a nice little stop, and it was before the station. So, instead of going into the station and being spotted by the company detective or the RCMP officer, I would get off the train.

I didn't travel with much baggage, only an overnight bag. I would climb up the little rampart and get off on the street. Right across from that spot was a comrade who lived in a certain house. He knew I was coming. They all knew because my name would be advertised in advance—that's why the police would be looking for me. I would go to his house rather than have him come looking for me because that would connect me with him and we'd be followed. So I would just knock on his door and he'd open. I'd sit there all during the day and people came to talk with me and took up all sorts of matters. But once I appeared at my public meetings, I couldn't be seen talking with these people. They could listen because it was a public lecture, but I wouldn't contact them or they'd lose their jobs.

The late Charlie Sims was the editor of the *Clarion* [the Communist weekly] and he worked very hard at exposing another form of discrimination. The private detective agencies or the RCMP would hire people in Toronto and send them up to Sudbury and have them sell door-to-door. These people were trained to ferret out information about people. They would get themselves invited into a house and make note of all the papers which they could see in the house. For instance, if you received the *Vapaus* in a Finnish house-hold, your name was put on a list and you'd lose your job. *Vapaus* was the radical Finnish paper. If they found a Ukrainian left-wing paper, that would be taken down and that man would also lose his job. And when you lost your job at INCO, you lost your livelihood. You had to get out of town, sooner or later.

Charlie Sims worked hard at this story. He found one Ukrainian man who was very upset because he was offered a job doing this sort of spying. Charlie asked him to stay on and get all the information he could about this. He did. Later, that information was given to Charlie who made a big splash about the whole business in the *Clarion*.

In Sudbury, I was told by many of the Ukrainians and others that they had to belong to the church because that was one of the questions asked of job applicants at INCO. So, they belonged to the church in order to get a job, but they didn't go. They packed a hall on Sunday nights for left-wing meetings. They held concerts and lectures and danced the national dances Ukrainians are famous for. Some of them would joke with me and tell me, "We pay the Ukrainian priest but we come here." Those were the conditions at the time. Was that discrimination? Violent discrimination.

In those days, if you were involved with unions you had to work underground. I was the person who laid the foundation for the automobile workers' union. I was in charge of trade union work for the Communist Party. Once a week, in the evenings, I would head out to

Oshawa. I was told which house to come to, and I'd leave my old jalopy outside and go in. Small groups of men were inside. These were autoworkers who wanted a union but couldn't do it because they would lose their jobs, so we met secretly. It was taken for granted that that was the only way to do it. No wonder so many workers became left-influenced and radicalized in the process. It was a denial of an elementary right—the right to form a union.

Left-wingers were discriminated against in unions dominated by right-wingers. My own estimation of that very unhappy period was that the bad influence came from the United States. They were, at that time, on a rampage against communism, and most of the international unions were led by American representatives who were sent up here. This happened particularly in the craft unions like the bricklayers and carpenters and so on. They fought organizations like the Committee for Industrial Organization (CIO) because they saw them as a danger to their existence. The CIO was industrial unionism and the craft unions felt under attack and in danger of losing members and prestige, which they did soon after because the industrial unions became the dominant force in labour.

So, you had within the unions a rampaging sort of anti-communism. Give you an example. There was a convention of the Canadian Trades and Labour Congress, as it was known at the time, which was the spokesman for Canadian trade unionism. The bulk of their membership had once been craft unions, but when the CIO came in the industrial union members quickly came to the fore. They were younger and more dynamic, and they knew what they after. But there was a split in the American Federation of Labor: they expelled the industrial unions, which then became a trade union centre on their own.

In the beginning, the CIO was headed by one of the most prominent American trade union leaders—John Lewis of the Coal Miners. He was a very forceful personality, not a radical whatsoever. Politically, he was known to be a Republican Party member in the United States. The head of the Canadian Trades and Labour Congress was a gentleman named Paddy Draper. As far as his political thinking goes, he was a member of the Presbyterian Church

Layman's Association. A fine, old-type gentleman. He was against expelling branches of the union movement. His position was that, as far as Canada concerned, whatever the rank and file did was their business. But no one was going to split up the Canadian congress. He and I became very close. He knew I was the spokesman for the Communists and the left-wing in the union, and very much intertwined with the CIO groups in Canada.

There was one day I'll never forget. It was at a convention in Niagara Falls, I believe, and the pressure came from the United States to expel the CIO unions from congress. Some of leaders of the craft unions, like the carpenters and so on, were pressured by the Americans and threatened to pull out. But the membership didn't want a break and Draper represented the best interests of Canadian labour by opposing a break.

Because of our close relationship at the convention, we would meet every day and he was certainly no red—he wasn't even a CCFer. I shall never forget one morning when he said to me, "You know, J.B., I trust you. Everything that you say to me you will do, you really do."

And I looked at him and said, "Why? Did you ever doubt it?"

He said, "No, but I've been told by an RCMP man who is in your caucus about everything that went on there." I smiled because it was so outlandish that he should receive information every day from an RCMP man who would be in the left caucus and report back to him. So when Draper asked the undercover man what I had said, he was told everything. That's why he said, "I realize that whatever you say you will do, you really do."

SUFFERING QUIETLY

There was discrimination against people going to the States. That kind of discrimination was virulent. For instance, I never experienced a refusal of entry into the United States but I found out that many prominent business people were suffering from this. They were suffering quietly, except they had lawyers who were trying to remedy their miserable situation. These people *needed* to go to the States for business purposes.

I knew one Toronto businessman, and I won't mention the name because the family is still carrying on, but he was stopped at the border. I dropped into his place and said, "I heard you were stopped?" He said yes and told me his lawyers were looking into it. He found out he was on the list because he donated money to the Spanish Civil War. This was the same cause to which even the head of the Eaton family had made a contribution.

Another man, a very prominent individual who was the recognized spokesman for the Jewish community during that period, decided to investigate. He decided he was going to find out why a certain person was on the blacklist at the border. He knew that person and just couldn't understand it. Figuring that he was safe, he went to see the RCMP and told them, "If this thing goes on, my name could be on the list. By the way, could you check?" The RCMP checked and his name *was* on the list. Why? Because he had contributed money to a popular cause at the time, but it was considered a red cause by the powers that be.

OUT OF THE GIRL GUIDES

Norman Penner is in his book-lined office at York University's Glendon College, where he is a professor of political science. He is also a former functionary in the Communist Party of Canada.

I was a full-time officer of the Communist Party for ten years, from 1947 to 1957. I had social contact with people in the area where I lived, such as the ratepayers' association and the home and school association. I participated in those activities although I was always conscious that some people in the community deliberately gave me and my children the cold shoulder. For instance, my daughter joined the Girl Guides. After two weeks, she was expelled because it came to their attention that she didn't attend Sunday school. We sent a letter of protest to the Girl Guides and they sent down two of their people to see us. They told us that "under no conditions" would they allow anybody into the Girl Guides who didn't go to church and

Sunday school. My daughter was eight years old and it left a bad mark on her for a long time.

My brother Roland came back from Yugoslavia in 1947. He was part of a 100-person delegation from Canada who had gone over to help build "The Beaver" railroad. They called it "The Beaver" because it was built by Canadians, you see. There were one hundred people on this boat, the S.S. *Radnik*, when it pulled into the dock at New York. Everybody was allowed to leave but Roland. They told him he would have to stay on the boat while it docked in New York because he was barred from entering the US. He was incarcerated on that boat until it got to Montreal two weeks later!

Roland was a student and he was already late for the fall term, so I visited the American consulate in Toronto and told them that he had to get back to school. The consul said to me, "Well, we don't want any Communists in our country." I offered to put up a bond which would be forfeited if he got off the train from New York to Canada before it reached the Canadian border. The consul just looked at me and said, "You're a member of that *Penner* family. Your father is a notorious, world-wide Communist revolutionary!*

"We wouldn't let you, your brother, any relatives in your family, or any friends of yours in or around or near the United States of America!" he added. That stuck because when Roland became the attorney general of Manitoba he couldn't get into the United States. Finally, through pressure from the Manitoba government, who had a lot of dealings with the US consulate in Winnipeg, Roland was issued a "waiver," but only for as long as he was attorney general.

FOLLOWED

I was followed by the RCMP at times. I was twenty years old in March 1941 when I led a delegation of the families of interned men. These men were confined in Petawawa, near Pembroke, Ontario, with Italian Fascists, but later were transferred to the Hull jail.

*Jacob Penner was a noted Communist Party leader in Winnipeg and had run for mayor in 1931 and 1932. He was elected alderman on November 24, 1933, and was re-elected for the next twenty-five years.

I noticed when I got off the train in Ottawa there was a guy there who was 6'5", weighed about 300 pounds, and was wearing a bowler hat. I kept seeing this guy everywhere. One night, when I was coming home from a party around two a.m., who did I see? This man, who was the only other person on the street where I was.

There was also the time I was sent from Toronto by the national executive of the Communist Party to be their main speaker at my father's birthday party in Winnipeg. The party was celebrating his seventieth birthday. For whole sections of that trip from Toronto to Winnipeg there was one person who got on and off whenever I got on and off—it was definitely the RCMP. They were probably concerned over the dangerous message I was bringing my father: it said "Happy Birthday from your Comrades!"

A Closed and Smug Society: Analysis

Reg Whitaker *is a professor of political science whose office is one of many located in a narrow and impersonal hallway in the Ross Building at York University in Toronto. "I grew up in Ottawa and the cold war was being played out around me. A teacher in our school had been named during the Gouzenko affair and I was a babysitter for a woman who was the daughter of a Communist. I discovered later that the RCMP had amassed thousands of pages on this guy, yet he wasn't even high up in the ranks of the party."*

Canada is changing a bit now, but during the '40s and '50s we were a much more closed society than the United States. The Americans did things openly on television. For example, the inquisition into Communists in Hollywood, which began in 1947, was launched under klieg lights, with cameras snapping and reporters everywhere. There were headlines in the papers the next day with revelations about so-and-so, and denials by so-and-so, then naming of so-and-so. It was all out there, upfront. The Canadian equivalent, which was the NFB, was handled so quietly that most Canadians weren't even aware that anything was happening. It was easy for Canada to be smug, but Canadians were simply not aware that equivalent things were happening here.

The Canadian government made a conscious effort to keep things quiet here. First of all, the Liberal government in Ottawa was very careful about it. They didn't want to let things get out of control. The Liberals were smart enough to realize what was happening to the Truman Democrats who had built up the "red menace" to scare hell out of the American people. It was Harry Truman's idea because he thought this was the way to get money to implement the Marshall Plan, build up NATO, and defeat isolationism. But too many others took the ball away. Along came right-wing Republicans, like McCarthy and so on, who accused Truman of being soft on communism. Canada's government looked at this and said, "No, we're not going to allow this to happen here." But they still used anti-communism, while making sure it wasn't politicized.

George Drew, the leader of the Conservatives in the late '40s, was a prototypical would-be McCarthyite. He came from the far right of the Conservative Party and thought a lot of members within his own party were pretty soft on Communists. He tried to be a McCarthy. He would get up in the House of Commons and try to talk about the Communists who had to be cleaned out of government. The Liberals would say, "We're taking care of this problem. We're in control, but we're not going to allow names to come out because it's not the Canadian way."

But they were doing it. Quietly, our government was carrying out security screening in the public service on a massive scale. You really see the RCMP taking control of this. I think it's also part of the Canadian way—the RCMP didn't like the way that J. Edgar Hoover at the FBI quite consciously used the congressmen and senators who were witch-hunters. Hoover would feed them material from his files and set them up. The House on Un-American Activities Committee had nothing except the information they received from Hoover. The RCMP did not like that at all and in their internal documents would criticize the "American style." The RCMP always wanted control—it's the Canadian tradition of law and order under the Crown. Except in Quebec, where the RCMP was thin and relied to some degree on Duplessis and his Red Squad. Even then Quebec wanted to be a "distinct" society.

In the western provinces the provincial police were contracted to the RCMP, so the RCMP was present in large numbers. During labour disputes the RCMP would "maintain order," make sure plants stayed open, infiltrate the unions to try and stop them, and also the security service who were amassing files on left-wing trade unionists.

The RCMP were responsible for screening all federal civilian employees, except for the military, which did its own. The RCMP also screened military contractors. Basically, the Mounties' files were the primary source for who was a security risk and who wasn't. This justified wide-spread infiltration by the RCMP into everything from trade unions to ethnic organizations. The RCMP also handled all the immigration screening and were responsible for advising the government on all matters of security, such as counter-espionage.

The Security Panel was a civilian group in Ottawa, housed with the Privy Council Office, that co-ordinated the government's security intelligence policy and operations. Represented on the Security Panel were the RCMP, defence intelligence, various senior civil servants, and a few people who were full-time security bureaucrats acting as a kind of secretariat. This was the government's attempt to centralize and to keep everything under their control. That's very much the Canadian way. The RCMP liked that better than the American way, which had a Hoover running around, fomenting and setting up witch-hunters who went out of control, eventually attacking the office of the presidency, and permitting a McCarthy to attack the US army and so on. But we had our victims here too.

Was there a blacklist here?

Sure there was. The whole security screening process for the government constitutes, in effect, a blacklist. The screening was to identify those who were security risks. We're talking about tens of thousands of names of people who were screened every year and had to be "cleared" during the cold war. In 1950-51, they began to security screen sailors who worked on the Great Lakes. The

Canadian Seamen's Union was Communist-led and Americans didn't want "red" seamen running amok on weekend leave when they stopped at US ports. People who worked for private companies on defence contracts were screened. You could lose your job this way.

The Liberal government was very politically astute and didn't want to appear to be attacking the labour movement directly as had happened in the United States. The US had a Taft-Hartley law, which demanded that people sign affidavits to attest they weren't Communists or they couldn't hold union office. It was a state intervention into the affairs of unions. The Liberals were much wiser and said, "We'll let the unions clean up their own houses." Thus, particular people within unions were blacklisted here.

I've seen documents from the Security Panel and senior bureaucrats which revealed that people had to be let go because they were security risks and couldn't be transferred to any other job. These people weren't fired publicly, but it was indicated to them that they should probably leave because their careers were really at an end. They were told they could go into the private sector and nobody would know. The RCMP would nod and say how liberal this is; however, we found out afterwards, the RCMP would dog these people everywhere they went. Vindictively. The person would get a new job and suddenly the RCMP would land in the employer's office and say, "You really ought to know who this guy is. . . ." Of course, he or she would lose the job. That's another quasi-official blacklist.

I found files on left-wing ethnic organizations. This is very important material that doesn't exist anywhere else. The RCMP had people inside these organizations who were informing and regularly reporting to them. How else would they know what a bunch of Ukrainians were saying in Ukrainian to each other?

One of the RCMP's uglier practices was to find something on someone and then go to them and say, "You're in trouble. We've got the goods on you. You won't get citizenship or the job you want. However, there is a way to save yourself: be of assistance to us." That's how they built their network of sources. It was like Hollywood where they wanted you to "cooperate," which meant naming names. But it was worse here because it was hidden. In the

States, you knew who the stool-pigeons were because the evidence was public. In Canada, it was all going on quietly behind the scenes.

SAVING THE RCMP FILES

In the end, the McDonald Commission [the 1981 McDonald Royal Commission of Inquiry Concerning Certain Activities of the RCMP] estimated that the RCMP had files on about 800,000 Canadians. CSIS [Canadian Security Intelligence Service] inherited them, but in 1986 the government ordered CSIS to close its counter-subversion branch and to get rid of the files. Except for a small number which were transferred to counter-intelligence and counter-terrorism, the bulk of the files were supposed to be destroyed. Fortunately, some of us who cared about the historical record pointed out they had no business getting rid of these papers. Certainly, they could be taken out of operation, but the national archivist should decide whether files should be disposed of and what should be maintained as part of the historical record.

As a result, I've got 300 pages of listings of subject headings of files which have been physically transferred to the national archives. I'm in the process of requesting some of these files. These 300 legal-sized pages are listings of material just on labour unions and Quebec separatists. There are files on the usual suspects like the United Electrical Radio and Machine Workers of Canada (UE), the Mine Mill, right down to the Ontario Secondary School Teachers' Federation. I'm sure the RCMP had far better information on labour unions than Labour Canada ever had. There are also boxes and boxes of files on the Parti Québécois, which was the elected party of that province.

Can the RCMP's actions during the cold war be justified now, since communism in the USSR appears to have failed and the role of the RCMP was for the overall health of democracy in Canada?

The argument that we spent the Soviet Union into submission by forcing them to carry on the cold war is one thing, but was there an internal threat to Canada? I have no difficulty in saying this argument is a crock. It's such a joke. Nobody ever took the Communists as seriously as the Mounties. The notion that one Communist within a trade union could transform it into an instrument of Moscow doesn't hold up. The organizers knew damn well they had to deliver contracts and put bread and butter on the table or else they'd be on the street the next day. Most of the people didn't give a shit about the Soviets, they just wanted a good union. The government talked a lot about sabotage but nobody ever came up with a single instance.

THE WATCHERS

*"**Bernie**" is an advertising executive in the Toronto area. He "grew up" within the left-wing movement in Toronto. "The majority of the young people in this milieu were active in the peace movement and in election campaigns for Communist candidates like Joe Salsberg, A.A. MacLeod, and Stewart Smith. I was expelled from my grade eight class over this once. Tim Buck was running in the Trinity riding and I came into class with a sweatshirt which said 'Tim Buck For Trinity.' My teacher said, 'You can't sit in the class with that sweater.' I asked why. 'There's such things as freedom of speech and freedom of expression.' Then he said, 'Not that free, not that expression, and it's my classroom.' I said, 'No, it's my class and you're here teaching me and it's got nothing to do with what I'm wearing.' After two days of being out of the class, I took my sweater off." That was the first of many confrontations over political beliefs.*

I was working in a radio station when the RCMP came to check on me and someone else. The RCMP told the station manager about parts of my background and history that gave the impression I was a dangerous subversive. The manager was strong enough to say to the RCMP, "Look, these two guys haven't said anything or done anything. This is a country in which people are free to think and I'm not going to fire them."

That was the first time. The second time was when I got a job in private television and someone I knew from college, who was already working at the station, came up to me. "OK, you're going to keep quiet. You're not going to say anything," he told me. "I know all about you because I was assigned to watch you for three years." Now, who assigned him to watch me for three years? He gave me the impression that the RCMP had, and he told me he was a reserve lieutenant in the army. This brought home to me the very fact that there was a system of "watchers" who observed the actions of particular individuals.

If you were living in a left-wing milieu you accepted blacklisting and the possibility of blacklisting as part of the adventure of "progress." You felt part of an army that was leading the world to a better tomorrow and you knew you had to live with blacklisting. It was like a folk-singer having to pay his dues. It gave you strength yet it made you quite fearful because you had no idea who was spying on you, and I use the word "spying" very deliberately. You assumed someone was watching and you became very careful. At the same time, you were very open in your own milieu. But every time you went outside that environment, you stopped to look back.

You understood that in the future you might have some trouble getting certain jobs—anything that involved government or a security check, or anything that involved dealing with the United States. For example, you had to be careful in applying to the CBC because it was a government corporation and you would be checked at certain levels.

As a kid, I knew people who had been blacklisted and had seen actors come up from New York to Canada. I saw [singer] Pete Seeger come up to our camp, which was called "Camp Naivelt" [new world], for a "rest." Although delineated as a "Communist" camp, it reflected a secular, non-Zionist, socialist perspective. It was a community of like-minded, working-class people, largely, in the needle trade. There were people who were active in union affairs and, yes, there were people who followed the Communist line. But did that make every one of their children a subversive and in need of watching?

This was a terrible part of Canadian history. It made the kids of these people paranoid, schizophrenic, and adventuresome at the same time. You knew there was the possibility of danger because someone out there was watching you; yet, you had a vision of a new world to win and it gave you strength—like the strength of a religion. We knew that we had to be careful and we couldn't even jest about it.

There was this classic story and it's true. A young couple was just married and someone said, "Let's phone immigration at the airport and tell them that two Communists are trying to get into the States and see what will happen?" It happened—they got stopped and it took years for them to clear their names even though no one investigated them. All on the strength of that phone call. It was that easy to incriminate.

There was a relationship between left-wing movements in different cities. That made me aware of problems in Montreal, where there was a Padlock Law and a Red Squad. The Red Squad very carefully investigated all the left-wing venues. We also knew that the Red Squad had spies who used to come to Toronto. When there was a general meeting of the National Federation of Labour Youth, which in effect was the Young Communist League, we knew for sure that at least one person from the Montreal delegation would be a spy reporting back to the Red Squad. And it did happen. One day, I brought home a young man from Montreal to have dinner with us. We sat and talked. Later, I found out he was the son of one of the policemen of the Montreal Red Squad. We lived with those kinds of close calls all the time and you thought, "Shit, you're going to get in trouble."

We took precautions when we visited Montreal for a conference. We always drove in separate cars, arrived at different times, and dispersed to different homes very carefully in the dead of the night. You have to realize we were only kids, only fifteen or sixteen years old.

The break for everyone took place after the Twentieth Congress of the Soviet Union and Khrushchev's secret report.* That devastated thousands of young Jewish people in the Communist movement. But was my adventure in the left worth it? Absolutely. It gave me a set of values which were humanistic, positive, and critical. It carried on the Jewish tradition of social justice. It was a different left-wing movement then—it had vision, ideology, clear principles, and

* Khrushchev's speech to the congress exposed Stalin's history of purges, executions, and mass arrests.

felt it was going to win. One could join that kind of army because there was certitude. Today, it's very hard to become a true believer in anything. I believe there's still a need for a life where social justice and not materialism or selfishness is the leading principle.

FOLLOWED BY THE RCMP

*A printer by profession, **Sam Lipshitz** became an editor and leader of the Jewish left in Canada during the '40s and '50s. He was the national secretary of the Jewish bureau of the Communist Party until he had misgivings about Stalin and the policies of the Soviet Union. He eventually broke with the party after a trip to the Soviet Union.*

I was followed around by the RCMP. In 1949 I went to Poland, where a Yiddish cultural conference took place. I was the editor of a left-wing paper that was invited and I was selected to go there. When I came back, I toured the country—Winnipeg, Edmonton, Regina, and Vancouver. In every single city there was a squad of RCMP following me everywhere. I recognized them right away. For instance: one Saturday evening in Winnipeg at 11:30 p.m., when I was going home to a friend's house, a car followed me. I realized who it was. The next day, they again followed me everywhere I went. I went into a coffee shop and the guy from the RCMP came in too and sat next to me. I turned to him and asked him if he wanted me to buy him a coffee. He was a bit embarrassed.

I went to Edmonton, where we had a number of good friends who supported the paper. Most of them were storekeepers. I met them in the evening and the next day I went into their stores to solicit contributions for the paper. When I went into the store of one man, who had been a very loyal supporter for many years, he suddenly told me, "Get out! I don't want to see you!" I was shocked because he was a good friend and a very nice person. Then I went into another person's store and he told me that the RCMP had come in to a number of stores and warned them about me. I went into the Eaton's store and the RCMP even followed me there, but I gave them the slip. In the evening, when

I came to the railway station, they were there! I suspect there was an informer who gave them information about my schedule.

I went to a place outside of Edmonton to see a friend and, sure enough, they followed me all the way. I turned back and deliberately stopped my car in front of the office of the Communist Party. I told the RCMP, "Why do you waste your time? If you had asked me, I'd have told you where I was going." I couldn't be intimidated. It was a matter of standing up for your rights and expressing your disgust at their behaviour. Why the hell were they following *me*?

THE FILES

Don Wall *is a former civilian employee of the Royal Canadian Mounted Police who analysed files collected during the cold-war period. Born in Saskatchewan of Swedish heritage, he started out with the communications branch of the National Research Council, which handled communication intelligence and listened to international short-wave broadcasts to decipher codes and messages. He believes his efforts helped prevent the witch-hunts from getting out of hand in Canada.*

We were in the civilian research section of a special branch of the RCMP, which was the Security Service. We assembled briefs on organizations which were Communist-oriented, like the Peace Council or the Association of Ukrainian Canadians or the United Jewish Peoples Order (UJPO). Most of the work involved pack-rat burrowing in files. Old and dusty files.

We spent a lot of our time pulling stuff together and trying to analyse it and make some sense of it. One of things we decided very early on was that the assessment of sources was absolutely essential. We persuaded the then head of the special branch, George McClellan, who later became commissioner, that this was a directive that he had to insist upon right across the country. Sources had to be assessed for reliability. When you got a report from Winnipeg that said "source absolutely reliable," you knew it was a wiretap. "Reliable" was good. If it said "reliability unknown," you'd have your doubts. They were required to make that kind of assessment.

We dug files out and went through them. I remember there were up to three volumes of files on certain persons and organizations, and each file was about six inches thick. One third of the file came from newspaper clippings, and interviews with friends were also recorded. Sometimes the file was in chronological order, sometimes not. We got to the point where we had a sort of intuitive sense about the person in the file. The files have a way of taking on a life of their own and you have to bloody well be aware of that.

It was my job to assess the files and boil down that mass of information into something which made sense. There were sources who just kept sending stuff in only because they were paid at the end of the month. An amazing number of immigrants were sources. They were profoundly anti-Soviet and also unnaturally voluble. They gave names, pages and pages of data. A lot of it was gossipy and highly tainted.

The files on people like A.A. MacLeod and J.B. Salsberg were thick. Salsberg was generally regarded as a humane, genteel, and intelligent Communist. We also had a file on a Welsh guy who was in the party who was an absolute drunk and we knew he liked martinis. The force had a string of informers inside the party. They had sources. They talked to Leslie Morris [an executive of the Communist Party] one time. They went to known Communist members cold and said, "Look, we know who you are and what you are. Do you want to come and talk to us?" They tried this on Morris and he told them to fuck off.

We knew there were informers to the force who made up things. That was one of the reasons we insisted on the very careful assessment of sources. The assessment was usually done in the divisional headquarters by the special branch guy. Usually, they were at least corporals and they had to have about fifteen to twenty years' experience. Some of them were quite good. They used their professional judgement.

Some hated the job but were required to do it; some kept files for years and years and wanted to prosecute—that's what they thought police were for. We were civilians and constantly regarded with suspicion. We were allowed to eat in the sergeants' mess but not the officers' mess.

We weren't operational but, once, a group of us did go to a meeting that Tim Buck (the head of the party) held in Ottawa. There were four or five of us and we went as a lark more than anything else. It was funny as hell. And dull as hell too. We all put on old clothes so we'd look like proletarians. Buck was a funny little guy and he talked endlessly. We must have listened for two hours. They looked at us a bit askance because they couldn't recognize us as party members, but we recognized a lot of people in the place because we'd seen pictures of them in the files. Finally, we got up and went away. We couldn't take notes, that would look too suspicious. Our function was essentially research and we weren't in any sense operational.

In the research branch, we started with a staff of three and it included a Czech diplomat who had defected from Ankara, Turkey, in 1948. The staff eventually grew to seventeen civilians and all had university training in various disciplines. Did we find anything consequential? Generally, we found that the aura of the cold war was exaggerated. There was far less to fear than the public and the politicians seemed to think. Our view was that a solid democratic system is its own best defence. We tried to reduce the basic fear that people had at the time. It seemed to us that that fear was dangerous.

There were guys in the House of Commons who were raging mad. I guess we were fortunate in those days in having a fairly sensible minister of justice in Stuart Garson who was a balanced sort of guy, not a radical in any sense. Some of our briefs went to him through his executive assistant, Gordon Blair, who eventually became a member of Parliament himself. I liked Gordon very much.

I was asked to do a report based on what the RCMP had on file on the CBC's International Service. I found that there was really nothing there. Someone in the House of Commons was raising a hell of a stink but not naming names. I went through the whole of the Mounted Police files on the international service and found maybe two or three guys who had some questionable association with some Communist organization in the past. But there was absolutely nothing to be concerned about.

There was close collaboration between the RCMP and the FBI. There was a guy from the FBI who had an office at Mounted Police headquarters that he occupied full time. The force was closer to the FBI than the CIA, which was new in those days. Actually, the FBI guy was a civilized guy, a balanced guy, and anti-McCarthy. But he had to fulfil the orders they gave him. He would get names from the force and these people would then have trouble getting across the border because their names went to the bureau.

I feel satisfied that we in Canada avoided what somebody called "the worst excesses of the French Revolution." We had some sense of balance and civility. There were a lot of others who were "rarin' to go get the goddamn red Commies." And hell, we got into fights with them. Once, I wrote a report and Sergeant McLaren said, "This is a criticism of the force." I said, "Mac, you're damn right it is, because the force is wrong on this!" He didn't speak to me for four months.

When I looked into the NFB I found again, as I had with the international service, that there were two or three questionable people who had long since gone. In order to deserve the reputation it had as a damn good film-making organization, the NFB had to have people like Norman McLaren and John Grierson. Christ, Grierson was a genius! The man founded the damn thing. Was he a spy? No, absolutely not. There was very little to the scare that the NFB was red. Certainly not on Grierson's part. He was just a tough-minded, left-leaning Scot.

THE VISIT

Gilbert Levine lives in Ottawa, where he spent many years as director of research for CUPE (Canadian Union of Public Employees). Canada's largest union represents municipal employees; hospital, education, and public utility workers; flight attendants; and many CBC employees, among others. Levine, a peace activist, is recently retired.

I had always assumed that there was an RCMP file on me, but I got quite a shock a number of years ago when I was in Halifax meeting with the research director of the Nova Scotia Government Employees Union. We used to exchange information from time to time regarding different public-sector research issues. When I sent him material, I would also attach my business card to it. He told me that one day a full-time grievance representative of the union came into his office, saw a document that I had sent with my card attached, and said, "Oh, I know that guy." The research director asked how and for some strange reason he answered, "I was his agent for the RCMP."

Normally, the RCMP are sworn to secrecy, even after they leave the force. This guy had left the force after eighteen years and, lo and behold, he ends up getting a job as a union rep, of all things! Anyway, he told my friend, the research director, this whole story about how he trailed me from time to time. He really spilled the beans. For example, he told stories about me during the Liberal leadership convention in Ottawa in '67, the year Trudeau became leader. It was during the Vietnam War and I was part of a group that had staged all kinds of peace demonstrations around the Civic Centre where the leadership convention was going on. One of his jobs was to keep an eye on me.

The next time I was in Halifax, I decided to pay this former RCMP guy a visit. I went up to the union office and asked for him. I was told that he was not in but was expected shortly, so I asked if I could wait in his office until he came. After five minutes, he walks in. You should have seen the expression on this guy's face!

I confronted him and told him, "I understand you know quite a bit about my life and my activities." First he denied it. To try to get him talking, I related a little true story to him. I said, "You probably know I am Jewish. When a new Jewish community is formed, one of the first things that is done is to put up a synogogue. But, even before that, a cemetery is prepared because Jews have to be buried in their own Jewish cemetery. Because of the Jewish experience—particularly in Eastern Europe under the persecution of the Russian tzars—an informer (a 'masser') was always considered to be the lowest of the low. If an informer ever died, he didn't have the right to be buried in a Jewish cemetery and that was a terrible sin to befall anybody. So, I feel strongly about informers and I want to know why you did that work."

At first he denied doing anything. Finally, he said he was assigned to me and he did follow me around to certain demonstrations and so on. But he could not elaborate because his wife was still on the force. I wasn't there to punch him out, I only wanted to extract as much information as I could. He had trailed me in the '60s when peace activities were considered by the Mounties to be synonymous with Communist or pro-Soviet activities. Therefore, they believed peaceniks were dangerous people. The Vietnam War was on and Canada was allied to the United States in that effort. The RCMP collected a lot of information—mostly from phone tapping. It bothered me a lot because I knew the RCMP was passing this information on to the president of my union and he was trying to use it to harass me.

My wife had a friend. The two of them used to spend an hour a day on the phone, talking about art and feminism and so on. I learned indirectly from another RCMP agent that all of that conversation was being recorded. Because she was involved in the feminist movement, my wife was considered by the Mounties to be even more revolutionary than me.

I graduated from university at the end of the '40s and worked at various social work jobs until '56 when I got my first job with the union. I had also been active politically from '45 to '56 and was a member of the CP. When I left school, I worked for four years as a research assistant for what was then the Toronto Welfare Council, which is now called the Social Planning Council of Toronto. A friend of mine who was living in Regina learned about a job opening as research director in the Saskatchewan Department of Health. I had the support of the deputy minister of health to get that job. Just as I had handed my application in, I took a temporary job in Toronto in a trade fair exhibition displaying Indonesian crafts. I was in my booth when a guy came along, sat down, and started asking me questions all about Saskatchewan. I found it strange. How did he know I had an interest in Saskatchewan? Eventually I said, "Why are you asking me all these questions?" He replied, "I'm doing an investigation on you." He must have been a Mountie.

Anyway, in the end I didn't get that job and I was told that for political reasons I wouldn't be accepted. Saskatchewan had a CCF government and, at the time, was supposed to be a better place politically than the rest of Canada. I don't feel Tommy Douglas would have done that, but somewhere in the bureaucracy there were people concerned about people like me.

CHAPTER SEVEN

THE QUEBEC EXPERIENCE: THE RED SQUADS

THE DUPLESSIS BRIDGE AND THE COMMUNISTS

Jacques Pigeon is a deputy minister in the department of communications of the province of Quebec. On June 6, 1948, the town of Trois Rivières opened a new bridge and named it after Maurice Duplessis. When Duplessis cut the ceremonial ribbon, he stated that the bridge was "solid like the Union Nationale." In the morning of January 31, 1951, the structure collapsed and eight people were killed. Duplessis and his cronies in government were quick to blame others for this disaster. Jacques Pigeon's father discovered the truth.

I was a teenager in 1951 when the bridge collapsed and I remember very vividly when my father travelled to Trois Rivières. It was quite an event. Duplessis had inaugurated that bridge in 1948 and made it one of the focal points of his regime. There was great pomp and circumstance when this "masterpiece" of a bridge was opened.

But Duplessis had handed out the contracts to build the bridge more on the basis of patronage than on qualifications, so the bridge was built with faults in it. Some years later, in 1951, the bridge just collapsed. People were driving on the bridge and there were some deaths. The bridge was in a riding adjacent to Duplessis' own. Since it was quite close to his electors, Duplessis had to blame it on somebody. With McCarthyism rampant throughout North America, Duplessis decided to blame it on the Communists.

His minister of public works claimed it was sabotaged by Communists. He couldn't admit that it was their people who were responsible. They had built this wonderful bridge but denied their people were at fault. They had to find somebody to blame it on, and that somebody was the Communists.

There was an enquiry following the collapse of the bridge. My father, Louis-Philippe Pigeon, was very strongly anti-Duplessis and he was known as such. At that time, he was a lawyer freely advising Georges-Emile LaPalme, the leader of the opposition. He would go over just about every piece of legislation and prepare the notes for LaPalme. My father was almost an engineer and was well known for his competence in that field. He could easily have passed any exams to be an engineer. He was the one who found out exactly what went wrong with the bridge.

My father, acting on behalf of the Liberal Party, demonstrated that the bridge was badly built and that Duplessis' engineers had just screwed up. One of the steel beams of the bridge was of such cheap quality—it was supplied by a contractor who was a bagman for Duplessis. That brought the bridge down. My father had many photographs of the collapsed bridge and the story was all over the papers. I remember seeing pictures of cracks in the steel beams.

THE POWER OF SILENCE

*Born in Napierville, Quebec in 1925, **Denis Lazure** is a prominent politician. A leading member of the Parti Québécois, Lazure was first elected a member of the Quebec National Assembly in 1976, representing the riding of Chambly. Also a prominent child psychiatrist, Lazure holds a medical degree from the University of Montreal and received specialty training from the University of Pennsylvania, McGill, and Temple University. In 1950 he was a student leader.*

By the spring of 1952 I was a medical intern in Montreal and had applied to study psychiatry in Boston and Philadelphia. I planned to travel by car to Boston and Philadelphia for interviews. I travelled with two friends, who were also interns, and we reached the border in Lacolle, Quebec. My two friends were cleared very readily. When my name came up, they found it in a big book and called me into an office and asked me questions for a half an hour. They finally said I would not be authorized to cross the border, but the US authorities would not give me their reasons for keeping me out. It was a Saturday morning and I had no way of calling a lawyer, so we went back to Montreal. I checked with all my contacts and, finally, was told by the Department of External Affairs that it was because of the trips I had taken to visit countries in Eastern Europe, namely Czechoslovakia and Poland.

In 1950 I was president of the University of Montreal student body and, for one month, I attended an international students' service seminar in France. After the seminar I travelled to Prague, Czechoslovakia, with William Turner, who was then president of the student body at the University of Toronto. Incidentally, Turner later became chairman of the board of Consolidated Bathurst and I have still kept in contact with him—he's one of my few capitalist friends. He and I were selected by the National Federation of Canadian University Students to be observers at the Congress of the International Union of Students. We were open about this. As a matter of fact, we even sent a report to Lester B. Pearson, who was a deputy minister of external affairs, about it.

The following year, 1951, I was again delegated by the National Federation of Canadian University Students to be an observer at the annual council meeting of the International Union of Students in Warsaw. I believe the information the RCMP had about me was transmitted to the FBI. In fact, I'm sure about that.

One day in 1951 the RCMP came down to my basement apartment in Côte-des-Neiges. I was still in medical school then and I recall these two big fellows in civilian clothes knocking at my door and they had their RCMP badges. They came to question me, and they inspected my books and papers. After an hour, they left and didn't say very much. They had a file on me and were building up that file. I sort of expected their visit because I was one of the few people who travelled behind the "iron curtain." Not too many people went there in 1950. There were students who were very much against our going to visit these countries.

In those days, I was tagged as a Communist by the Jesuit magazine *Relations*. I remember they carried a big article denouncing my acquaintance with the Communist regimes. They attacked me personally and it affected my medical career. During that year, 1951–52, I was an intern in St. Jean de Dieu hospital in Montreal which was then run by nuns. In mid-year I was expelled. This was because I was suspected of having Communist convictions. It happened in November 1951. The medical director called me in and said, "My poor chap, I like you a lot but you cannot come back after Christmas." I asked why. He said, "I can't tell you why but you cannot come back."

This went on for a few minutes and I told him I couldn't accept that and I would have to see the Mother Superior. This I did because the director was not the number one person in the hospital, but number two. So I went to see the nun and she was sitting behind her desk. She just said, "You cannot come back here and I don't have any reasons to give you." Sitting there with her, I understood the power of silence. I never really received a reason, either verbally or in writing, of why I was expelled from St. Jean de Dieu in November of 1951 but it was a "secret de Polichinelle," or an open secret, that I was expelled because of my trips the previous summer.

It was mid-year and I had to finish an internship in psychiatry in Montreal because I was planning to go the US the following September. I went to the Verdun Protestant Hospital [now Douglas Hospital], and this very pragmatic, English institution didn't delve into my convictions. They told me they didn't have any salary for me, but if I could come free of charge then they'd accept me. I did go and was without any salary for six months, but I was fed and lodged at the hospital.

PEACE ACTIVIST

I participated in a large gathering in Toronto in 1950 when I was president of the University of Montreal students. The peace movement had a big rally at Maple Leaf Gardens and I was one of the many speakers. I was sincerely taken by the peace movement. During my first trip to Prague in the summer of 1950, I was very impressed by people who were there, like Olaf Palme who was then president of the Swedish students. The Prague meeting was also attended by many other well-known pacifists. I remember Picasso was there. The Korean War had just started and there was a large delegation of Korean students and I was also impressed with the emergence of the colonized peoples of Africa and Asia. In that sense, I was what you would call "leftist," but I was never a member of the Communist Party.

When I ran for the first time for the Parti Québécois, Camille Samson of the Créditistes, who was a candidate in Témiscamingue, called me a Communist on the air. He half-retracted that allegation because most people didn't take him too seriously. Being called a Communist didn't harm me then but it did when I was a student. When I was refused entry to the States I became the centre of controversy, and the refusal became a big issue in student newspapers and campuses all across the country. Very, very big.

At the same time, when I came back from the second meeting in 1951, I proposed that Canadian students and Soviet students set up an exchange. There was a referendum on each campus over this. The yeas won by a large majority, but it didn't materialize because there was a special clause in the constitution of the National Federation of Canadian University Students that we needed a consensus. "Consensus" was interpreted as meaning unanimous. Fifteen years later, there was finally an exchange between Canadian and Soviet students.

MONTREAL BATTLES

Lea Roback *is a long-time union organizer and party activist. She learned Yiddish at home, English at school, and absorbed French on the streets of working-class Montreal.*

I was running the party book shop on Bleury, not far from the Armoury. It seemed like Duplessis' Red Squad came in every five minutes. We knew when they came in and we'd wink at each other. They were always buying books but I'm sure they never read them. One of our best customers was Monsigneur Lionel Groulx. He wanted to read them so he could tell the poor French Canadians who buy those books that they were going straight to hell. He must have had quite a Lenin library!

The church was worried because many French Canadians listened to what we were saying. The church didn't want change—especially that person called the "little Cardinal." It got physical once during the time of an election. The French local of the movement was at 2544 Ste. Catherine East. I was sent there because I spoke French. At that time, students from l'Université were on St. Denis street. They had no use for our "locale dans l'est." So they came down wearing velvet berets, with ribbons which identified the faculty they were in, and canes. One of them threw "une balle" through the window and broke it. I walked out and saw the man I called "little Cardinal" there. He had red hair and I knew he was a high-ranking member of the religion because he wore a purple sash and was leading the students. One student pushed me and I fell and hit my head. I screamed, "Can't you watch your dirty gang?"

He said, "Your tough luck. You should have stayed indoors."

That little red-headed "Cardinal" was leading them and with him was a Red Squad man, Ennis, who hated my guts. It was mutual since I hated his too! I played it tough. You see how lucky I was to know French—it got me bashed in the head.

The Red Squad came to our house on Querbes Avenue. As Mama would say, "Zonnen vider dah" ("They're here again"). Neighbours would wonder, "Look at all the cars in front of the Robacks'." There were six cars. "What could be the matter?" they'd ask.

We didn't have much money in our house but we always had books. The Red Squad would take the books and Mama would tell them, "You have no right to come to my house!"

The Red Squad guys would tell her, "Go away, don't bother us!"

My mama would respond, "You want me to go away? This is my house." Then she put a book with a red cover under the Red Squad man's nose and said, "Why don't you take that?"

He said, "Are you through laughing at us?"

Mama was a very determined person. As she used to say, "If something is not right, you change it. Don't allow it to carry on."

It was tough when Gouzenko happened. He wanted favours from

the Canadian government and got after the most vulnerable persons, like the the people who were active with Fred Rose. It was tough because you never knew when you were going to be taken in. I worked for Fred Rose during the elections and got a taste of it. The police came around.

Once, when those "Cossacks," as Mama called them, came tramping up the stairs to my bedroom, I had some very confidential lists in my possession. What did I do? I threw them out the window and I went out the back stairs. Outside, the concierge on our Querbes Avenue building told me, "I think you threw this, and the wind blew the pages down." I said thanks and grabbed my lists. Before I went to bed that night I found a safer place. We kept moving stuff all the time.

I still say we were right. Maybe our methods were not what they should have been but, by jove, our instincts were good! What hurts many movements is when people go in saying, "I'll go in because I'll be able to get a job out of it later." Then you're sunk because you're going in only for yourself. I don't mean to be heroic but we never went into it for ourselves. The times were tough because so many of our people were blacklisted and couldn't get jobs.

There was a wonderful couple, Bella Gauld and her husband. That couple looked after those who were blacklisted and had nowhere to sleep and nowhere to go. People would come to Bella Gauld's home and she'd take care of them. There was always a couch, a rug, or the floor for them to spend the night. We were always helping one another.

DUPLESSIS' FOES

Madeleine Parent *was a union organizer for forty-one years. She and Kent Rowley, a colleague and later her husband, led many of the great struggles in Quebec labour history, including the fight by textile workers to organize and improve the conditions in their plants in the 1940s and early 1950s. Blacklisted by Duplessis, she was harrassed by the Quebec provincial police Red Squad. Today, she's retired but is still very active as a feminist and Quebec representative to NAC (the National Action Committee on the Status of Women).*

What did being on the blacklist mean to you?

We were followed, especially in time of strikes such as the Lachute strike and the Valleyfield and Montreal strikes. They knew where we were all the time. I was physically frightened at times but you had to depend on the people you were working with—the cotton or woollen mill workers and their families. They were very helpful and protective. For example, I was arrested about five times during the Lachute strike, yet I could go into the houses of many families and hide there until I was ready to go out on a picket line or to a meeting.

After the strike of 1946 in Valleyfield, the police were hunting for me on the eve of a vote. It was a trumped-up charge by Duplessis who wanted us to lose. The police were searching all over town for me. I was in hiding in a workers' home and she would get reports from other women who would tell her, "They're searching on our street."

They would all warn each other. They were courageous people who didn't cower in their homes, and they were proud of their own contributions and knew what was meant by solidarity. Even today, I meet people who are forty-five or fifty years old and who were children of those parents who were in our strikes and organizing campaigns. Many of them are activists today in Quebec.

TAPPED PHONES AND LIES

I once got a phone call from another trade unionist who was sympathetic and was calling me on behalf of his union president, who was also sympathetic. He told me that we were under such terrible attack that their own union had to be very careful in spite of their sympathies. I knew our phone was tapped and I tried to convince him not to talk but to meet me instead. But he kept talking for about forty-five minutes. I didn't hear from him afterwards, so I sent two of our strikers to see him. And he said to them, "Did Madeleine report what I said to her? Because Cardinal Leger repeated to my president, word for word, what I said to her on the telephone."

It was all taken down during our phone conversation. In those days, tapped phones were more obvious than they are today. There was a kind of a buzz at certain intervals; it stopped until a tape got around again, then there was another buzz. So it was a familiar warning.

I'll tell you another event which took place during my third or fourth arrest in Lachute during the strike of 1947. The police came to pick me up along with another colleague at the union hall around two o'clock in the morning. We knew they were going to arrest us. One of the strikers and his two daughters stayed with us so we wouldn't be alone when the police came. The police put us under arrest and Paul Benoit, who was the policeman in charge of that little detachment of provincial police, went nosing around the hall and picked a paper out of the garbage bin. Paul Benoit was the Red Squad man.

When I had my trial for seditious conspiracy, he presented this paper. It was a series of notes about a meeting that the president of the local chaired and I sat next to him as organizer. The paper contained an agenda, along with his notes and my notes. Benoit forged incendiary expressions into those notes. He tried to imitate my handwriting and added words to the note, things about "beating scabs" and so on, things I would never say.

Benoit testified and presented this document as a piece of evidence. He read it aloud. My lawyer got this paper from him before he cross-examined him. I circled all of the words he had forged, so my lawyer cross-examined him on every one of those words. That pretty well destroyed his testimony. But he had the nerve afterwards, at noon break when the judge and jury were out, to come over to my lawyer in my presence and brag, "Well, it wasn't a bad try, was it?" It was that blatant.

Ours had to be a fairly militant union organization because the big textile companies were absolutely adamant about not having a union. They had fought unions successfully in the '20s and '30s and they were still determined not to tolerate them. So any union organization which was the least bit militant was deemed communistic. That was especially true during the time of the Valleyfield and Montreal strike of 1946, when we had 6,000 members out. We were not members of the party, but we would not refuse to work with other trade unionists such as Alec Gauld from the Plumbers and Steamfitters Union or people from the Fur and Leather Workers' Union or the Seamen's Union who were considered leftists. They were union people too, and they were involved in a struggle for their own members and generous in offering solidarity to other organized workers.

DUPLESSIS' GREAT TRIAL

Five of us were charged with seditious conspiracy in the Lachute strike of 1947. There was Kent Rowley, myself, another union organizer, and two of the striking workers of the Ayers Woolen Mills. Subsequently, the charges against the two mill workers were dropped—that left three of us. Duplessis planned it as the "great trial." Mine was a three-month trial—the longest that had ever been held in Quebec at that time. The judge who presided was a Duplessis man who had been the president of the Conservative Party of Quebec at the turn of the century. He was in his seventies by then. Every day during the trial, Duplessis would put in a phone call to the Crown prosecutor, Noel Dorion [he later became a minister in Diefenbaker's cabinet], to enquire how the trial was going. There would be a hushed silence in the courtroom and the judge would signal to the Crown prosecutor that Duplessis was on the phone waiting for him. The proceedings were adjourned temporarily while Noel Dorion reported to the premier and then came back to his work.

"Seditious conspiracy" turned out to be a question of our conspiring to ruin businesses these generous enterprising men had brought to industrial towns where people could earn a living and live happily. As they saw it, we caused trouble and defied authority and religion; we were defying these great, generous industrialists. We were said to be breaking down the fabric of society. The Crown had a professor of philosophy who was in the witness box for three to five days, just explaining how it was a Communist act to have a strike in a situation like that. He was a lay professor of theology who was treated with great respect by the Crown and judge.

Most of the other witnesses were provincial policemen, including Paul Benoit who I mentioned before. Benoit also repeated my speeches in the court. During the strike, we used to have meetings every Sunday night. These were public meetings so not only strikers came but also their wives, children, and the whole town. Benoit repeated my speeches in court but he distorted things at every opportunity to make them sound more revolutionary, more anarchistic.

How did the trial end up?

I was sentenced to two years in jail by a jury that was intimidated and/or bought. We found out that one of the jurors, who owned a grocery store and had a beer licence, was told that if I was not condemned then he would lose his licence. Another juror owned a couple of taxis in Ste. Agathe and one of his drivers had recently been in a serious accident. He got a visit from the provincial police who told him, "If she's acquitted you're in real trouble, but if she's convicted you'll be OK." The foreman of the jury once owned a small hotel/beer hall and had lost it. He was told that if I was condemned then he'd get his licence back so he could buy another business, which he did.

We went to appeal and won on a technicality. The court stenographer died before he was able to enter the three months of testimony into the record. After the appeal, we went back to the courts every year at the opening of the assizes to ask for a new trial. We were refused and the charges were left, pending orders from Duplessis. The information came down that the procureur general [attorney general], who was Duplessis, felt it was not in the public interest to proceed at this time.

Finally, in 1955 Judge Caron, who was no friend of Duplessis, was sitting. Caron had presided over the public investigation into corruption in the Montreal police and the premier disliked him greatly for that. When we came before Judge Caron and asked for a trial he asked the local Crown prosecutor for his opinion. He answered, "We can't proceed because the senior Crown prosecutor, Noel Dorion, can't be here at this time."

Then Caron said, "And where was he last year?"

The local prosecutor hesitated but found another excuse for Noel Dorion.

"And the year before that, where was he?" asked Caron.

There was no answer to that.

So Caron said, "I am fixing the date for trial—two weeks from now."

He then gave notice to both sides that he would accept no excuses or delays. Two weeks later, we showed up in court. So did the same local prosecutor who brought a note from Duplessis which said it was not in the public interest to proceed. Caron read the note and threw it down with contempt. I still remember the way that sheet of paper floated slowly down in the air. Then Caron said, "We will proceed."

He had twelve men sworn in for jury service. There were no women on juries in those days. The charge was read by the court clerk, then the judge ordered the Crown prosecutor to make his case but the prosecutor had nothing to say. Then the judge instructed our lawyer on the best way to proceed. He said, "You've got three choices. If you do it a certain way they can still get back at your clients. If you do it another way something else could result. If you do it a third way, they shall be acquitted and there's no chance to renew the charges."

Naturally, our lawyer did it the last way. The judge turned to the jurors and said, "Gentlemen, you have been witness to this case. The Crown has no evidence against the accused and you have no choice but to declare them not guilty." So they all said not guilty in chorus and the judge asked them to repeat their verdict individually, which they did. And we were acquitted—eight years afterwards!

It wasn't even reported in the newspapers. They had reported all the publicity against us without really reporting our defence to numerous attacks. When the news was in our favour they didn't write about it at all. As a matter of fact, people would meet me later and say, "I thought you were in jail." They claimed to have lost track of me and didn't know what happened, except that they had heard I was going to the women's penitentiary in Kingston. The *Gazette* and *Le Montreal Matin* were the most vicious dailies of all, reporting on the strikes and anti-labour trials.

THE BLACKLISTED SPORTSWRITER

Bess Shockett *is a former activist of the Communist Party's youth wing who, along with her family, felt the stings of the infamous Red Squad in*

Montreal during the era of the anti-Communist Padlock Law. Today, she's a prominent executive in Jewish cultural organizations in the Toronto area and promotes the revival of the Yiddish language.

In 1947 I had my own introduction to the Red Squad when I went to Europe to attend the International Youth Festival in Prague. We went to work in Yugoslavia as volunteer labour to help build a youth railway from Samac to Sarajevo.

We worked for three weeks, were given a tour for three weeks, and then hung around waiting for our freighter to take us back home. We were able to get a transit to take us through Paris into Prague but we weren't allowed to get out in West Germany whatsoever. And then we received a transit visa to get into Hoboken, New Jersey.

When our ship came into Hoboken there was a bus waiting for us. The only way we could get back to Canada was if the people in Toronto (the Communist Party and the youth movement) had a bus waiting for us. They put us right in the bus to take us straight to Toronto. We weren't allowed to "contaminate" American soil. But the poor bus driver was tired out as he reached Buffalo and he was going to seal us in the station because he had to go to the washroom. We all started yelling, "Hey, we also have to go to the bathroom." I threatened that we'd all pee in the back of the bus. Then he opened the bus door and said, "You've got half an hour."

When I came home to Montreal I went to work immediately the next day because I was so flat broke. As I returned home at 5:30 in the evening, I saw neighbours peeking through the doorway. One of them whispered to me, "There's big guys in there!" I walked through the door and there were these four guys from the Red Squad just going through all my books in my house. There were five of us whose homes were raided that evening. I didn't fare that badly. The wife of leader of the youth movement was home with the kids when the Red Squad raided their home and they terrified her. They actually tore up her chesterfields and pillows and so on with a knife.

In my house they dumped things to look through them and they took a lot of my books. Interestingly, most of my books were non-Communist books, but they didn't discriminate and they took those too. First of all, I asked them if they had a search warrant and they said they did. I asked to see it and they said, "Well, you can't." I said, "I will get *you* arrested if you don't have a warrant." So they went to their car and got it.

Then I said, "Listen, I want a list of all the books you're taking—everything. You're just going to have to stand here and wait till I list all these books or, again, I will have you arrested for stealing."

I was scared silly but I figured that I had to take a stand. They couldn't intimidate us. I was living with my parents, and my step-mother was frightened. She kept saying, "There's nothing in the rest of the house, it's all in *her* bedroom."

I took the list of the books and kept haunting headquarters and going back and back. I told them, "You've taken an awful lot of books which have nothing to do with politics and I have a right to have them back!" So eventually they brought most of them back. For me, that was a victory of some sort. I felt I had harassed them as they had harassed other people.

In the Red Squad, there was a man nicknamed "Scarface" and another man named Benoit. Their boss was named Ennis, and would appear, occasionally, at special meetings. We knew two of the Red Squad in particular because they were there all the time. They showed up at all our meetings, which were pretty well advertised. They read the *Tribune* and so on. Eventually, one of the sons of a member of the Red Squad infiltrated our group. We didn't know at the beginning, but eventually we thought he was an infiltrator but we said, "What the heck."

Fact of the matter was that all we did was get together to have programs and we weren't going to overturn the government. The United Jewish People's Order (UJPO) was basically a social group which organized and handed out leaflets during strikes and helped strikers and so forth. You have to remember, the Padlock Law was in effect so we couldn't march openly. You went out during the night and gave out leaflets at factories and tried not to get picked up by the police.

I remember once I got to Winnipeg in late '49. It was around the time we were collecting signatures to "ban the bomb." I kept looking behind me to make sure there wasn't anybody following me. In Montreal you just didn't do that. You just went door to door or were very careful. In Winnipeg they had their Red Squad too, but I didn't feel the oppression I felt in Quebec.

My younger brother worked for [airplane manufacturer] Canadair. He was not being moved up in his job and was stuck. He found out that it was because of me and my reputation as a party person. Therefore, he was a "risk." He eventually quit and went elsewhere because he would have been sitting and doing the same job ad nauseam.

A very close friend who worked in the administration of Canadair told him why. My brother spoke with him and said, "So-and-so got a job here after I did and yet he moved up and I'm still here. He's not much brighter but I'm still sitting. Is it because I'm Jewish?" His friend told him, "No, it is because of the risk factor."

My older brother wrote for the *Daily Tribune* and got blacklisted in every newspaper in all of Canada. He just couldn't get a job. This was in 1948 and 1949. He was a sportswriter who used to write for the *Montreal Herald* and when the *Tribune* became a daily he was asked to join them. Interestingly enough, I told him not to take the job. I felt the *Tribune* was an iffy situation because it takes a lot of money to run a daily paper. He had a family and I thought it was too risky financially for him.

He was a very close friend of Jackie Robinson's. When Jackie Robinson was signed up [for the farm team of the Brooklyn Dodgers, the Montreal Royals], it was Paul Robeson who phoned my brother and said, "Sammy, one of our own is coming to Montreal and he'll need a lot of help. Try and give it to him." My brother did and became close friends with Jackie and even profiled him for the paper.

Eventually, though, the *Daily Tribune* went under and became a weekly and he went into insurance because he just couldn't get a sportswriting job—not even on a small newspaper. He died a young man about thirteen years ago. It's too bad because he was such a good sportswriter for the *Montreal Herald*.

Looking back on it now, do you think you were naïve in your early years as an activist? Were those days a waste?

No, I don't think so. I think young people should have ideals. Very good things came out of the left-wing movement as a whole. Progress was made, such as the organization of trade unions and getting better conditions for workers. Unemployment insurance would not have come about without a big fight.

I'm a good organizer as a result of the training and skills I got from the Communist Party. I know a number of people who, after leaving the party, went into business and did extremely well because of the training they got.

PADLOCKED, INTERNED, AND FIRED

*Muni Taub was an organizer with the Fur and Leather Workers'
Union, a job he eventually lost to right-wing forces in his union. When
he lived in Montreal, his home was padlocked by the Quebec Provincial
Police. He was also interned during the war at a camp in Petawawa,
Ontario, because of his political beliefs. Recently, he was one of the people
who helped found a co-op apartment building in Toronto.*

PADLOCKED

The forerunner for McCarthyism in Canada was the Padlock Law in Quebec during the time of Premier Duplessis. It started in September '38 and the fight went on and on and on. In January 1939 the house that I lived in was supposed to be padlocked. The house was owned by my father-in-law. "Padlocking" meant that people were moved out and a lock was put on the door. That's what they actually did to a number of houses and institutions in Quebec.

The Padlock Law was actually passed to stop the spread of communism. Duplessis claimed communism was a threat and he felt he had to do something about it. One of his measures was to introduce and adopt a law, a piece of legislation, popularly referred to as the Padlock Law. The law allowed him to padlock all such houses from which communism and communism propaganda emanated. As a matter of fact, his spokespeople referred to such houses as being similar to houses of prostitution or brothels.

How did I get caught up in it? I was an officer of the Communist Party of Canada and so they picked a few people like me against whom they could apply the Padlock Law. The first person was another Communist Party officer in the city of Quebec. Later on, they threatened some institutions—radical and progressive institutions, even the home of the United Jewish People's Order which was then called "The Kanader Arbeiter Ring."

The Quebec Provincial Police were instructed to try and padlock our house. We lived on Laval Avenue. The address was, I think, number 24. That's where all the drama took place. The house itself belonged to my father-in-law, Louis Fineberg. I lived in the house with my family, but my father-in-law didn't actually live there. When the police would come to raid our home they would take away books and tell us to get out. Then the police wrote us to say that if we didn't leave by such-and-such a date they were going to padlock the house.

As a matter of fact, after they made the raids nobody knew who they would evict and whose house they would actually padlock. The Communist Party was officially legal but it was persecuted. The police would keep on raiding their meetings and the Red Squad was always present. It was hard to rent a hall because the owners would be threatened with loss of business, etc. The Communist Party operated as a semi-legal organization in Quebec, contrary to many other provinces where the party was wholly legal.

One time, following a series of raids they made in the weeks beforehand, the police said they were going to padlock the house I lived in with my family. In the raids, they mainly confiscated books which we never got returned—books which they thought were of a Communist nature. As a matter of fact, they were so intelligent that they once came across one of Balzac's novels which was bound in red paper and they said, "That must be a Communist book." They took it away.

They also raided other people's homes and collected their books. Once my wife didn't let the police in because she had to tend to our baby who was only a few months old. She just didn't open the door for them. They climbed up the back stairs onto the balcony and stepped right into the kitchen and shoved her aside. Then they told us, "We have here instructions to see what you have in this house and we have to take away all the Communist literature that we may find." That's what they did. That happened on a couple of occasions.

On one occasion, members of the Civil Liberties Union and friends and sympathizers of the Communist Party decided that we were going to sit in the house and let them padlock it with us inside. It was one of the first sit-ins I experienced. The police arrived and found the house full of people. They left. It worked.

Naturally, the Civil Liberties Union played a role at that time, and they and many liberals claimed the law was unconstitutional in the first place and that Duplessis could not and should not padlock these places.

Eventually, the law was considered in court. The Civil Liberties Union suggested that my father-in-law take legal action against me and that he ask me to vacate the house because his property was threatened if they did padlock the house on Laval. After all, what was he going to do if the law says the house had to stay padlocked for at least a year? He was going to lose a year's rent and who knows if he would be able to rent it after that to someone else.

So what did my father-in-law do? He sued me for staying in the house and for threatening the value and his income. I, in turn, engaged a lawyer to fight *him*. My poor father-in-law. Some people thought he really wanted to evict me. He once came back from a stroll on the mountains, where he proudly went for a walk with his grandson. Some of his friends, either seriously or half in jest, asked him, "Look, Mr. Fineberg, what have got against your son-in-law and your daughter? Are you trying to evict them with this little baby? Your own grandson!" He came home and said to me and my wife, "What do you people want from me?"

Nevertheless, he was astute enough to understand that it would benefit the cause of simple justice by bringing the Padlock Law to court. So he sued me and I opposed him and that brought it to court as a civil case. Eventually, it went to provincial court and there they ruled that the law was constitutional and that the government had a right to padlock.

My father-in-law was a bystander, although, formally speaking, he won the case. But he didn't want to win the case—not against his own daughter! The chief justice was Greenshields and he wrote two pages on the Padlock Law. Our lawyers appealed the case, and my father-in-law was happy we were appealing. It was appealed, but by the time it got to the higher court the Second World War broke out and this whole issue was put on the back burner. In the meantime, Duplessis was defeated in the elections and the new provincial administration came in and stopped the raids. They were much more concerned with fighting the war.

INTERNED

Of course, as a result of the war and my political activities, I was interned. At the outbreak of the war, the Communist Party was waffling over whether or not to support it. As soon as the war broke out, the Communist Party and all other progressive-minded people in Canada were ready to fight against Hitler and Fascism. We had already participated in the Spanish Civil War, which was actually an invasion of Spain with the assistance of Mussolini and Hitler. That happened back in '38. We supported Dr. Bethune's mission and I was, personally, a member of Dr.Bethune's committee and collected assistance for him. We were all ready to join ranks and fight the war.

At the same time, the Communist Party was affiliated with the Communist International, which was, in turn, dominated by the Soviet Communist Party. And the Soviet Communist Party, which ruled the Soviet Union and their government, for its own reasons and as it claimed for "its own protection," concluded a pact with Hitler, the non-aggression pact.

Their side of the story was that the West was trying to come to an agreement with Hitler and that is why they allowed him to invade Czechoslovakia and that is why Chamberlain ran to see Hitler and came back with a piece of paper saying "Peace is assured, peace in our time." But instead of attacking the Soviet Union, Hitler attacked Poland and then France, England, etc. The Communist Party was, historically speaking, towing the line of the Communist International. As soon as the International declared that this war against Hitler was nothing but an imperialist war, the Canadian Communist Party was outlawed and declared a "disloyal" organization.

I was an officer of the Communist Party, and the RCMP was looking for our leadership in order to arrest them. They found very few of the top leaders and, in Quebec, the leaders all went underground. But the RCMP was desperate to find somebody, so they arrested three people, none of whom had gone under. One was Kent Rowley, a trade unionist, another was Sidney Zarkin, a business agent for the Amalgamated Union. And me.

All three of us had been functioning quite openly because we had a job to do with the unions. I was working in a shop and they knew exactly where I was. Yet, they raided our homes in the middle of the night, around three o'clock in the morning. They arrested us and splashed it all over the newspapers that they arrested three prominent Communist leaders. That, of course, wasn't true but it suited them. We three were sent to the Petawawa internment camp and I spent twenty-one months there.

It was like a prisoner-of-war camp. We were under the jurisdiction of the army and treated as POWs. In fact, there were barracks there with POWs such as Italians and Germans. It was quite a large camp. There were also Italian-Canadian Fascists, German-Canadian Fascists, and the mayor of Montreal, Camillien Houde, who was against conscription and wasn't the greatest supporter of the war. There were also French-Canadian Fascists like Adrien Arcand and his gang. His barrack was right across from the one in which I lived.

The atmosphere was strained. We claimed, rightly so, that we had no business being there in the first place and certainly we shouldn't be kept together with Fascists. But, as far as the army was concerned, whoever was sent up there was treated like prisoners. We were all alike to them. It was rough. The main work all the prisoners of war did was chopping wood in the forest. We demanded a trial but were denied. Finally, they did send up a judge to have a hearing behind closed doors. Nobody was there on our behalf. We had no right to bring our lawyers there and the RCMP was present. It was a sham and we said so.

All the judge did was listen to the police and to the records and then sent a report, which we never saw. All we knew was that there were protests, inside and outside, and demands that we should be given a fair trial or be charged. They said, "No, we're doing this under the War Measures Act."

During this time, my wife had it very rough. She had to go to work and my mother and father-in-law took care of the baby, who was named Norman after Norman Bethune.

But life was tough in the camp. When the Soviet Union was attacked by Hitler after June 1941, there was no rhyme or reason to keep us there. Gradually, the pressure brought by the community was pretty strong and the Communists were transferred to Hull and started to be released.

At my personal hearing, the RCMP brought out all the files to show the judge my record. I didn't make many comments because I knew I was just talking to a wall or allowing the RCMP to take further notes. The one objection I made was when I said, "Your honour, could you or the RCMP explain to me what this picture is doing in my file?"

The judge asked, "What's wrong with that picture?"

I said, "Well, if you notice, that picture is of my wife and myself and there's a third person there. That's my six-month old baby. Why would a six-month-old baby be in the files of the RCMP?" So the judge told the officer to take that picture out. I still have the picture.

We took these hearings as nothing but a sham. Of course, Mayor Houde came out of that hearing and he told us about the speeches he made there about the government. But we told him, "All you did was give the RCMP additional information."

There were incidents in the camp, like fights between the Germans and the Italians which ended up in broken legs and arms because they threw each other off the roof. They fought over who was going to control the kitchen, which was very important to them—both because they could receive graft and also because they could eat better if they controlled the kitchen.

Later on, I didn't have to go to chop trees because I was taking care of the sick as a nurse. I had TB many years earlier, in the late '20s, I knew how to take care of a person who had tuberculosis and how not to contract it. I took care of a Finnish Communist who was editor of the paper. He eventually died and they took him out of this isolation hut where I lived with him as his nurse. In the middle of the night, they snuck him out. I also helped Sidney Zarkin, who was suffering from Buerger's disease. He asked to be released because Buerger's disease made his toes rot—like gangrene. It's a rare disease and the doctors were not acquainted with it. They did not take it seriously. Eventually, Sidney lost his foot and he had to be released. They had amputated the foot and I remember when I took him to see the colonel. Sidney had a temper and was banging on the table. He demanded that he be released. But Sidney was fighting for his life.

Later on, we called a strike. We demanded to be moved or else we would not go to work. As a matter of fact, we threatened to break through the gates. We knew they couldn't ignore us because we might have done that. Finally, we were transferred to a prison in Hull. It was empty and they gave us the run of the prison and life became quite easy.

FIRED

After the war I was sent to Winnipeg by the International Fur and Leather Workers' Union, of which I was a member. I spent nine years there. We organized a number of shops—in some we had to call strikes. Working conditions, pay, and hours were gradually improved.

One of the things I remember was when a delegation was sent to Europe in order to screen people who were in the displacement camps. We called them DPs. My name was submitted by the union to be one of the delegates to go to Germany's DP camps and screen some people who were able to work in the needle trade and bring them here where there was a shortage of skilled labour. At the same time, it would help these people who otherwise would have to go back to wherever they came from. For Jewish people it meant going back to Poland which, after the Holocaust, they weren't willing to do. They wanted to come to Canada.

However, the government refused to allow me on the delegation on the grounds that I was too much of a radical. My name was rejected and then another name from our union was also rejected. Nobody from our union in Winnipeg went. Other trade unionists did go and, indeed, did help a few hundred people come to Canada. Later on, we found out that no progressives, socialists, or communists were allowed to come as immigrants. As a matter of fact, ex-Nazis didn't have as many hardships coming over here. The government even adopted a policy that being a member of Hitler's army in itself was not considered a crime. If you were just a member of the German army you were quite kosher.

In Manitoba I was discriminated against because of my radicalism. Our battle was to combat the cold-warmongers but we suffered. The cold war brought about a split within the trade union movement. Some of the leaders played footsy with the reactionaries and helped them aggravate the cold war. They worked very hard and eventually expelled some unions from the CIO and from the AFof L on the grounds they were Communist-dominated unions. This was part and parcel of the cold war.

Personally, I suffered in 1953 when I was transferred to Toronto from Winnipeg. I had continued to work for the union, was an elected officer, and my wages were paid by the local in Toronto. We decided to merge with the American Federation of Labor (AFof L) because we felt it was in the interests of working people and in the interests of getting a better agreement. I was democratically elected but the president of the AFof L, who was [Bill] Green at the time, gave instructions that a number of officers had to be expelled—not only removed from office, but also expelled from the union. And I was one of them.

I was removed by an edict from Green in head office in Washington. In Canada, Max Federman, the organizer of the fur local affiliated with the AFof L, went along with that. He should have protested and insisted that, since it was a merger, officers who had been elected by the union should remain. In the United States all officers of the Fur and Leather Workers' Union remained.

In some ways, Canada was worse than the United States during the cold war. The Seamen's Union was broken up by the measures taken by the government—the famous Hal Banks was brought in. Everybody knows the record he had.

I had to look for another job. I went into selling products to builders of homes and apartments. It was tough for a while because it was very unjust. The feeling of someone who loses a job is interesting. You are going through a tough, traumatic experience. People talk about being unemployed and you become a statistic. I knew people who were unemployed from my younger days in New York when I worked in the needle trade shops, so it was nothing new to me to see the suffering of people. But until you personally face that situation you don't feel the burden that is thrust upon you. Particularly when it was unjust. And it was new to me.

I had two children and my wife had to go get a full-time job. It was very tragic and I felt discriminated against.

THE PADLOCK TRIALS

Albert Marcus is a lawyer who practised in Montreal. He graduated from the McGill University law faculty in 1934. Among his firm's clients was the Soviet consulate in Montreal. "On one occasion, when I was asked to come for a consultation, I borrowed the automobile of a friend of mine and parked the car at the entrance of the consulate. Sometime later, my friend received a visit from the RCMP inquiring what business he had with the Soviet consulate. I am happy to report that my friend told the RCMP it was none of their damn business." From 1937 to 1957 one of his priorities was the fight to remove Quebec's repressive Padlock Law.

Very soon after he was elected in 1936, premier Maurice Duplessis of Quebec enacted what was popularly known as the "Padlock Law." This act provided that the attorney general of Quebec had the authority to padlock any premises which were being used for "Communist purposes." This applied to a residence or a business and, of course, did not define the meaning of a "Communist purpose."

Throughout his term in office, Duplessis was both premier and attorney general. A number of homes and establishments were padlocked. A section of the Padlock Law allowed the police [the Red Squad] to enter any premises and seize any books which were "Communist propaganda." This was the most troublesome and most-often used section of the law.

There were hundreds and hundreds of visitations made by the Red Squad. They'd knock on the door, look at all the books, and remove those which, in their wisdom, they thought were Communist literature. Usually, they were quite illiterate and didn't have the slightest idea of what they were looking at. A book with a red cover was most suspicious. For a short period, all *Time* magazines were confiscated. They must have seized and destroyed many thousands of books.

This had a disastrous effect on any liberal-thinking person. It was an obvious attack upon fundamental rights, and my partner, Abraham Feiner, and I were interested to see what could be done to attack the validity of the Padlock Law, but there were difficulties in doing this. One, the Padlock Law, stipulated that no one could take any action against the attorney general. Thus, we had to attack the validity of the act itself.

It must be realized that Canada was constituted as a country in 1867 merely by an act of the British Parliament. While it established Canada as a country, the British North America Act did not, in any way, deal with civil liberties. It merely divided the various powers between the federal government and the provinces. It was understood that the matter of our civil liberties depended on those of Great Britain where they were unwritten and varied from time to time according to precedent. So the difficulty in attacking the Padlock Law was how to show that it was a basic infringement of our civil liberties since we did not have a written declaration of those civil liberties.

As the Padlock Law specifically provided that no action could be taken against the attorney general, we felt that an action directed against him as the principal defendent would be defeated. At the time, there was never a strong movement to have the Padlock Law declared unconstitutional because the anglophone community in Quebec felt the law was a useful tool in fighting what they considered "the red menace," small and insignificant as that menace really was then.

We became involved in the attack upon the validity of the Padlock Law when a client, by the name of Muni Taub, rented a room at the home of his father-in-law, Mr. Feinberg, on Laval Street in Montreal. To enforce the Padlock Law, the Duplessis government created a special squad, called the Red Squad, whose function it was to enforce the provisions of the law. The Red Squad had received orders to padlock the premises of Muni Taub. When the squad arrived they discovered he merely had rented one of the rooms in the house. Not having the authority to padlock the entire house, the Red Squad served notice they were going to do so.

We were consulted on the matter and saw an opportunity of attacking the Padlock Law and surmounting the prohibition against an attack on the attorney general. We did it this way: it was arranged that Fineberg, proprietor of the house, take an action in damages against the son-in-law, Muni Taub, claiming that he was being threatened by the attorney general who was going to padlock his house unless he, as landlord, evicted his son-in-law.

We appeared on behalf of Muni Taub and brought the attorney general into the case on the grounds that his law was unconstitutional. The case came to trial about a year after the event. It came before the chief justice of the Superior Court of Quebec. He was a fabulous character named Greenshields who had actually been in a regiment which had fought in the Riel Rebellion. At the trial, when Judge Greenshields learned the essence of the case, he showed great impatience with the attorney general's lawyer and indicated in a judicial fashion that he thought the attorney general's case was very weak.

We were very much encouraged at the end of the hearing. But six months later, to our great disappointment, the judge declared the Act valid and dismissed our case. We inscribed an appeal. It was 1940 and the war was on. We found that we had no clients available to consult with because the Communist Party of Canada had been declared an illegal organization and its leaders and other prominent spokesmen had been interned. Our appeal lapsed because our clients were arrested or had gone underground and we had no money to pursue it.

I would like to indicate the position of the federal administrations during this whole period when the Padlock Law was in force in Quebec. The BNA Act provided that, within a year's time of the enactment of a provincial law, the federal government could disallow any provincial law. A campaign was conducted to persuade the Mackenzie King administration to disallow the act. But he and succeeding prime ministers never took any position on the matter.

Duplessis was defeated in 1944 and succeeded by the Godbout administration of the Liberal Party. This Godbout government was in power for about four and a half years. During this period they did not repeal the Padlock Law but, in practice, they did not use it. After Godbout was defeated in 1948, Duplessis came back and re-established the Red Squad at an increased rate and began padlocking places which were "Communist" or being used for Communist propaganda. The arrest and conviction of Fred Rose under the War Measures Act heightened the activities of the Red Squad.

In all the cases, the Red Squad descended suddenly, and without any notice, upon a person's home, searched all their books, and confiscated such books which, in their poor judgement, they considered to be "Communistic." There was no recourse against such actions and we could not attack them in the courts because, under the Act, the attorney general who ordered these searches was protected.

In the early 1950s, on the instructions of Premier Duplessis, the premises of John Switzman were padlocked. The Padlock Law provided that when premises were padlocked it extended for a period of one year. Switzman's landlord sued him for damages on the basis that he was losing rent for a year. We appeared on Switzman's behalf and required the attorney general to enter the case and defend the validity of the Padlock Law.

The case came up for trial before a judge who was obviously not sympathetic to Switzman. It did not take long for this judge to follow Greenshield's judgement and to declare the Padlock Law valid. We went to appeal, and in due course the case was argued in front of the Appeal Court of Quebec. The Appeal Court of Quebec held that Duplessis' Padlock Law was valid. Of the five judges only one, Judge Barclay, dissented and held that the Padlock Law was invalid. The appeal court of Quebec took about two years to render that judgement. I believe this was a record time for a Court of Appeal.

Our final alternative was to take the case to the Supreme Court of Canada. The procedure was that if a party lost its case in the Appeal Court of Quebec and desired to appeal to the Supreme Court of Canada, it required the consent of any single judge of the Appeal Court of Quebec. The Appeal Court designated one of its members, on a rotation basis, for a period of a week to hear applications for leave to appeal to the Supreme Court of Canada. Four of the five judges of the Appeal Court had already declared the Padlock Law valid. We felt that if we asked for leave to appeal before any of these judges we might be refused. Fortunately, within the period allowed to make such an appeal, Judge Barclay was sitting, and he had declared the Padlock Law unconstitutional. Without hesitation, he gave us the necessary authorization to take the case to the Supreme Court.

From the beginning of the time when we undertook to contest the

Padlock Law, we were anxious to engage the services of a prominent legal figure to act as counsel. We agreed that Professor Frank Scott, who taught at McGill University, would be the best counsel we could have. When we met with him, he declined the request to act and said if we were associated with the case it would be injurious to the best interests of McGill University. Scott said he had already been informed that if McGill had appointed him dean of the faculty of law, a position to which by seniority he was already entitled, the university would lose many of the grants or subsidies which should come to it from the Quebec government. It was only when we appealed to the Supreme Court of Canada that Scott found his way clear to become associated with us as counsel in the case.

When you appeal to the Supreme Court it is necessary to file a précis of the argument you are going to make. Frank Scott prepared this précis. It was very thorough and quite convincing. The question was whether the Padlock Law was, by its nature, within criminal law. If one agreed it was criminal law, then it was beyond the jurisdiction of the provincial government. Under the BNA Act only the federal government has jurisdiction over criminal law. If, on the other hand, one argued that it was not criminal law, then the province had jurisdiction.

The Padlock Law was an attack upon a political party and a political philosophy. To us, it was quite evident that it was a criminal matter and it was beyond our comprehension that the various judges in the various courts of Quebec ruled otherwise. The case came up for argument before the Supreme Court around 1957. It was argued by Frank Scott and my partner, Abraham Feiner. After a delay of around four months, the Supreme Court rendered its decision. By a majority of six to three, it held that the Padlock Law was invalid because it was a matter of criminal law and, therefore, beyond the jurisdiction of the provinces.

Incidentally, if such a matter had come before the Supreme Court nowadays when we have a Charter of Rights and Freedoms there would be less of a problem. After the judgement of the Supreme Court, the Duplessis administration had to find other means to harass left-wing movements.

PART THREE

PAYING THEIR DUES—UNIONS AND THE BLACKLIST

CHAPTER EIGHT

ORGANIZE NO EVIL:
WE'RE STICKIN' TO THE UE

PARTY LINES

Mike Bosnich *was born in Yugoslavia. During the cold war, he was an organizer and official with the UE, the United Electrical Radio and Machine Workers of Canada. During the "hot" war, he fought in Europe in 1944–45 with the Canadian army. He was also elected councillor in the Welland area, where he still lives. There were numerous strikes here in the 1930s. "This area, Crowland Township, is a rural township which was called 'the red spot' on the map of Canada. It had the biggest steel plants, was a large industrial area, and had transportation by canal and railroad." It's now part of the city of Welland.*

Because of the Gouzenko business, the RCMP decided that the whole country was full of Communist spies—"reds under every bed," as the old expression went. So the RCMP expanded their security surveillance and kept a dossier on most left-wingers, particularly known Communists and leaders in the left-wing unions such as UE, Mine Mill, Fur and Leather Workers', and the Canadian Seamen's Union. According to them, we were all agents of the Kremlin. They would intimidate people we knew.

For example, I had a habit of going to eat in a particular restaurant in Hamilton on my way from Welland to Toronto for union meetings. The restaurant was owned by a Yugoslav man who I knew. One day he asked me, "What have the RCMP got against you?" I wondered why he would ask.

"A couple of them were here and they showed me your picture and asked if I knew you," he said.

He told them he knew me, but that I only came in for breakfast and that he didn't know me well. Then he asked me again, "What have they got against you?"

So I told him that I was involved in the left-wing movement and was a member of the Communist Party and was active in the UE which was known as a left-wing union. I added, "They're letting you know who I am. In fact, they're not so much worried about me, but they're contacting you to let you know to shy away from this guy—that you're treading on thin ice associating with guys like Mike Bosnich."

There was no question the RCMP knew everything they wanted about me. I was open about it. Welland is a small community and everybody knew me. They had my army history and knew I was a campaign organizer for the Labor Progressive Party. They weren't worried about me, but went around intimidating others to show they knew all the so-called Communists and agitators and that they knew who was associating with them. Therefore, they went to friends of mine or acquaintances and tried to scare them. Because of that some people shied away from me.

Another example involved my father-in-law, who lived in Welland was active in the left-wing movement and was a member of the Communist Party. He had fought for Canada during the First World War as a volunteer, but every time he applied for citizenship he would be rejected. They never had to supply any grounds. They never gave reasons and you couldn't appeal. Even to this day there is no way to appeal if you are rejected. They're a law unto themselves. I presume he was rejected on the grounds he was a Communist and the fact that he fought for the country was immaterial.

The RCMP had approached a number of people in my community and one fellow told me openly that he was solicited when he applied for his Canadian citizenship. He, like some left-wing people, were told, "Look, you could be very valuable to us if you could continue attending these left-wing functions of your ethnic organization while your application for citizenship is being processed and report to us anything that happens. If you do this we'll facilitate your application for citizenship." If you said no you never got your citizenship.

In one case I knew a guy who told the RCMP, "Look, you are asking me to spy on people who are my friends and associates, not enemies of this country. They are simply disgruntled citizens who may have had hard times during the Depression. They don't believe in capitalism but they're not spies or agents. They may be 'parlour pinks,' socialists, even Communists, but they are not spies!" His citizenship papers never came through.

When I left the party it was public knowledge. I even wrote articles in the Communist papers expressing my dissatisfaction. But they [the RCMP] still kept tabs on me because I was a union official. I knew my line was tapped. There was this peculiar experience one time when I was in Alberta in 1961 organizing the Camrose Tubes plant, which was part of Stelco. After I got back to Welland I called the local's president in Alberta. The long-distance operator connected us and he said, "Hello," and I said, "Hello, Rudy. How are you?" All of a sudden the line goes dead.

It wasn't five seconds later that I hear him say, "Hello" and I hear my own voice answer, "Hello, Rudy. How are you?" And then suddenly it went dead again. Somebody pulled a boo-boo or did it deliberately to let me know that I was being recorded.

The RCMP was watching all left-wingers, I'm sure. They claimed they had files on hundreds of thousands of Canadians. When they switched the Security Service to CSIS [the Canadian Security Intelligence Service] they were supposed to destroy all the old files and start fresh with a new approach. That's whistling Dixie. Anybody who thinks the old files were destroyed and that the new service was starting from scratch has gotta be naïve and I have a Brooklyn bridge to sell them!

The national officers of our union, like president or secretary-treasurer, were automatically on the international executive board of the United Electrical Radio and Machine Workers of America. But when the McCarthy era began in the States our executives were asked the same question when they were crossing the border: "Are you now or have you ever been a member of a Communist or totalitarian organization which advocates the overthrow of the government?"

If you said no and were a member of the Communist Party, they would warn you to get back to Canada. If they caught you over there again it was an automatic five-year jail sentence for coming across the border under false pretenses. Our officers refused to meet those conditions and didn't go over to the States. Our union and the Communist Party was not illegal and our officers considered it an infringement of their democratic rights. But they couldn't participate in the affairs of the international union.

In 1956 we were campaigning to have our union be separate from the American one—we wanted our own constitution and to be able to elect our own officers. Mainly, we didn't want to send our finances to the States. There was an international convention coming up to discuss this question of independence for the Canadian union. The officers couldn't go over, but we needed someone to go and explain to them why we wanted our independence. I was approached to go down with four others to explain our case because for some reason my name was not on the watchlist and I've never been banned from entering the States.

At the border I was asked, "Where are you going?"

I said, "I'm just going to the restaurant."

Once over, I got a train to New York City. When we got there we were cautioned by certain people not to appear at the convention and not to get up and make speeches because there were FBI agents there. So we had to have a back-room meeting with the constitution committee to express our point of view and to explain why we wanted our independence. So, while we were not delegates and not officially there, we *were* there to represent the interests of the Canadian union.

At the meeting, a man there who was an executive of one of the union districts made a point of contacting me and the Canadian delegates (although we weren't really delegates). He came to my hotel room and sat down, talked with me, and said he was favourably disposed to our position and that he would put our point of view before the constitution committee and would facilitate our Canadian independence. I thanked him and explained to him we weren't trying to bust up the union and that we would still be affiliated with them fraternally but we wanted to run our own show.

Well, lo and behold, some years later I was reading an article about hearings before the House Un-American Activities Committee, when they were investigating some of the UE locals in various areas of the United States for communistic activities, and who I did read was testifying before the committee but the same fellow who befriended us. He testified that he was an officer of the UE union for many years and was in the pay of the FBI the same time! Then I realized why he supported our position—as an agent of the FBI he was interested in busting up the left-wing UE in the States and anything that could contribute to that was part of his cause. Therefore, if the Canadian section left the UE in the United States that would be part of a breakup of the union. The FBI, through this agent, wanted to facilitate the dismemberment of the UE.

ELECTRICAL SPARKS

Ross Russell is a retired union organizer for the United Electrical Radio and Machine Workers (UE). He fought in the Spanish Civil War. A shrapnel wound in a lung kept him out of the army in the Second World War. Russell joined the UE in 1941 and within three years was elected its director of organization in Canada. He held that position until he retired in 1976. I had the privilege of meeting with him a few months before he died in May 1990.

Canadian General Electric had two big plants on Dufferin Street near the Canadian National Exhibition grounds in Toronto. One plant made incandescent light bulbs. The Radio Valve plant made tubes for radios. There were thousands of people making radios in plants those days. Among the things they made was the "peanut" tube which was about half the size of my little finger. Inside that tube are little wires finer than hairs. Each of the women workers had magnifying glasses as big as a steering wheel on an automobile. They worked underneath that and used tweezers to pick up these fine hairs to build the tube. You do that for eight hours a day for a year or two and you wouldn't be much good any more.

The company had these young women with good eyes working on this stuff and after they were there for a couple of years the company would get rid of them. The eyes of these girls would go and they got very little pay for what they did. It was different when they got organized. We got seniority and so on. Seniority was a big thing in those days because if you didn't have seniority you would be in and out.

Until they got organized, they had no protection of any kind. When I organized RCA in Montreal the girls who were making the same radios were paid around half as much as they were in Toronto. We brought them up to equal status. Then Duplessis took all our certifications away and we were driven out of Quebec on the grounds that we fought for Ontario rights and had won them. Bang! Duplessis just took away our certifications. A lot of other unions moved in and made deals with the companies. Quebec was our worst example and we lost our whole membership. It's only now that we're building back.

You have to understand that UE, from day one, was known as a left-wing union. We had to fight the boss *and* our own union movement. In the States, my union walked out of the CIO [Congress of Industrial Organizations] convention in 1947 because of the pro-company position taken by the leadership. In Canada we took an altogether opposite position, which was to stay in and fight. So the congress here were very clever, instead of expelling us they suspended the officers.

In the States a man named James B. Carey had been the original president of the UE, but had been voted out after his first or second year in office for being too close to the bosses. After he lost his job with the UE in the States, he was brought in as the secretary-treasurer of the CIO. Then in 1947 or '48, he was made the president of what we called the imitation UE. They gave themselves the name the International United Electrical Workers or IUE. The proof that this was a phony deal was when the two largest corporations with whom we had collective agreements in the States and Canada, General Electric and Westinghouse, immediately allowed the IUE to move in. The result was that our union's losses in the States were substantial. Of course, the IUE set up an equivalent in Canada.

A Catholic clergyman in the States wrote numerous pamphlets against communism, the UE, and why the members should switch to the IUE. In Canada, we had an experience in Peterborough, Ontario, at the mother plant of General Electric. At that time, there were about 5,000 people in our bargaining unit. We had a collective agreement the IUE challenged and a vote was called. The bishop of Peterborough, who had tremendous power in the Catholic church, spoke on the radio and called upon the Canadian General Electric workers in Peterborough to vote for the IUE. Fortunately, they didn't follow him and we succeeded by a very narrow majority in holding that plant.

In Niagara Falls a monsignor called on the members to do the same. We had a committee of Catholic members who visited the monsignor and asked him not to interfere. They said, "Look, we're good Catholics but this is our bread and butter." The workers didn't vote on his recommendation.

Were you ever personally harassed?

In Stratford somebody put a fake bomb in my car and smoke came out. I never knew who did it. The thing that happened to me which was most serious took place in 1956. The UE was still out of the congress [having been kicked out in 1950] when the AF of L and the CIO decided to merge. But we still had the right to have two people from the Canadian UE attend the executive board meetings which were held a few times a year in the States. The head office was in New York. Since the AFL and the CIO were merging the question was: "Should the UE continue as an independent union or should it dissolve itself and go into another union such as the IUE or what have you?" The union was split on this issue.

Our union in Canada had a strong position: there was no way we would dissolve. We'd stand and fight as an independent union! They had executive meetings every ten days in the States because of this. When C.S. Jackson, the head of the Canadian UE, arrived at the executive meetings, the powers that be simply put him on a plane and told him not to come back again. They warned him that he'd be barred if he came back. So George Harris, the secretary-treasurer, went but he was barred from the States. So I was appointed to go. These special executive meetings were almost always held Monday mornings, so I would drive to Buffalo and take the train to New York on Sunday.

I attended a number of these executive meetings. The fight was on. I'd never seen anything like this in my life since it became very clear that our union was full of FBI agents, some of whom were even on the executive board. You could tell by the speeches they made. It was so bad that in order to have a discussion with someone I trusted, we didn't dare go to the hotel room or even the lobby. We would go on the subway and drive to the end of the line and back again as we had our discussion. The place was so full of spies.

On my way to one of these meetings across the border, the customs inspector never asked me my name or anything but he told me to pull over to the side. They kept me waiting for a half-an-hour and then they came out with a card and told me I was barred from the States. They said I could appeal it if I wanted to but that was it. Eventually, I got a letter which said I would be subject to five years in jail if I was found in the US. This was all a part of the cold war. For me, personally, the cold war meant that I never went back to the States.

It was an uphill fight for my union. We were constantly being raided. At our peak we had 25,000 members. The UE was put in a defensive position and it was difficult for us to organize. Steel [the United Steelworkers of America] was raiding us whenever it could. These things occupied a tremendous amount of our time. The harassment was with us throughout the whole cold-war period from 1947 till we finally went back into the new Canadian Congress of Labour.

From various employers we learned that the RCMP would supply them with information. When the Labour Relations Act came about, groups of lawyers learned how to fight unions. They had contacts with the RCMP and through them the companies would be supplied with information. We could tell because they had no other way of getting it other than the RCMP. For example, I had changed my name and they knew this.

In Simcoe, Ontario, I discovered an informer. We had organized the mother plant of Canada Wire and Cable in Toronto. They opened another plant in Simcoe and the company set up a guy who was in the shipping department and he set up a company union. We had our own committee headed by a young fellow who was eighteen and we applied for certification. This young fellow had an uncle who was a night caretaker in a fourth-rate hotel in Simcoe. The uncle told our young man that the head of the company union was living in that hotel. The guy who set up the company union had come from out of town. We found out later that he came from Montreal and that he had been strikebreaking in Montreal and led a back-to-work movement in a plant there. It turned out he was getting a cheque every week in an envelope with an open window. We eventually looked and it was from Canada Wire in Toronto, so we knew that the company had set this up and that it was all done through a law firm.

It was all part of the cold war. Secret deals were made. Once, we caught Canada Wire making deals. They were paying fifty bucks for people to come break our strike. They didn't succeed. We had guys who turned over the cheques to us.

We had a great many cases where our members were discharged from companies due to their union activities. We tried to protect our members from this. We won some cases and lost some. In earlier days, employers were crude and we could prove it. Later on, they got advice from these lawyers I mentioned. The number of lawyers grew and grew so that, today, there are dozens and dozens of lawyers who live off the trade union movement. Incidentally, in our union we didn't use lawyers. They decided to use me. I represented our union in all of our cases before the Labour Relations Board.

It's not easy to organize. Any union organizer will tell you of the difficulties. Practically no employer wants his company's workers to be organized. So they fight, some harder than others. You expect to have to fight the employer, but we had to fight the employer *and* other unions moving in. When other unions tell workers we're a no-good union and the employer is telling them the same, then we had quite a battle on our hands.

The only reason we succeeded was because we had some of the most able people. We had unity at the top among Jackson, Harris, and I. We fought out questions and came in with a single position. Two out of three had to carry the day and that was it.

But in 1950 we almost lost our own union. We came out with a "Ban the Bomb" petition. "Peace" was a very dirty word and one of the worst things you could say in that time. Anybody who put forth a proposition of peace was considered a Communist. We printed a "Ban the Bomb" petition and met with our stewards throughout the union. We said, "Take this ban the bomb petition into the plant."

Well, we had a hard time convincing our stewards to do it. Some of them put the petitions in their pockets and didn't do much with them. Those who took the petition into the plants were met with terrific resistance. It went to the point that some people thought we were going to lose the union. "We'd better back off," some members told us. We said, "No, we've gotta explain this thing."

Today, it's hard to imagine this because there are leading clergymen and a conglomerate of people taking a position on world peace and ban the bomb. At that time it was just the opposite.

We had written into our constitution that the officers could not be paid more than the highest worker in the industry. Things of that nature were why we were called a left-wing union. We had Communists in the union and it wasn't hidden. George Harris, who, in my opinion, was one of the finest trade unionists in the history of this country and one of the best orators, was a leader in the Communist Party.

CHAPTER NINE

OF MINES AND MEN:
THE MINE MILL STORY

MINING DISCRIMINATION

Ray Stevenson is a former organizer and elected local and national executive officer for the Mine, Mill and Smelter Workers Union in Northern Ontario and the rest of Canada. He is a Communist.

There was no law in Canada as there was in the States that you couldn't be a member of the Communist Party and still be elected to the leadership of trade unions. I suppose the thing that really does stand out in my memory is Senator Taft [who lent his name to the repressive Taft-Hartley Labor Relations Act] standing on the floor of Congress in the United States and saying that Northern Ontario had been invaded by Communists who were trying to get away from his Taft-Hartley Act and who had come to carry out subversive activities against the people and government of Canada by organizing the gold miners into unions.

There was a great deal of job discrimination here, and the RCMP and the so-called security forces openly tried to intimidate people who were identified as Communists, of whom I was one. I remember being shadowed by the RCMP in the town of Timmins in Northern Ontario. In 1949 a peace committee had been established in Timmins and I was a member of it. The peace committee was informed that the dean of Canterbury was going on tour in Canada to establish a public position for what later became the Canadian Peace Congress and an affiliate of the World Peace Council. He was called the "Red Dean" and was a famous dean of

171

the Anglican Church at Canterbury. He had written a book called *The Socialist Sixth* which was quite pro-Soviet and anti-cold war.

When he came to Canada his meetings were attacked in Toronto and Hamilton but in Timmins we said, "There's no way he's going to be attacked here." We tried to book theatres and tried to engage the McIntyre arena where Barbara Ann Scott did her skating and where George Drew, the premier of Ontario, held meetings. Of course, the theatres and other premises were witheld from our use for purely political reasons. Finally, we were narrowed down and had to have this meeting in the Ukrainian Hall, a left-wing hall which seated approximately 450 in the upper deck and in the basement you could perhaps get another few hundred people.

We wired the upstairs and downstairs and put loud-speakers outside. As well, we blanketed every window on the inside for fear of flying glass. We organized about one hundred and fifty of the biggest, toughest miners we could find and we set up our own security force. We then told the police we would work in cooperation with them. Nevertheless, on the night of the meeting we found out that a corporal of the RCMP had come all the way from Toronto to Timmins to organize an anti-demonstration. They did manage to smash every window in that hall with stones.

I met this guy after the meeting and asked him, "You are Corporal so-and-so of the Mounted Police?" He said yes.

I then asked, "Why the hell don't you have your uniform on? When I was in the Canadian army I was proud to wear my uniform! You're in plainclothes. Did you organize this?" He walked away.

The fact was there were 2,000 people outside the building, most of whom were there to hear the dean. It was a rather strange sight because here was the dean with his long black coat and long, flowing, white hair addressing this crowd and quoting the Beatitudes and saying, "Blessed are the peacemakers," and "smash" would go another window. The hoodlums outside were stoning the hall.

We found some of these people carrying rocks and eggs trying to get into the hall, but suspicious-looking characters were frisked by our "security" miners. Most of these did not enter the hall. The meeting was a success and they couldn't smash it. Of course, I was named as the main instigator of the rough stuff at the affair.

WANTED POSTER

Blacklisting was wide-spread. I know of at least ten or twelve people from that area who suffered job and other discrimination in one way or another—either they had to change their names or had to go south for employment and so on. There was anti-communism from every angle. From the church to the newspapers to employers, you had to stand up and take your lumps or cave in.

One Finnish woman applied for Canadian citizenship and when she went before the citizenship judge in the town of Cochrane was asked, "Do you know or have you ever known Ray Stevenson?"

"Yes, of course I know him, " she replied.

The judge said, "Then you are denied your citizenship."

One other incident had an amusing aspect. I was travelling from Hearst to Timmins and in Kapuskasing some workers close to the party told me, "You know your picture is up in the police station."

I asked, "What's it doing there?"

And they said, "Well, there's a most-wanted list over there."

"You have got to be kidding. Where did they get my picture and is it a real glossy?" They told me it was from a newspaper and I was on the board with four other "most-wanted" people.

I decided that this wasn't a very nice thing to be happening to Mrs. Stevenson's little boy Ray, so I went over to the police station. And sure enough the damn picture was there right alongside some criminals of every description! So I made the chief of police, who was really a company stooge, take it down. The reason he took it down was because I said I would sue and told him, "You are placing me in the company of wanted criminals and you cannot show me where I am a wanted criminal under any statute in Canada. If so, you can arrest me right now. If you can't do that, I will sue you!" It was pure open discrimination not only against me, but also against anyone who dared to think for themselves, or oppose the status quo, and the bankrupt policies of the cold war.

STRIKES AND FIGHTS IN THE WEST

Tom McGrath is the national vice-president of the Canadian Brotherhood of Railway, Transport and General Workers (CBRT). Originally a sailor from Saint John, New Brunswick, he joined the union movement as a ship's delegate for the Canadian Seamen's Union (CSU). He spent part of the cold-war years in British Columbia.

In 1953 I had an opportunity to go to work in Kemano, British Columbia, when the Kitimat project first opened. They were building an aluminum smelter. I was at the labourer's union hall and heard there was a strike on up there. A lot of miners were living in Vancouver. Many of the miners had come all the way from Sudbury and Timmins, Ontario, to work on the Kitimat project. Craft unions were building the tunnels and they didn't have qualified people so they had recruited in industrial towns like Sudbury and Timmins where miners came from.

The Ontario workers were brought out to British Columbia with promises of a good job and good conditions, but signed an agreement which had no bonus system or shift differentials. Because of this poor agreement, the miners shut down the project and just wouldn't work. Then the company tried to import scabs and run the miners off the project.

I was in the labour hall in Vancouver at the time and looking for a job as a chock tender [miner's helper], but I knew there was a strike on. I got called into the back office of the union hall and offered a job.

I told a guy there, "I can't go up there because there's a strike on."

"Nah, you can go up there. Here's a list of three hundred people—all Communists—who were just fired! The strike is settled and everybody else just got a raise so you can go up there."

So I phoned up Harvey Murphy of the Mine, Mill and Smelter Workers Union, who was co-ordinating the campaign for the strikers. I asked him if I should go up to Kemano to look around because his miners weren't allowed on the property. Harvey said, "It's a good idea for you to go and to take up a bag full of leaflets that we want distributed."

I decided to go up but not do any work. There were twenty-seven people hired to go to work—all B.C. residents who the company just picked off the street. None were qualified miners. We went up to Kemano by boat, a thirty-hour trip. I pasted leaflets wherever I could, but couldn't convince too many people not to go to work.

When our bus arrived at a camp, a guy got aboard and called out– "Is there a McGrath or a McGraw here?" They took me off and sent me to Rupert by ship and I went home to Vancouver by plane. In the meantime, the miners negotiated and settled because the company just couldn't get anybody to do the job. The miners got their bonus, shift differential, and a wage increase, along with a local to represent underground workers.

If you happened to come from a union which was labelled left-wing then your opportunities for finding a job were not that easy. There was a campaign not to accept people who were left-wingers and to kick them out of the unions. It started early in British Columbia.

The first big purge happened in the carpenters' union where they kicked out Jack Stevenson, who was the president, and several other members. They labelled Jack Stevenson a Communist, but I was told that he was a front-line Freemason who sided with the other members and just didn't agree with what the international head-quarters of the union said. Another union, the International Brotherhood of Electrical Workers (with headquarters in Washington), local 213, eliminated some of the Communists and left-wingers. All left wingers were pretty well scrutinized within all the craft unions.

STRUGGLES IN SUDBURY

Mike Solski is a former smelter labourer, blacksmith, and plateworker at INCO who became an officer of the Mine, Mill and Smelter Workers Union. He's retired and living in a two-storey family home in Coniston, Ontario, a town a couple of miles from the eastern border of Sudbury, a mining centre. He's been living in the same house since the late '40s.

Discrimination against left-wingers in the mining camps around here goes right back to the 1930s. Red-baiting was a convenient way to get rid of people. In this area you had to be a supporter of a church. If you weren't then that was reason enough to put you on a blacklist. The church played a real rotten role here. Many were stool pigeons for the companies. That can't be disputed.

I started working at the age of seventeen in 1935. My first job with the union was as a volunteer plant organizer just as the union first started up. In 1942 the church took the side of the company when the union started to organize. There were pronouncements from the pulpits urging people not to join the union, but the churches had very little influence on the men because the men were fed up with working conditions and really wanted a union.

The church warned about the "red menace" and Communists coming from the States to take over. We started to organize despite the pressures from them and we were fairly successful. We improved conditions on the job for our members, built meeting halls, bought and improved a summer camp. We did something that had never been done before—we provided cultural activities for members and their children. There were ballet classes for students; big bands were brought in to play dances.

Our recreation director, Weir Reid, was responsible for bringing in different groups and he invited the Royal Winnipeg Ballet to perform. The Winnipeg Ballet was a jewel of a company and booking them was considered quite an accomplishment. The hall was sold out but, three days before the performance, they called from Winnipeg to tell us the main dancer had the flu. The story we got later was that the State Department applied the pressure and told the Winnipeg Ballet it wouldn't receive a visa to dance in New York and other places in the States if it didn't cancel Sudbury.

There were all kind of things which happened locally. Two radio stations cancelled our programs. We had shows about union news and labour reports. We sponsored the shows and paid the radio stations but when things got hot, usually around bargaining time, the programs were suddenly cancelled.

When I was president I had two public relations people on my staff. One of them prepared the program in English and another chap, a French Canadian, did the French news. He and his wife performed skits on the show. Today, news about labour is very common but not back then.

There was a movie called *Salt of the Earth*, which we wanted to show in Sudbury. We had one heck of a time when we tried to show that film. All the forces in this area got together to try and block its showing. The church warned its parishioners not to see it. We finally found a small theatre in which to show it. It ran only three days.

Another incident took place in 1948 when we were organizing Ontario gold mines in the Timmins and Porcupine area. We got to the stage where we could negotiate but we had very few people who were capable of bargaining so we brought in a fellow from our union in the States, our international vice president, Reid Robinson. Before things got going, there was a deportation order and Robinson was returned home.

As a matter of fact, every one of our organizers who came from south of the border had their visas cancelled or were deported. It was all right for the government to allow Hal Banks and his goons in but when we brought in somebody competent and respectable, it was stopped. When our members from Canada were going to conventions in the States, they were also stopped at the border. The left-wing unions were all targeted.

Guys like my father, who had big families, couldn't afford to fight. If you fought, you were blacklisted. I have files under my name at the Ontario Public Archives and in those you can find some of these blacklists. People were fired for no reason at all. When the union came along, it was a godsend. That's why I didn't give a damn who the leadership of our union was. If they did a good job they were elected, but they were booted out if they didn't.

In our union everyone, from the top international president right down to the board member, had to stand for office every couple of years and be voted on by the entire membership. This talk about "communist" domination was always B.S. You were elected on what you did for the people. Somebody did a survey about how many party people were actually in the leadership of our union in Canada. The percentage was negligible. Many times I was a hell of a lot more militant than the guys who were members of the Communist Party. I did it because I was a trade unionist.

CHAPTER TEN

WAR ON THE WHARVES:
THE STORY OF THE SEAMEN'S UNION

I KNEW THE WATERFRONT

Dan Daniels *is a Montreal playwright and former sailor. A number of his plays were performed and won awards, including the Dominion Drama Festival, Quebec western region. From 1947 to 1950 Daniels was the editor of the* Searchlight, *a newspaper put out by the Canadian Seamen's Union (CSU). The Ottawa government at the time, as later admitted by a cabinet minister in the House of Commons, imported an American union to break the CSU. The attack was led by the notorious Hal C. Banks of the Seafarers International Union (SIU). The CSU was accused by the right of being Communist-led and under Moscow's control.*

As editor of the *Searchlight* I would go after information. There was this chap who was an agent for the scabs and was ready to let us have us some information dealing with the scabs and the RCMP collaboration. I got a confession from him about the RCMP collaboration with the SIU [Seafarers International Union]. The day after the story appeared in the media he called me, claiming he had new information. I arranged to meet with him at a restaurant/café. Suspecting that all was not on the up and up, I arranged to have two seamen drop in, just in case I was being set up. They were not to sit with me or show any recognition when I entered.

There were two floors to the café and I agreed to accompany the informant to the second floor. I turned my head, for a minute, to admire a woman who was passing by. He then hit me, but good, yelling as loud as he could, "Communist! Moscow spy!"

I was wearing glasses at the time and he cut my eyes. I was badly stunned too, not having been geared for the attack. As he was launching his assault on me, I recognized members of the Subversive Squad [Montreal Police in this instance, not provincials] coming on the double to help him. They had been hiding in the restaurant. I let out a yell which brought the two seamen aroaring up the stairway as well. If it hadn't been for them I would have been badly clobbered. Fortunately, they got in between the cops and me. The cops were yelling, "Don't hit us. We're police!" The three of us were arrested and charged with assault.

Later that week, I met up with the manager of the café. He told me the police had been in to see him earlier that day and told him that a fight was going to take place, and to mind his own business. When I asked him if he'd testify to this, he backed off, saying he didn't want to risk losing his licence.

There was a rumour that those who wanted the SIU to win had brought in Murder Incorporated. This was in 1949, during the deep-sea strike. Sometime after we heard this rumour, I was contacted by a person who was trying to be a double agent. He claimed to having contact with the Montreal Red Squad (aka the Subversive Squad). He tells me a decision has been made to knock me off and to dump my body in the drink. There was going to be a coroner's hearing, but it had been decided in advance that my death was to be recorded as "accidental death by drowning while intoxicated."

It had a ring of authenticity to it because that was exactly the decision that was rendered in San Francisco about one of our other seamen, a brother-in-law of one of our members, Jerry MacManus, our secretary-treasurer. Two other seamen who had been picked out of the drink in San Francisco also had their deaths recorded in this manner. That made it sound possible. On the other hand, it might have been a form of intimidation.

Once, when I was in need of some sleep, I went over to my mother's, which was still officially my residence. I was stopped by a neighbour who said, "Don't go. There's a car parked outside your mother's home and there are thugs inside the car." I went into his house instead and through the back went to my home. For a while, I packed a gun. But I thought, "What am I playing with a gun for? If they're really professional gangsters, how can I compete with that?"

I was cautious though. When I was out in the streets I was only with other seamen. I only walked alone at two or three in the morning when I knew the thugs wouldn't be around. And I knew the waterfront, they didn't.

There are certain industries, and the shipping industry was one of them, in which the form of exploitation goes back to ancient times. Both the mines and the ships have a similarity—the people who were sent into work the mines and sent on the ships were often considered those who are really outside society. Prisoners would be sent to ships to do their term. They were shanghaied. The authority on the ships is a dictator, like a king. There's no such thing as democracy or rights there.

The conditions of the ships were geared so that the comforts of the crew were the last thing which was taken into consideration. In Nelson's fleet—in which the mutiny against Captain Bligh took place and in which, two years later, the entire fleet mutinied—the conditions were as follows: the living quarters were so compact that no seaman taller than five-foot-four could stand up straight. He had to crouch all the time because there was no head space. This does two things to you—first of all, it makes you hunched over all the time and, psychologically, when you are hunched over it does something to your manhood. Not that it succeeded all the time —aside from the mutiny on the *Bounty*, there were constant rebellions taking place.

Then there's the food. Your food is never the same as that given to the officers. For your sleeping quarters, no attention is given to warmth or comfort. Look, I sailed on lake ships where there would be steam pipes over our heads. Water would be dripping down on us. If you were in extremely cold weather and your hand touched the bulkhead, your flesh could bloody well be attached to it.

You had four to six guys sleeping together on one cabin. How much space could you have for your self? I liken it to prison cells because, from the few times I've been arrested and put into jail, the quarters on ships at that time were far more crowded and uncomfortable. They were worse than the cells I saw in prisons. Then there was the attitude of the officers. They are exploited themselves but they are given authority and made to feel that they have power.

Each time we have had a merchant marine our government has sabotaged it by the way they have operated. This attitude goes back to the time of Confederation when our clipper fleet was eliminated—we then had the fourth-largest merchant fleet in the world. We had a merchant marine during the First World War and then they got rid of it. Hence, when war breaks out you need ships but they haven't enough seamen from the lakes. What about officers? They can't get enough officers. Well, Britain comes to the rescue. But Britain isn't going to send us the best officers, Britain is going to give us the castaways. And what we got *were* castaways—some of them were certainly mental.

Aside from that, the British officers weren't accustomed to Canadians—we were colonials to them. They were not accustomed to the type of union we had because, at that time, the British Seamen's Union was collaborationist. Later, it turned out to be one of the finest unions but this didn't happen till the '60s. During the time I am talking about, every time there was a strike it was done outside the union. It was organized by Trotskyists usually.

On one ship, where I was the ship's union delegate [equivalent to a shop steward ashore] I was asked by the captain, who was from the UK, "Who do you think is running this ship? You're here amidships as often as I am." Since he was frequently tanked up and subject to the shakes, I told him, "Well, Captain, someone has to run this ship and you're in no condition to do it." He was furious and ordered me out. I didn't get the beef settled but I felt good. Yep, we Canadians were snotty. Many of us were very young and we had the strength of our organization. It gave us a feeling that we could stand up to this kind of authority and it infuriated the officers even more.

THE RAID

I had been living in Toronto where I edited a youth paper which was the organ for the National Federation of Labour Youth which was, in effect, a Young Communist organization. After leaving the editorship we came back to Montreal. My wife's grandmother had had an accident and we were staying with her grandfather while her grandmother was in the hospital.

I came home one evening to work on a manuscript I had been writing in Toronto. It was a history of Canada through an examination of our technology—as our technology changed so did our social mores, etc. I also had with me a book I had been writing off and on with stories about the '30s and '40s, about childhood, the Cartier district, and seafaring.

I had differences with the Communists before leaving Toronto, and although I was still with them, mentally I wasn't. But I wasn't yet ready to leave the party and after living over one year in Toronto I was a bit careless. Also, I figured that the police intelligence were more informed than they actually were. They shouldn't be too interested in me at the present, I thought, for surely they knew about the troubles I had with the party leadership in Toronto. So I lowered my guard.

A functionary of the Labor Progressive Party, who was a close friend of mine and also a former CSUer, also figured the cops wouldn't be interested in me. So much so that he had me hide some of his best books: he was fearful that his home was going to be raided by the police. Well, one particular evening, I decided to go home and do some work on my manuscripts. Also, I wanted to write a letter to my mother-in-law who, at the time, was writing letters to my wife which weren't doing our marriage any good. She particularly wasn't able to understand why I wasn't yet in business or seeking to better myself economically. My Jewish mother, she told her, must be very disappointed in me. I sat down at my typewriter and started to write a letter to her, trying to explain what moved me, why I wasn't interested in acquiring wealth, and that I was far more concerned with helping to better the living conditions of my fellow Canadians. It was a very personal letter, not of the kind that you care to have strangers look at. I had also laid down on my desk the copies which I usually secured elsewhere. But as I said earlier, living in Toronto had made me careless.

For some reason, which I can't remember now, I called Harry Binder, who was with the Labor Progressive Party in Montreal. Harry must have been very near the phone because he grabbed it and yelled out, "Police. They're raiding!" Then the phone was grabbed out of his hands and was plunged down.

Well, the police are raiding and I have nothing to fear, right? So I sit down to phone everybody I know who might possibly be raided—Communists *and* Socialists. I'm phoning as many people as I can since I have nothing to fear and there's no reason for me to hide anything. Then my door bell rings and the police come in with a warrant from the Padlock Law. That was approximately 8:30 and they did not leave my home until 12:30.

The raid was a joint operation of both the Provincial and Montreal Subversive Squads. Unfortunately, I had not yet unpacked much from Toronto and a lot of the books were in boxes. But I told them that, according to the Padlock Law, they could not take anything unless I had a right to note everything they take.

They said, "Yes, of course." It was bullshit because there's no such thing in the Padlock Law but I kept them busy. I figured, "Hey, they're playing games with me, I'll play games with them."

Well, they ended up playing the best game with me because after they left I looked around for the list of the books they seized. They took it with them. The manuscript I had been working on for over a year was seized. The stories I had been preparing off and on for five years were seized. Plus numerous little stories, lots of files, and the personal letter. AAAGGHHH!!

The interesting thing about this was that I phoned the head of the Subversive Squad in Quebec and I got back four books, including one on horsemanship, and I asked him about the manuscript.

He said, "Oh, you should get a gold medal for that one."

"Did you like it?" I asked.

"I didn't say I liked it. The Communists will give you a gold medal for it."

He told me it was going into the fire. The reason I mention this is because a year and a half ago I asked the minister of justice, or he might have been the solicitor general at the time, to conduct an enquiry into the raid. The provincial police, after some time, reported that as far as they were concerned the raid had been legal. When asked what happened to my writings and library—over 2,000 books—they reported that they had been destroyed. When I looked at the time which they gave for doing away with my works I noticed that they had done so after the law was declared unconstitutional. I have it all in black and white.

There's a footnote to this. There was one story in the collection I wrote called "It Shouldn't Happen to a Dog." I said, "Look, leave that story alone for goodness sake! If there's political stuff, take it, but that's a commercial story. It's one I can easily sell. You are really interfering with my livelihood."

The cop read it. "Aha," he said, "You see both dogs are arguing over hydrants and this dog wants this hydrant for himself and the other dog says we should all use the hydrant because every dog has a right to a hydrant. This is Communist propaganda," he said and he confiscated it. About two years ago, when I was moving my workplace to my home, I unexpectedly came across a copy of the story. I had no idea that I had somehow secreted a copy of it. I was going to throw it in the garbage—after all, it was something I had written back in 1954 and was not up to whatever quality of skills I've since learned. But my wife, Anne Marie, who is my main critic, read it and said, "Don't. Just make a few editorial changes and send it out." I did and it was immediately accepted by a quarterly in Regina. So what could have been with the rest of the material that I had written—especially those two volumes? I don't know.

How did you survive and make a living through all of this?

My hands. Working at whatever jobs I could find. Like so many others, the alternative would have been to go to the United States but there was the McCarran Act. It was a mistake. I should have gone across. Years later, when a play of mine was going to be produced in New York, they stopped me from crossing the border when I was with the crew. The theatre crew came here and then I drove back to New York with them. At the border they just nonchalantly checked us. We had a guitar and they said, "Oh, you're a band," and they were very friendly.

Stupidly, the driver said, "No, we're not a band. We're a theatre group."

They said, "Theatre? Out!"

The very word "theatre" triggered that reaction and they put our names through on the computer. He came to me and said, "You're un-American."

And I said, "Of course I'm un-American. I'm a Canadian."

He said, "You know what goddamn thing I mean and you're not crossing."

A friend brought me back home and when he got back to the border the same immigration man was there. He told my friend, "You can tell your friend Daniels that the only way he can cross the border is in a coffin."

Of course, he was wrong and I did cross the border more than once. Each time, however, I was worried about either getting turned back or being arrested when I was in the US because I had been warned by immigration that if I crossed the border without their permission I'd be jailed. It meant I was hesitant to do any work in the States even though I had some possibilities and some contacts.

THE MAKING OF A RADICAL

Bud Doucette *is a former merchant seaman and organizer with the Canadian Seamen's Union (CSU). Doucette was born and brought up during the Depression in the Miramichi River valley, near Newcastle, New Brunswick. Too young to enlist in the armed forces during the Second World War, he was eager to join the anti-Fascist effort, so he headed off to Halifax where he began a career as a merchant sailor and ships' organizer in tankers and dry-cargo vessels.*

If you ask me of a single incident that convinced me the system we lived under in the 1930s was unjust and cruel to workers, I'd cite the tragic case of a poor fellow named Joe McGinnis. As a very young man, Joe went to work in a sawmill on the Miramichi. The principal industry in the upper reaches of the river, then and now, is lumbering and related mill work.

One day Joe was snagged by a piece of wire stitching on one of those broad belts which powered the mammoth wheels that spun the saws that reduced logs into lumber. He was whipped into the machinery, 'round the wheel, and smashed to the floor. He was mangled; I believe almost every bone in that young man's body was twisted, broken, and misshapen.

Joe never walked again. As a matter of fact, he never stood thereafter. His only means of mobility was to drag himself through the ditches in the summer months by grasping bits of sod and small clumps of twigs or weeds and pulling himself forward, painfully and with agonizing slowness, on his way to visit friends.

During the wet and cold months, Joe couldn't venture out from his parents' home. One year, around Christmastime, my mother sent me to deliver a small gift to Joe and family. It was a molasses cake, flavoured by molasses and sultana raisins. Since most local houses were heated by wood-burning stoves, a wood storage house was attached at the rear of the building. I walked in and saw Joe lying on a mat that had been fashioned together from burlap potato sacks, sewn together, and placed alongside the wood stove. A kerosene lamp dimly lit the room. There, like a pathetic animal, huddled for warmth, lay this gentle man, uncomplaining. The smell of poverty was inescapable. This family had no income, no employment, little food, no comfort, and no hope.

Vague rumours circulated, from time to time, that the mill-owners whose machinery had crippled Joe for life might be intending to buy him a wheelchair. But no wheelchair ever materialized. I began to wonder about these mill owners and their "Christian" friends. They led good lives. They were well nourished, finely clad, lived in comfortable homes, often replete with "serving girls" and other hired help. Yet, none of them had any time or charity to waste on the likes of Joe McGinnis.

Joe's fate was burned into my consciousness forever. In a way, I'm grateful for having known him. He died sometime in the '40s. That experience taught me about the social class system; it told me about which side my fellow workers and I were morally destined to fight for.

I went away to sea and became a member of the Canadian Seamen's Union where I found a philosophical course to steer and a bright, steady light to guide me. During the long days and nights at sea, questions arose and answers were sought. How was it possible that, for the whole wasted decade of the 1930s there was said to be absolutely no money—no funds for schools, for health care. The whole country was reputed to be broke. Canada could not afford to alleviate the misery and suffering of desperately poor people like Joe McGinnis.

Then, miraculously, it seemed, following the outbreak of war that might have been avoided or its enormity lessened by an earlier confrontation of Fascism in Spain, money flowed from all directions. The able-bodied unemployed who had "rode the rods" by boxcar from east to west and back again in search of non-existent jobs, suddenly found themselves in great demand as soldiers, sailors, and airmen.

Of course, a large merchant fleet became a vital necessity. Our prewar ships, thirty-seven in total, were mainly small, obsolete, and slow. Canada built a merchant navy of over 180 ships, manned by about 12,000 seamen. Over seventy of our vessels were lost to enemy action. The death rate of wartime merchant seamen was calculated at 9.55 per cent, compared with 3.9 per cent overall for the three armed forces. One hundred and ninety-eight were taken as prisoners of war, most of them averaged four years in enemy concentration camps.

THE BLACKLISTING BEGINS

I was first blacklisted by Imperial Company in 1944, for having the audacity to bring on board their tanker, *Trontolite*, some copies of the union paper, *Pilot*, published by the then militant National Maritime Union (NMU) of the United States, as well as a few leaflets picked up from the CSU hall in Halifax. When accused of this heinous crime I readily admitted guilt and was informed that I would not be required on the next voyage. The Imperial ships were anti-union and never organized.

The merchant fleet had begun steadily dwindling in numbers. It started in 1946, when shipping operators began to transfer registry of our ships to "flags of convenience," replacing Canadian crews with seamen recruited in Asia and other cheaper labour markets around the globe. No longer were we remembered as the "heroes of the North Atlantic." Now we were portrayed as Communist subversives, fanning the flames of revolution at home and abroad.

Canadian seamen were handed over like chattels to the infamous thug, Hal Banks, and his henchmen. The Louis St. Laurent government had negotiated a sell-out deal with an American gangster organization called the Seafarers International Union. The shipowners and Banks' mercenaries had the active support of governments and police, at home and overseas. A reign of extortion of dues, intimidation, and coercion settled over the Canadian maritime industry.

A blacklist known as the "Do Not Ship" list (DNS) denied most of our veteran seamen the right to sail Canadian ships. The sale and flag transfers accelerated. The fleet was doomed. From a position of third-largest merchant navy in the world, we now have no ocean-going Canadian flag carriers at all. The government in Ottawa considered this a victory over a confrontational, fighting union of Canadian sailors. Victory? Who were the winners and how much did the people of this country lose?

For CSU activists, the long arm of the blacklist extended to other industries. Right-wing labour unions wanted nothing to do with ex-CSU members and we were barred from employment from AF of L unions when our previous occupation became known.

It was extremely difficult to find work and that blacklist remained in effect. For example, I got a job with Dominion Bridge on a construction job putting up a warehouse. I was on the job for only three hours when somebody from the Dominion Bridge personnel office came by car to tell me, "There's been some problem with your paperwork." They gave me two days pay, I believe, for my efforts and told me there was a problem with my union membership and that I couldn't be employed any longer.

CHAPTER ELEVEN

OUT OF THE UNION AND CIVILIAN WAR

FIRED BY THE UAW

Paul Siren was born on a homestead in the Port Arthur area (now Thunder Bay) in a two-room log cabin built by his father, an immigrant from Finland. Paul Siren became an international representative and Toronto director of the United Autoworkers of America. For seventeen years he had been a top union negotiator, but was fired from his position by the UAW's Canadian director, George Burt. The union boss claimed Siren had attended a meeting where Communists were present and that "he had no right to discuss union matters with Communists present." Six months later the UAW became even more vindictive and barred Siren from "holding any office, elective or appointive, anywhere in the union." Siren stayed in Toronto as a labour consultant and later joined the fledgling performers association, ACTRA, which he helped build into a strong force.

My experience in the UAW is an illustration of the McCarthy period and the willingness of the international trade unions primarily to adopt in their constitutions the provisions whereby no person who had any participation or affiliation with Communists would be allowed to hold office. While the UAW was not among the first to adopt such policies, it eventually developed the same kind of attitude whereby everyone was suspect if they didn't profess and expound the particular policies of the moment.

I think my first indications of real problems in terms of UAW policy was with the Marshall Plan. I had made the terrible statement in the District Council of the UAW that the Marshall Plan should be administered by the United Nations rather than unilaterally by the United States. Very shortly after that there was a meeting of all the staff called in Windsor at which time we were read a very stern lecture about questioning policy. At that meeting I don't recall any one pointing a finger at me personally, but it was clearly intended to explain to the staff that this kind of disservice would not be tolerated.

The cold war had emerged at that point and the United States was the major proponent of cold-war policies. In that sense, there was a desire to make sure the Americans had control. It was not limited to the State Department. It became a matter of general policy adopted by most of the international unions of the time.

In 1947 there was a cleanout of the staff of the UAW in Canada. It was in that period that the Reuther forces gained ascendancy.* And Burt was willing to adopt the policies of the international at that point. To be fair, up until the end of the war in 1945 George Burt had associated with the left in the Canadian labour movement. He was not an outright left-winger but his policies were certainly supportive of a left-wing attitude in the labour movement. I had a good relationship with George. Then in '47 we had some changes. A number of the staff were let go. I understand my name was among those being considered but I was not dismissed at that time. I was international representative for the union, which meant you were really one of the staff organizers or representatives of the union. But because it was an international union you were part of the international structure.

As the policy clashes developed in the labour movement generally they were reflected in the UAW. After the war many returning veterans became active in the union movement. They sought office and were willing to take their place in the ranks of leadership in the union. This was manifest, particularly, in Oshawa. In 1959-60 things became rather tough. In the late '50s Cliff Pilkey ran against George Burt and that was interpreted as a challenge by the "young turks" who were being led around by the nose by the Communist Party and who were either members of the party or were associated with the party.

I was directed as was the other staff international representative to

*Walter Reuther, president of the UAW from 1946 until his death in 1970, was an anti-Communist who tried to suppress their influence within the labour movement.

undertake measures which would lead to the defeat of these newly elected young turks that were raising Cain in the organization. In early December of 1959 I had a discussion with George Burt and made it clear to him that I was not prepared to carry out that policy, which meant I would have had to spend considerable time in Oshawa trying to defeat the elected leadership of that local union. I happened to be in charge of the region from Brantford to Oshawa.

I believe that once George Burt swung to the policies of the international union he did so completely. He did not question them at all. He expected the rest of the staff to do the same. We had a meeting and he raised these questions to see what I could do to defeat the leadership of the Oshawa local and some other locals in the Toronto area. He indicated to me that there were members of the staff who believed that the area over which I was director contained a good deal of the left in the leadership of the UAW, and I had something to do with it.

I had already started to think about what my role was going to be in the union. Burt and I had a long relationship and had worked together through many fights. George was somewhat sorry to have this situation develop. There was pressure on him and he sincerely accepted that pressure. And he saw no way out.

By 1960 I had three children. My eldest was in university. There's always a concern about looking after a family. But I had always felt that I would be able to manage somehow and I had made up my mind that I was not going to succumb to a situation where I would be placed in a position of having to fight an elected leadership of Oshawa and other local unions to support a policy which was primarily developed in the United States and was a spillover, in my view, of the McCarthy type of fear of Communism and the left. Clearly, the intention was to remove Communists and fellow travellers.

A great many people in the UAW were not connected in any way with the Communist organizations but reflected a very militant position. One must remember that in the mid '50s there had been the long General Motors strike. It lasted five and a half months and 18,000 workers were out on strike. I had a great deal to do with that strike, including its negotiated settlement, and I ran the strike fund for the union at the time. Many of the right-wing leaders of the

UAW felt that much of the militancy exhibited was clearly promoted by Communists and that these workers were Communist influenced. They didn't come out and say it to your face but there were statements about "Communist influence."

The most strident attacks came from the right-wing CCF people. The right-wing CCFers within the UAW took a very ardent position in respect to supporting international policy. Dennis McDermott, who later became president of the Canadian Labour Congress, was a supporter of CCF policies and was just so close to the American leadership and wanted to be identified with the American leadership. Many of these people were not only intolerant but were, in almost a fanatical sense, concerned that the left would take over.

The feeling was "that unless we smash these people they were going to take over." It was made quite clear in district council meetings of the union and at staff meetings that there was this paranoia about the left having undue influence.

In 1959 I had my meeting with George Burt and told him I had no alternative but to resign from the staff, if those were his instructions. George Burt repeated those would be my instructions as a staff member and I offered that I would write to let him know. I then wrote a letter saying that I was going to resign effective February 1, 1960.

I received a telegram on the 8th of January saying that I was dismissed. They didn't wait for my resignation. The accusation was that I attended a meeting in Oshawa during the General Motors strike at which there were Communists. I have no hesitation in saying that in the course of the strike, which lasted five months, there were pressures from left and right, from skilled workers and assembly line workers, and I attended many meetings. Some of those meetings must have had Communists in them, but I didn't know why I should have been worried about that. As long as they were concerned about the strike.

This meeting happened years before during the GM strike. Why weren't you fired in 1956?

Or any other period. You must remember these accusations were made some years after the strike. A chap named Gordon Wilson ran to be chairman of the General Motors negotiating committee of Oshawa and got defeated. Rising out of his defeat were these allegations and George Burt examined the allegations and took them to the international executive board and they obviously supported the decision of my dismissal.

I appealed to the Public Review Board established in the constitution of the UAW. This board was comprised of a Catholic bishop and some church officials. There were some academics from the United States and one Canadian magistrate from Windsor. At my insistence, the hearing was held in Toronto. The international union was represented by legal council from Washington—a very prominent lawyer. I appeared by myself. The unanimous decision from the Public Review Board was that I could be reinstated. However, I had made up my mind not to go back under those circumstances. I would have been sent to Moosonee or some other place and been safely out of their way. I had no intention of being put in that position.

I had spent seventeen years at the UAW. Leaving was a little wrenching because I had taken part in the development, formation, and organization of the automotive industry. I think I organized as many workers as any person in Ontario. Many shops have disappeared like the CCM plant and Russell Industries.

I organized de Havilland, Massey Ferguson, and Frigidaire and helped in the organization of the Oakville Ford plant in the early '50s. In the course of those campaigns, many thousands of people joined the union and I negotiated their agreements. It was not an eight-hour-a-day job. I recall one summer when I had only one weekend off. It was a rich experience and I don't regret it. I freelanced for five years before joining ACTRA where I spent twenty-two years.

Did you ever have trouble getting into or travelling to the United States?

I don't know how many UAW people were barred from the United States, but in 1949 I received a letter from the American immigration department which said "you are barred for life" from entering the country. Of course, they didn't give you any reason.

I didn't go across and have been across only with permission. I came to the conclusion that it's not worth my while to spend money on legal challenges. I travelled a good part of the world without having to go to the United States even though I would like to have gone there from time to time. It was not imperative to my life style. It was a handicap in that I couldn't participate in UAW meetings held in the United States, so I had to send someone else over to represent me.

DIS-UNITED NATIONS

Lukin Robinson is a researcher with Ontario Public Service Employees Union (OPSEU). He is over seventy but he looks fiftyish and strides across the union staff room with amazing energy. Toronto born, he was employed as a civil servant in Ottawa in the '40s when he felt the sting of anti–left-wing discrimination.

I enlisted in the air force in 1942. The main reason I didn't get into uniform before then was because of a ski race in March 1940 in which I ran into a tree and broke my leg. It took a long time for me to get well enough to be physically fit for a uniform. I was posted to air force headquarters for eighteen months and I made a number of friends during the war in Ottawa. Most were left-wingers who were politically active as well.

I got out of the air force in the fall of 1945 and I started to work in September at the Dominion Bureau of Statistics. I was also involved in a civil liberties organization which arose as a result of the fourteen or sixteen people in the famous spy raids—the Gouzenko business. As you've probably heard, the police came to them at night and took them off to the RCMP barracks somewhere in Rockcliffe where they stayed incommunicado for a number of weeks.

Later on, I got involved with the Civil Service Association in Ottawa, which was essentially the rudiments of a trade union representing civil servants. I was elected to the executive of the CSA in 1947 and the next year I became one of the leaders of a campaign to increase civil service salaries. Salaries were generally low as a holdover of the Depression years. If somebody earned 2,000 dollars a year that wasn't bad. I was a statistician when I started and my salary was around 2,800 dollars per year. But the cost of living was getting higher.

In the fall of 1947 the people who were in the Ottawa-based CSA took a leading part at a convention of what was known as the Civil Service Federation of Canada. Outside of Ottawa, civil servants were organized by department Canada-wide. So there was a postal union of internal postal workers and a postal union of letter carriers and a union representing all the employees of Revenue Canada and so on. This was a thoroughly antiquated and employer-dominated outfit at the top. And we set about to dislodge the incumbents and make it into an effective somewhat democratic organization which represented the interests of the employees and we were successful in doing that.

Interestingly, the two components of the federation on which we largely relied were the two unions of the postal workers—the inside workers and the letter carriers. And, as history shows, they have become the most militant of all federal workers in the years since. We took a significant step towards that.

Then in 1948 when we mounted a second campaign for civil servant pay increases it was a Canada-wide campaign led by the Civil Service Federation. It had quite a significant resonance throughout the country. One result was that the government began not to like us very much and they mounted a "red scare." This was shortly before the election for the executive of the CSA which was to take place in December of 1948.

The result was we had two slates running for the executive—I was the leader of one and the other slate was run by other people centred mainly in the department of labour. The red scare was that some of us were members of the CP, even though we hadn't admitted it, and in any case were certainly under CP influence and this was a dangerous thing. And if the CSA wanted to remain in the government's good graces and be able to speak effectively for the employees it represented, the best thing to do was to elect a slate which was in no way contaminated.

This came out in a resolution which was presented to the council of the CSA which met every month. This was hotly debated in the council of about one hundred people. Then it was published in a flaming editorial of the CSA newspaper and it was picked up by the Ottawa papers in flaring headlines. The *Ottawa Journal*, which was very conservative, was very hostile, and the *Ottawa Citizen*, which tended to be liberal, felt it was an undemocratic and unnecessary way to go about things.

Only one person whom we recruited for our slate decided to withdraw from it because of pressure from his department. He had reason to be frightened because of what his superiors told him and he was genuinely shaken by this because he didn't have experience with red scares. I too was shaken because I realized it was effective and scared a lot of people. All the other nominated people on our slate stayed firm.

Anyway, the left-wing slate was defeated and that ended my participation in the CSA. Then I was told it was, more or less, wise to concentrate on my work. The principal reason for the red scare was to defeat an effective and, what in trade union terms would be called, "militant" organization. There's no question about that in my mind.

The political atmosphere of 1948 was poisoned because anything that was tainted, or made to look red, was in bad odour. Anybody who was accused knew that his or her job was in jeopardy. Certainly, I was very clearly told that my career prospects were zilch from then on. It was only because my boss at DBS was relatively enlightened that I was able to stay on at all.

In 1949 the attack began against the people who were working at the film board in Ottawa. I knew many of them and they felt their houses would be raided. Gouzenko happened three years before but world events reinforced the general anti-red feeling. There was the Berlin blockade, the Communist takeover in Czechoslovakia.

I can tell you a funny story about the RCMP and me which happened later on. There were stories that the RCMP had been investigating a number of MPs, including CCF MPs. Of course the RCMP denied this. My brother, who was a fairly prominent lawyer in Ottawa, happened to know the deputy commissioner of the RCMP.

One day, when he was having lunch with this gentleman, my brother asked him whether there was any truth to these stories. Of course, the deputy commissioner wasn't about to say yes or no. My brother wanted to pin him down so he said, "Well, let's take a specific example like my brother, Lukin Robinson, do you have a file on him?"

And the guy's jaw dropped and he said, "Lukin Robinson? Is he your brother?"

My brother said, "Yes, he's my brother."

The RCMP fellow answered, "My God, we have a file on him this HIGH!"

I know this because my brother, in great distress, told my mother. She thought it was a big joke. The RCMP didn't advertise what it was doing but it was very active. I left Ottawa in 1950 to go and work for the United Nations. Essentially, I wanted to leave because I was told there was no future in Ottawa in terms of promotion. Basically, I was on a blacklist.

THE DIS-UNITED NATIONS

During the first six months of 1950, [Norwegian diplomat and Secretary General of the United Nations] Trygve Lie went on a famous peace mission to see if he could cool the cold war a little bit. Some people thought it was a good thing but some people in the government thought it was not. When the Korean War started it took a different turn. From documents which came to light later on it appeared that the US government determined to purge from the UN staff everybody who it thought was tainted "red" in any way.

Eventually, this spread to all specialized UN agencies. Strictly speaking, the staff rules and regulations prohibited that—people were to be recruited completely independent of political affiliation. Once they started to work for the UN they were in no way beholden to their respective governments. They were to act wholly in the interests of the UN. When the US government told someone in the UN administration to get rid of a person because of a feeling about his political affiliation, they weren't allowed to do that overtly. When the US government pressed the UN and asked, "Why aren't you acting on this?" a reply would come back, "It's not as easy as all that because we have these rules and regulations which we have to abide by."

Nevertheless, they started by firing six people in the fall of 1950. I was, at that time, on the executive of the UN staff association. The staff association decided to take up the defence of these people. I became rather deeply involved in this—unsuccessfully, as it turned out, because the dismissals were upheld during the appeals. But we hired some prominent lawyers—in particular, Telford Taylor, who was famous because of his role in the Nuremberg trials. The fact that we had these lawyers and were making a lot of noise caused the administration a lot of stress.

I was on a one-year fixed contract for 1950. That was up for renewal in the fall of 1950. The department where I was working wanted to give me what was called "a temporary indefinite contract." It didn't mean I was permanent but my contract didn't have to be renewed every year or two.

But the administration said, "No! He's already a thorn in our flesh and we'll give him one year because you've asked us to, but make it clear to the so-and-so that if he doesn't behave himself then that's it."

When I got my next one-year contract I didn't have to be told what the implication of that was. I knew because it was just at this time that we were getting into the defence of those people who had been fired. Three of them had been on the executive of the staff committee no less. It was both a political purge and a purge of the staff committee which was the executive of the staff association. Anyway, at the end of my second contract I was told it would not be renewed and it wasn't. So I went through an appeals procedure with the support of the staff.

The US was asking why aren't you getting rid of these red-tainted people in a hurry. One of the results was that eventually the staff regulations were changed and it became much easier to purge people. After the initial six and the change in the rules, there was a massive purge. It extended to detailed investigations of US citizens who were employed by the UN's specialized agencies.

For example, in the International Labour Organization and the World Health Organization, which were both located in Switzerland, the Swiss government said, "We're not going to let your FBI people come here to investigate people who are international servants and who we have welcomed." So the investigators set up shop in Paris. Each individual, including friends of mine, was called to Paris as part of an investigation. One of the things which was held against one friend of mine was that he had sent a telegram from my house when he came to visit me for one day!

When he was interviewed he was asked, "Did you ever spend a night at Lukin Robinson's place?"

"No, I didn't," he said.

So they hauled out a telegram which he had sent from my house to his wife in Geneva and asked him—"Well, how about this? Doesn't that show you spent the night there?"

My friend said, "No, I spent the day there but not the night." And that's the kind of investigation it was. The telegram was sent in 1951 and this interview took place three or four years later. They had it on file.

Anyway, the result was that I was ousted from the UN and that's when I started to work for the Mine, Mill and Smelter Workers Union.

CHAPTER TWELVE

ASSOCIATED PROBLEMS

Was There Really a Blacklist?

Pierre Berton is the best-selling author of numerous books, including the Governor-General's–Award winning books Klondike *and* The Last Spike. *A broadcaster of note, he's a regular panelist on "Front Page Challenge" and in 1978 won an ACTRA Gordon Sinclair Award for integrity and outspokenness in broadcasting. "I never had any problems with politics and said whatever I wanted. I was never a member of the Communist Party nor terribly sympathetic with it because it was too damn shrill. I don't like the way they wrote—the clichés—as a writer I couldn't stand that."*

It would have been very hard for anybody to prove they were black-listed in this country. If people were blacklisted it was on a personal man-to-man basis. It still goes on at the CBC—you hire your friends and you hire people you like. The only time I was ever visited by the RCMP was about Lister Sinclair when I was with the *Toronto Daily Star*. The Mounted Police came in and they asked me about him. I said, "For God's sake, I know him very well. I've know him since university. He's not a security threat or anything else. He was left wing like we all were. I was probably further left than Mr. Sinclair."

I was never a member of the party but I sympathized with most left-wing causes at that time. This was in 1960. It was a government job. I think they checked security for everybody in a government job. That's the only time I was ever asked about anybody. He got the job.

Now, I remember we were offered Ted Allan's book when I was working at *Maclean's* magazine. You know, *Bethune:The Scalpel and the*

Sword, the one he did with Syd Gordon. We tried to get it published but Arthur Irwin, who was the editor, was shrewd enough to know that the top brass at *Maclean's* wouldn't publish it. So he just pretended he hadn't read it.

We kept saying, "Well, look what are you going to do about this book?"

"I haven't read it yet," he'd say.

I think we paid for it and I wanted to run it very badly because I thought it was a good book. It was a little heavy on the propaganda side and I think if I'd had the editing of it I would have smoothed that out. It was not a very objective book, even Ted would say that now. Bethune deserved his place in Canadian history and *Maclean's* should have published it. But you could not do it back then.

—— —— was certainly a member of the Communist Party and a friend of mine. I helped hire him for *Maclean's* as our West Coast correspondent in the '50s. When the McCarthy thing got very tough, Ralph Allen said, "We cannot allow this guy to go around picketing buildings and making Communist speeches. He's supposed to be out writing objective articles in B.C. as a member of the *Maclean's* staff." And he said, "We can't keep him on the staff." I tried to argue that but they took him off staff. But I do say this: he continued to freelance for us. We just paid him for articles and he worked freelance for us. —— —— continued to write for us and as a freelancer he could write for anybody. I opposed the idea of taking him off staff and I thought it was unnecessary.

The interesting thing was the Gallup poll and I remember this because I thought at least we were escaping McCarthyism in this country. Then I read the Gallup poll and the Canadians were just as McCarthyite as the Americans, according to the Gallup poll. I think we were worse! Certainly just as bad. The approval rate, or something like that, for McCarthy, was just as strong as in the United States.

THE ACTRA CONTROVERSY

I remember the George Herman incident well because they were going to hire him as business agent for the union. I objected to it not because he was a Communist, but because he concealed that fact and because he was a member of a union which was very strongly under Communist influence which I thought was hurting the union movement and I still think it was. But mainly I objected because he was presented as "clean" and they went out of their way to hide the fact that he had been involved in a Communist union and was clearly himself, if not a member of the party, certainly a very close sympathizer.

He wasn't fired, he just wasn't hired. And the union voted against him when it was revealed, and it was a shock and a revelation when somebody got up and said, "Just a minute. You should know this guy's background is a very heavy background in the Communist Party and we haven't been told this." I thought, "Well, that's deception," and I didn't like it very much.

I don't think it was a plot. I think a good many union members, at that time, didn't want somebody who had been involved in the Mine, Mill and Smelter Workers. You have to remember a couple of the unions, the electrical workers and Mine Mill, were getting sweetheart deals from the bosses in order for the guys in charge to keep their jobs. And there was a good deal of criticism within the union movement by the non-Communist unions about the weakening of the labour movement by the Communists. As you know, they stayed till two or three in the morning and got their slates elected. I must say I don't think this was blacklisting; I just think this was self-preservation.

I thought it would hurt the union and I still think it would have hurt the union. The main thing was the guys who were in charge of the union then were not levelling with the membership. They were not telling us what George Herman's background was. And I think the union has a right to know about a guy's background before they voted on it. I think this deception was certainly what bothered me. I didn't know anything about his background until it was told to me. After that there was an enquiry which I went to, and George Herman went to, and which Barry Morse chaired. And they brought in a "Scottish" verdict—unproven or something like that. And he resigned.

THE ACTRA CONTROVERSY

Mrs. George Herman *is a Toronto resident who believes her late husband, George Herman, lost his job with ACTRA, a union for radio and television artists and writers, in 1954 because of the "red scare."*

My husband and I had lived in Los Angeles for four years when we decided to leave for Canada in 1950, with our eighteen-month-old daughter. My husband was working for the Mine, Mill and Smelter Workers Union and, as a Canadian, his status was that of "resident alien," as the term is used in the United States. The Taft-Hartley Act had been passed and the effect of it was to hunt out non-citizens who were active in what they called "Communist unions." We were afraid he would be deported, which would be very bad if we ever wanted to travel back again to the States. So Mine Mill posted him here.

I myself had been blacklisted in the States before we came to Canada. I was in Los Angeles during a time when the progressive movement was very strong. I remember a big rally on behalf of the Hollywood Ten in which Katharine Hepburn made a stirring speech which was written by one of Hollywood's top writers. I had been active in a number of progressive organizations, including the Hollywood Independent Committee for the Arts, Sciences, and Professions which was a left-leaning organization. Most of us were listed in a publication called *Red Channels*. As a result of this, I was fired from my job in the industry.

My husband worked for the union in Southern Ontario, and was doing a lot of travelling and servicing various locals, organizing and negotiating for the union in various towns. In 1954 he decided to leave the union, partly because he was tired of the travelling and partly because he was upset about certain practices he had observed. He had a few in-between jobs. There was a movie called *Salt of the Earth* which the Mine Mill in the States had been instrumental in producing. It was being shown here and my husband took on the job of publicizing that film. Later he worked for a television company editing film.

Then he heard about a job opportunity with ACTRA which was then called ACRTA. They were looking for someone with negotiating experience to be their business manager. My husband was interviewed several times by various echelons and I guess they liked him and hired him, knowing his experience as a union organizer. He was on the job for a few weeks and I thought he was doing remarkably well mastering the details of the ACRTA contracts because it was so different from his previous field.

Then the first membership meeting came up since he had started his job. George was introduced to the membership when two men, so-called civil libertarians, Lister Sinclair and Pierre Berton got up and, in what I felt was an orchestrated strategy, began to attack my husband because he had been a representative of Mine Mill, which they said was a Communist union and had rigged ballot boxes and done all sorts of unethical and dishonest things, which had nothing to do with my husband who had never been part of such practices, if they did indeed go on. But in a typical McCarthy "guilt by association" technique, they said it certainly wouldn't do any credit to ACRTA to have a former representative of Mine Mill working for them. By that point I left the room because I felt too uncomfortable in being there. Right then and there, they brought a motion to the floor to fire him. And they got the membership all worked up about it and the motion was passed and he was out. We were both terribly shocked. He had to change careers.

[George Herman died in 1966.]

UNION ORGANIZER

Ruth Weir is an elected trustee of the Etobicoke school board. As a young woman in Toronto during the '40s and '50s, she was a union organizer and member of the Communist Party. During those years she claims to have been followed by the RCMP, whom she believes also intimidated her employers and work colleagues. She was first blacklisted in 1942.

My first experience with the RCMP following me around and intimidating me took place when I was a teenager and joined the Young Communist League and led a delegation for free textbooks to the board of education. And then my poor mother started to get phone calls from the RCMP telling her that her daughter was keeping "undesirable company." Mother told them to mind their own business. She knew what kind of people I was associating with. After I graduated from high school I went to work at John Inglis to help organize the plant. My suspicions that the RCMP were keeping tabs on me were confirmed when I came in one morning to work without my pass, which I had forgotten. So I stopped in the office to get a pass and the girl brought out my entire file and written on it was, "Make copies of everything for the RCMP." I knew then they were on to me.

There was a slight disagreement over which union should be in the plant and when the vote was taken only 51 per cent of any workers voted for any union at all. When the day of the vote came I was escorted by two big guards, one on either side of me, to the voting booth so I wouldn't be able to influence any employees with my seditious ideas about wanting a union. Two unions had tried to get in. There was the International Association of Machinists, which I originally started out working for. They were raided by the steelworkers, which was an anti-Communist union.

I remember one day I went into the union office and the girl there asked me to show her my shop steward card. When I did she tore it up and threw it at me and said, "Communists can't be shop stewards in the steelworkers union!" That kind of thing went on.

That was during the war about 1942 and in September of 1943 I decided to change occupations so I got on a train and went to Vancouver and joined the Canadian army. I found out the RCMP was still following me around. At basic training they were giving us a little lecture about the fact that they had to send in a report about some people every month. They looked directly at me and I thought, "Oh, oh, here we go again!"

I belonged to the only girl mechanic motor unit in the Canadian army and we went to Edmonton and were shipped back to Vancouver for a ten-day leave. Because of my feeling about the justness of the war I said I didn't want a ten-day leave. I said that I would work in an office and I went into the office and typed. Then my equipment came in and I had to go back to my own unit but they said that I couldn't go back and that I had to stay and work in the office. So I folded my arms and sat in a chair. For two days I sat there and said, "I can't type and nowhere on any of my documents does it say I can type!"

Then the captain called me into his office and said to me, "You know you have a political record? Well, I have to send in a report on you every month and if you are a good girl and stay with this unit I'll send a good report. Otherwise, I'll send a bad report."

I looked at him and asked, "Is that all you have to say?" Then I walked out to my own officer, who was a very fine lady, and I asked her if she knew I had a political record. She said yes. Then I told her that now I knew too because the captain tried to blackmail me with it. So she took him up on charges and had him thrown out of the unit.

After the war I went into the factories. I worked for a factory and got fired from there for trying to organize a union. I was pretty young and green. Then I worked for the Small Arms Company. One day, they gave me a promotion because I was such a bright girl, and the next day, after a union meeting, they escorted me out and told me I was finished. After that I couldn't get a job in any other factory.

I tried but couldn't get any more jobs. The RCMP just quietly went to it and made sure that I wouldn't work in another factory. I suppose if I would have been the sole breadwinner it would have been a terrible thing. I was fortunate I had other skills, so I went to work in offices. I stayed in office work while my children were growing up and I became very proficient in office work.

My husband was a Communist organizer and he didn't make much money. If we wanted something like a holiday with the kids, we needed extra money. As a highly skilled worker, I made a lot more money than he did, though I worked on a part-time basis.

After I stayed at one office for a while, someone would come in and visit my boss. I remember I was working at a trust company and working for a lawyer whose secretary was sick. He called me into his office and he started telling me all about these wonderful Soviet films he had for his child's birthday. I just nodded.

When the children started to get older I did all the office work for a truck parts firm. One day I came in and one of my bosses called me into office and asked me what my husband did. I said he was a Communist organizer.

The boss said, "Doesn't he do something else, like work for a newspaper?"

I said, "Yes, the *Canadian Tribune*."

He said "Yup. That's it. I want copies of that newspaper because I've got a Cuban customer and I want to show him what a good guy I am." He just thought it was a good way to get in with his Cuban customers. The RCMP had obviously been in because I had never told them where my husband worked.

I got tired of office work and went to work for Stafford Foods in 1964. I'll never forget the first day because I went to the Unemployment Insurance Office and this was where they sent me and I was walking up the street and asked a girl where Stafford Foods was. She pointed and said, "Over there." Then she showed me her hands and they were all bleeding. That's a challenge I thought and went on in.

Because I didn't tell anyone I was leaving office work to go into a factory, they didn't find out I was a Communist until after the union was organized. I started in September, and by March we had a union. When we went to the board to certify the union we had 70 per cent of the workers signed up. But when I ran for president of the union I got red-baited. People called me names and shook their fists in my face.

You have no idea how bad some of these factories were. In the chicken coop department I worked on a sealer where the packages of soup are sealed by hand. One young woman on the line was going to have a baby and one day she was sick and she asked me if I could change with her so she could sit down. I said sure but then the forelady came in and was furious. So she put me in "purgatory": I was sent to pack hot chilies with no mask for two days: that was my punishment. But I didn't get sick because I was a tough little character.

Another time I was working with the stuff they sell to restaurants—the bleach they put on potatoes to make them look nice and white. We were supposed to take this stuff out of jars, but one of the jars just crumbled and fell into the pan. I said, "Well, I guess we'll have to throw this away." But no, I was told to pick the glass out. You saw a difference when the union came in. I was working with the maraschino cherry machine, which had jars going around and a trolley under a hole which gets filled up with juice and sealed. Once machines started to break jars. So I started to shut it down but the foreman shouted, "Keep it going, keep it going!" I had glass on my hand and said, "Shut it down." They shut it down.

During the cold war, it was difficult when you went out on a petition to abolish atomic weapons. I was once chased off a veranda by a guy with a knife. It was a terrible kind of period. I remember canvassing once during an election and going up to this clapboard house. This man came to the door and shooed me away, saying, "You go away, you Communists want to take over my house." Looking at this house, which was totally rundown, I said, "Who would want it?"

PART FOUR

TEACH NO EVIL

CHAPTER THIRTEEN

TEACHERS AND THE BLACKLIST

TORONTO'S HIGHS AND LOWS

Ben-Z. Shek is a writer/teacher who was shut out of a high-school teaching career in Toronto by the blacklist. He has written award-winning films for CBC-TV and for the forerunner of TV Ontario. A long-time professor of French language and literature at the University of Toronto, he was involved with left-wing activities as a young person during the '50s and he worked with Nathan Cohen on the Jewish newspaper the Vochenblatt. *His first love has always been teaching.*

My troubles started when I decided to go into teaching in 1959. At that time in Ontario we had an emergency teacher training program. They needed teachers quickly so they trained you in summer school and you started teaching in the fall, and could go back next summer to complete the training and that was considered the equivalent of a full year at the College of Education. So I landed a job at Harbord Collegiate in Toronto in 1959.

I taught a whole slew of courses—five different subjects. But when I had to go back to complete my summer training in 1960 I was told I was incompetent. Two inspectors from the secondary school system in the city of Toronto recommended that I not be allowed to finish my teacher training. They gave their report to my principal, and the principal told me about it. I suspected there was something more to it.

Late that spring, a veteran teacher I had befriended told me he heard rumours that I was involved with the Hungarian uprising of 1956. He claimed Hungarian Canadians had come to the principal and charged that I had opposed the uprising there. The fact is I was nowhere near Hungary in 1956. But there was evidently an unwritten rule that left-wing people, from the radical left, were barred from teaching in the city of Toronto.

When I lost my job at Harbord I was married and had just had a child. My wife and I were angry and worried, but we didn't want to make it a public thing. I didn't even tell my mother for a long time. In all these years, it has not been made public. I tried to appeal by going to Dr. Cannon, then director of education for Ontario, but he said he couldn't do anything about it. His office couldn't override inspectors. His advice was: "Go to the RCMP and try to clear yourself. Say *mea culpa*." But I wouldn't do that.

In the fall of 1960 I had enrolled in the College of Education full time. I completed my teaching qualifications in the college and I did very well, standing in the top ten of the five hundred students. I knew the mother of a young woman who worked in the dean's office and she told me that, one day, her daughter had overheard people coming into the dean's office and asking about six or seven of us who were at the college at that time. We presumed these people were from the RCMP and they wanted to know which schools were going to hire us. We had all been in the left at one time or another. One of the people on the list, who is a retired university professor in Ottawa, was followed around everywhere he went for job interviews.

My geography and history teacher told me that he too had been asked about my political views. He said he didn't care what they were, but that I was very competent.

I worked freelance for the CBC on such shows as "Tabloid," "701," and "Closeup," and had won the 1960 Canadian Annual Film Awards for best film on television for a program I wrote about the Canadian doctor and sculptor Robert Tait Mackenzie. I had a friend at the CBC who was working in children's TV and he told me there was a job-opening, so I applied. It was blocked. Apparently, being a freelancer was OK but staff was out for me at children's programming.

THE '80S

About eight years ago I had to go to Los Angeles to get a plane for

New Zealand, where I was going to an academic conference. I was supposed to be in transit in Los Angeles for only four hours. I brought a telex from the high commissioner of New Zealand asking me to give some lectures in universities there, and so I had this letter with me in case anything happened.

And something did happen in the Vancouver airport. US immigration authorities gave me quite a going-over. They looked in a big black book and then someone said, "Just a minute!"

They asked me questions like, "What organizations do you belong to?"

So I named some; for example, the Canadian Association of Professors of French.

"Are any of these affiliated with the Communist Party?" they asked.

"That is ridiculous, " I answered. "These are academic organizations."

With me on this trip was the Quebec writer Roch Carrier, and he asked me, "Did they quiz you?" He was also evidently questioned about his political ideas and his affiliations, which was surprising since he was not even that involved in Quebec politics.

The authorities put something in my passport, but I didn't look at it. Then they said, "OK, you can go now." When I looked at it, I saw "PAROLED UNTIL MAY 14th, " which was the day I was travelling. That meant I had to leave the US that day and hand in the form when I went on the plane in Los Angeles for New Zealand.

THE RCMP AND TEACHERS

Steve Endicott is a professor at York University in Toronto. He graduated from university when he was nineteen and immediately became an organizer for the Communist Party, a job he did for nine years. After a falling out with the party he lost his position, although he remained a member for twenty-one years. Then he began a quest to find another way to make a livelihood.

In the beginning, I worked in factories and other places. But eventually, I decided it would be best to take up the training I had in history at university and to get a job teaching high school. I was already in my thirties and had three children. This was in late 1959 and early 1960, when there was a great shortage of teachers. There were lots of advertisements.

I called the principal of a school in East York, which is in east-end Toronto, and told him that I was interested in replying to his advertisement for a history teacher. When I told him my name he repeated it and said, "Endicott—that's not a very good recommendation for teaching history in a democracy, I would think." He was going on the name of my father, James Endicott, who was a leader in the peace movement.

So then I tried my old alma mater, Vaughan Road Collegiate, where the principal had known me well. But his immediate reaction was to tell me, "Steve, I'm afraid you would have problems in relationships within the staff room." He had an image in his mind that I would be a radical leftist and would insist on my point of view and that I wouldn't fit in.

Eventually, I consulted a friend, A.A. MacLeod, who had been a member of the Ontario legislature for the Labor Progressive Party. MacLeod had made a great impression on Leslie Frost, the Conservative premier of Ontario, who appointed him to a little job deciding on historical monuments—what should be preserved for Canadian history. So I talked to MacLeod about my experiences with the schools. MacLeod suggested I go and see the director of education for the province, Dr. Cannon, and tell him what was happening to me and hear what he had to say.

I arranged that appointment and told the director of education about these incidents, and I asked him if he thought I should have an opportunity to make a contribution to teaching in the secondary school system. He called in his deputy ministers and asked them. They said, "Certainly, but we have one difficulty—we can't give you a job or appoint you. The system in Ontario is such that each local school board has the right to decide who it will hire. But we'll allow you to drop our names in an interview, if you can get one."

How did you finally get a high-school teaching job?

The thing that helped was that I had worked in industry after I left my party job. Part of that time, I had worked as a credit manager for an electronics company where I gained some commercial knowledge. There was a great shortage of commercial teachers; so instead of applying to teach history I applied to teach business.

I was hired by a school out in Port Credit where I mentioned that Dr. Cannon had suggested I apply. One of the things they wanted me to teach was economics!

After I got home, just after they hired me, I got a worried phone call from the head of the department who said, "You know, Mr. Endicott, economics has nothing to do with politics. Does it?" "Of course not, " I said. Somebody had recognized my name right after I got the job. Of course, the class included discussions on capitalism, socialism, and communism.

While I was teaching I had to take two summer courses. They were so short of teachers they allowed people to get their teaching certificates by taking two six- or seven-week summer courses. During the second year of this course, an RCMP officer came into the Ontario College of Education and asked to see the files of the "three or four Communists" which he said were students there. These files were apparently pulled out and given to him. What did he need them for? He wasn't in charge of our academic progress. Perhaps he wanted to find out if there was a chance we would fail. One of the secretaries in the office was very upset by this and told one of us about the RCMP visiting. It was a policy of harassment which was supposed to make it difficult for us to enter the teaching force.

In the classroom I had to lead the students in saying the Lord's Prayer and in reading a passage from the Bible. I remember feeling that the principal of the school where I got hired was doubtful whether I would do this. I didn't think that this should be done because there were people of different religious viewpoints in the classroom. What I actually did was to take the Book of Job as a piece of literature.

Later on in the year, I had the students conduct these opening ceremonies themselves. One day, as I was sitting in the back, the principal came tearing in, saying, "Don't you know you have to have opening exercises?" I said, "But nowhere does it say *I* must conduct them."

The first year I stuck close to the textbook. At the end of the year, I asked my students to evaluate the course. Some of the brighter ones said, "Well, it was interesting, sir, but couldn't we have deviated from the textbook a little more?"

I did the job and got along all right. I only stayed there one year and then went to a different school in the same system and became the head of the department—the director of the business and commerce section. I left high school teaching after eight years and decided to get a graduate degree.

TRAILED BY THE RCMP

There were things that happened which led me to believe the RCMP came to every job I had after leaving the party to try to let my employer know about me and make him feel uncomfortable about having me as an employee. The best example of that was my experience here at York University. After I had done my Ph.D., I got a teaching job here at Atkinson College. The dean was Harry Crowe, and he called me to his office one day and he told me a funny thing which let me know his position. He remarked that he had grown up in Winnipeg and that he learned his politics from J.S. Woodsworth and others. He said, "At the time, I was taught to fight the capitalists and to fight the Communists, and I've been doing it ever since." Then he added, "I want to tell you that after you were hired here, the RCMP came to see me. They asked me if I knew whom I had hired. I told them I knew."

Then they asked him, "Well, will you cooperate with us as others have done?"

Harry thought a minute and said, "Yes, certainly I will. If there's anything you want to know about him, just write me a letter and I'll send you a reply *and* a copy to Professor Endicott." And that was the end of that, I'm sure! It was an attempt to intimidate. The RCMP had no business coming here. I hadn't done anything illegal. This was in 1972.

Held in the States

In 1980, after I had been a professor here at York for eight years, I wanted to attend the American Historical Association's meeting in Washington. But I knew that the names of everyone in my family were in the black book and we were forbidden to go to the States. I went down to the consulate to give my name and see if there was any reason I couldn't go.

I was asked, "Have you ever been in jail?" I said no.

"Have you ever been convicted of a criminal offence?"

"No."

"Are you a Canadian citizen?"

"Of course."

He said, "Then you can go."

I asked, "Are you sure?"

He went to look, returned, and said yes again.

And I insisted, "Are you really positive?"

"You mean, " he said, "I should look in the political book?" He came back and said, "You're right, you can't go. In order for you to go, you'd have to give a statement to the FBI, get yourself finger-printed, ask for permission for some specific reason, and you'd wait up to three months and then, perhaps, the answer might be yes." That was just an indignity, a form of harassment.

I remember in 1952 I was working in Europe at the time. I was in Budapest at the headquarters of the World Federation of Democratic Youth acting as a journalist for *Jeunesse du Monde*. We lived there for two years. My wife was with me and our first daughter was born there. In the course of that work, I had to come back to Canada on occasions. Once I was on a plane, a Constellation not a jet, and it couldn't fly right through to Toronto but had to refuel at Gander. There was cloud cover there, so we ended up in New York, at Idlewild Airport.

When I got off the plane, a man suddenly came up and I was led immediately to a little area and put into what was really a cage—not chicken wire but a chain-link cage. It was something with a little place where you could sit down. There was a whole row of these cages. I was kept there for hours without anything being said. The other passengers had left a long time earlier. Then came some questioning; I was asked why I had the nerve to come there without any visa or anything. I said, "First, I don't need a visa to come to visit the States from Canada. Second, it was entirely accidental that I came."

They hadn't checked but just nabbed me off the list. A couple of hours later, they came back with a policeman. He got into a car with his gun and he put me in. I asked, "Where are we going?" He said, "We're going to La Guardia and we're putting you on a plane to Montreal."

CHAPTER FOURTEEN

A Peace Activist and his Church

The Red Squad and the Divinity School

Ted Baxter is a retired teacher in the Toronto area who was, for many years, head of the modern languages department at Victoria Park Secondary School. He was a peace activist while studying at McGill University in Montreal.

I guess I first became aware that there was discrimination when I became involved in the peace movement. I was living in Montreal from the fall of 1950 to the summer of '53 and was aware of the Montreal Police's Red Squad, the anti-subversive squad, which used to go around to peace meetings and union meetings.

They would take down names and see what they could find out to use against people. They were plain clothes police, but they were quite well known to people who attended meetings. Two of them in particular I remember—one was heavy-set and had a scar on his face and everybody called him "Scarface." His real name was Boyczum. The other was a tall, heavy-set, French-Canadian named Benoit. They were the original B & B of the Montreal Red Squad.

There was a law on the books of Quebec which was referred to as the Padlock Law. It made it possible for a building to be, literally, padlocked if the authorities felt the building was being used to promote left-wing causes. They said "Communist causes" but that included anything left of centre. And they did in fact close down buildings by just putting a padlock on them.

In the fall of 1950 I was enrolled in the faculty of divinity at McGill. I registered late because I had gone to Europe the previous summer on a trip organized by the World Federation of Democratic Youth, a left-wing organization. We spent time in France, Italy, Czechoslovakia, and Poland. While we were there we got visas and spent three weeks in the Soviet Union. This was long before it became the "in" thing to do—to spend a week wandering over the Russian steppes.

Naturally, the authorities at the divinity school were a little bit leery of this leftist guy who was appearing on their doorstep fresh back from Red Square. I remember they said to me, "Well, we know that you're involved with the left, but we just hope that there isn't going to be any trouble."

One member of our group who went on the trip had grown up in a missionary family in China and he detached himself from our group in Russia and went off with another group and spent a month or more in China. This was only a year after the Chinese Revolution in '49, so going there was a very new thing. He was also a theological student in Toronto and he came down to Montreal for a visit and I invited him to come and speak to the young people's group at the church in Montreal with which I was associated, St. James United. He agreed and a lot of people came to hear him because it was interesting to hear someone who was just back from China, especially someone who was not a Communist but was speaking from a Christian point of view.

Lo and behold, here come Scarface and his sidekick Benoit. They walked in, looked around, and we handed them hymn books and gave them a place to sit. They sat through the meeting at which I introduced my friend, who talked about his time in China and so on. But the young people in the church were really very frightened by these two burly cops. These kids were scared and wondered what they were getting themselves into. "Are they going to put a padlock on the church or are they going to take our names?"

At some point, these two cops reported that, "This guy Baxter is a Communist. He invited this Communist friend to come down to Montreal and talk propaganda to the young people of this church." I have a lot of respect for the minister of the church, Reverend Tom McLennan, who was quite incensed by this whole thing. He brought it up to the presbytery and his intention was to ask the presbytery, which involved a lot of churches in Montreal, to protest and say,

"Why are the police interfering with a peaceable meeting in a church? Can somebody tell them to please leave us alone?"

Somewhere along the way the whole thing got turned around and the question became "Is Baxter a Communist? The police say he is and where there's smoke there must be fire."

This was what the head of the theological college wanted to know. They kept saying to me, "Are you a Communist?" and I guess the simplest thing would have been to say, "No, I'm not," and forget about the whole thing. But I think I have a stubborn streak in me and I just thought, what if they next came around and asked, "Are you a member of the CCF and should a candidate for the ministry belong to an organization like the CCF?"

It seemed to me that if I played along with them and answered the first question, this could be the next step. So on principle I said, "I don't think that's a relevant question to ask." Not that I was afraid to incriminate myself because my answer would have been no, but I was indignant that the original reason for raising this issue by Dr. McLennan had been completely perverted and that nobody was asking the question, "Why does the Red Squad barge in on church meetings and frighten young people who are minding their own business?"

The question became, "Is this guy Baxter a Communist and should he be in the faculty of divinity at all? Is he subverting the government?" I didn't answer the question on principle and said, "I don't accept your right to ask me that question because a person can be a theological student and a candidate for the ministry and his political beliefs are his own business."

I remember the dean of the faculty of divinity told me, "We're less concerned about your intellectual beliefs than we are with your commitment to some movement which is un-Christian and un-Canadian."

My father got involved in it and I still have a letter which the dean sent to my father. To this day, my father believes that had I handled the situation more tactfully I would have finished my course at McGill and would have been ordained and would have become the moderator of the United Church.

Somewhere at the end of my first year at divinity school I came to the conclusion this was not the way I wanted to spend my life. I still don't regret leaving divinity school.

In 1955, while I was working for the Canadian Peace Congress, we bought our first car, a 1946 Ford named "Jonah," and we drove down East to visit my folks. We hadn't seen them since we got married. Naturally, I had to get car insurance and I arranged it all with an insurance agent who said, "OK, I'll look after it. Don't worry."

So down we went, but while we were there we decided to sell the car and fly back. I phoned up my friend and told him that I'd sold the car and to cancel the insurance.

He said, "Oh, I was going to tell you: I couldn't get insurance on your car." He told me that when the insurance company found out I worked for the Canadian Peace Congress they thought there was a possibility that the car would be used for illegal purposes. They refused to insure it. So here we had driven 1,000 miles and assumed our car was insured and, because somebody thought the Peace Congress was going to use my car to transport bombs or whatever, we were refused insurance.

"Peace," in those days, was not a good word, and it is a much different concept now. In the early '50s even to say "peace" was sticking your neck out.

My first teaching job was at Weston Collegiate and Vocational School in 1956. This was back in the great teacher shortage. You took a ten-week course in the summer and you became an instant teacher, as long as you could get a contract. In the spring I told the principal that because I now had a family I would stay another year. He raised his eyebrows and said, "I'm not sure the board will renew your contract."

I never knew whether there was anything political or if anyone had gone to him, but when the principal said the board didn't want to renew my contract he also told me, "The best thing for you to do is to write a letter of resignation because then it comes from you and can be accepted. And it's on your initiative, whereas if the board takes the initiative it would be a black mark against you." And then he added, "Like the case of this guy [Herbert] Norman who jumped off the building in Egypt."

Our friends thought he was saying that Norman and I were two of a kind, and that if you didn't want to end up jumping off a building like Norman then you resign before you have it on record that you were fired from your first teaching job. It was interesting he chose that example.

CHAPTER FIFTEEN

B'NAI BRITH AND THE "Y"

CLEARANCE BEFORE EMPLOYMENT

Henry Rosenthal is the editor of the left-wing magazine Outlook
("Canada's Progressive Jewish Magazine") and lives in Vancouver.
"I came out of a left-wing family and am a third-generation atheist.
That was par for my family and they stood behind me all the way."
A former social worker, he worked with the Young Men's Hebrew
Association (YMHA) in Montreal and Winnipeg. He retired in 1985
after twenty-three years at the University of British Columbia, where he
worked in the field of adult education.

There was discrimination, mostly in terms of employment. It was
an economic form of discrimination. I graduated from the School
of Social Work in Toronto and had been active with the left in
campus politics at the university, and my name was known. I had
also been working for the B'nai Brith on a part-time basis while I
was still in school.

I recall a job interview I had in New York City in 1951. I was called
to the States for an interview with B'nai Brith. This was for a job in
Canada but the hiring was done in New York. And the question was
asked, "Have you ever been a member of an organization that could
be considered un-American?" I replied, "I've never been in an organization that could be considered un-Canadian."

That was the end of that interview and I didn't get the job. It
made me aware of the role of the "establishment" Jewish organizations. First of all, you had to go to New York to get a job to work for
the B'nai Brith and groups like the Joint Distribution Committee

and others. Everybody knew clearance had to be obtained from the US State Department before these groups would hire anybody for work in the international field. They didn't tell you directly that you weren't hired because of your politics, but it was apparent because there was a pattern. I wasn't the only one; there were a number of other people in the same situation.

I had a lot of job offers in the States but I couldn't take them because I knew what would happen. I knew what the outcome would be, but it wasn't till years later that my name was put on a list of people banned from the United States. In 1980 I was denied entrance to the United States for the first time. There was somebody here in Vancouver who sent my name to the US consul. Anybody could just send names in.

I consulted a US immigration lawyer in Seattle who specialized in these kinds of cases and was told that the only way they would remove my name from the list was through a direct court order. You had to go to court to prove them wrong and also to prove that you were bona fide, to prove that not only were you not a Communist but also that you were anti-Communist. You had to name others. I finally said the hell with it.

There was another way to clear yourself. You had to fill in certain kinds of forms which they have for clearance. One of the things I can remember in the form was a blank you had to fill in. It read something like, "I believe I have been denied admission into the United States for the following reasons and no others." You had to incriminate yourself. This was wholly contrary to the US Constitution, self-incrimination. Of course, there was the danger of being charged with perjury if your definition didn't fit theirs because they never told you why you were excluded from the United States. If you asked them point-blank, they would claim that nobody is excluded from the United States and that there was no such thing as a list. They would deny the existence of the list.

There was a hysteria around the cold war. About a year after Fidel Castro came into power in Cuba, it was reported that a group of students from the University of Toronto had been detained by US immigration in Miami. It turned out they had been on a visit to

Cuba, mostly as a lark, I think. They returned via Miami. When they were apprehended by US immigration, it turned out that they were the officers and leaders of the U of T campus branch of the Progressive Conservative Party. The US authorities, of course, were not familiar with Canadian politics and had twigged to the word "progressive." The students were kept in jail down there for ten days or two weeks. Those of us in the left who had been active in campus politics got a kick out of that particular episode.

PART FIVE

THE BORDERLINE

CHAPTER SIXTEEN

TRYING TO GET ACROSS

KAFKAESQUE CARDS AND PASSES

*"**Harry**" is currently an arts administrator in the province of Quebec. In the '50s he worked as a trade union organizer for the Communist Party and was a writer for the Communist newspaper. He eventually severed ties with the party but, because of his background, he had difficulties travelling to the United States. His anecdotes reveal a tale of bothersome bureaucratic headaches and of a Kafkaesque system of cards and passes which he required to conduct business within the United States.*

For a number of years I got an annual letter which allowed me to cross the border by making an application for each occasion. That was finally replaced by a card which is, apparently, non-revocable, and allows me to cross each time. However, at times I've had considerable hassle even with that. Not necessarily out of any malevolence on the part of the customs and immigration people but because of a lack of awareness and knowledge on their part.

These "laissez-passer" letters have receded into the distant memory, so most of the people manning the border don't know what it's about. That has always been a source of embarrassment, especially if I was travelling with business acquaintances. At times, it's a source of inconvenience if I have an appointment somewhere because I have to anticipate rather remarkable delays on the way back and forth.

I knew I was on a list at the border. Under the McCarran-Walter Act, people who were members of the Communist Party, or had subscribed to Communist publications, were denied entry to the United

States for fear they would go to advocate the violent overthrow of the US government. I went down there a lot by car and also by plane.

It was not until 1976 that some problems arose. I was flying from Vancouver, where I had just opened a film of mine, to Los Angeles where I had an important business appointment. I got stopped at the Vancouver airport. It was the US bicentennial, and a Canadian tribute to the United States was opening with one of my films. I said, "Look, we're going down to pay tribute to your government!"

I showed him letters about it. Well, it didn't cut any ice, even though my luggage was already on the plane. So I couldn't take the flight. I called a friend of mine at Simon Fraser University who had been a colleague at the Canadian Seamen's Union. I rented a car and we drove to Seattle and told them we were going to have a beer across the border. He drove back home to Vancouver and I took a plane from Seattle to Los Angeles.

The funny part of this story is that the following week he really went down for a beer across the border and he *got* stopped! It became a big joke at Simon Fraser. At the time, Pauline Jewett was the chancellor of the university and the incident didn't have any effect. After that, I decided I wouldn't take planes anymore to get across the border.

A year later I was in Toronto and had to go to New York City. I rented a car and I was stopped at the Rainbow Bridge in a spot check. I spoke to an immigration officer, who was very sympathetic.

"I accept what you're telling me that you no longer subscribe to the beliefs you once held," he said, "but my superior isn't here and I can't really let you through."

So I waited for three hours but he couldn't get hold of his superior. Eventually he said, "OK, I'm going to let you through but see a lawyer because there's a way you can cross. But be careful because if you're caught violating the rules, there will be real penalties."

After that, I did go to see a lawyer in Montreal, the late Michael Berger, who used to specialize in immigration problems and after many months I received a letter from the US authorities which required the completion of a form each time you crossed the border. It asked where I would be staying in the States and when I would be returning to Canada. It seemed like a big relief at the time to get approval to cross but if you were travelling with someone it was embarrassing. I wasn't interested in discussing everything about my past with my travelling companions, so I sort of had to skate around that problem.

For several years, I had an annual paper which I had to renew every year and it cost me about eight hundred bucks a year. Then I got a border crossing card, which cost me three thousand bucks and which, apparently, I just needed to flash. Sometimes that was the case and, at other times, people were confused. They just didn't know and sometimes you would meet someone who was very hostile.

In one case, an immigration officer told my wife, "We're holding him up because he's got a criminal record." There was no criminal record, but this was the confusion that attached itself to the whole procedure.

The advantage to working with a lawyer to get a pass to go the States was that I didn't have direct contact with immigration officials. What I did have to do was aver that I believed in democracy and that I had not conspired or advocated the overthrow of the United States government by violence.

Before I left the party, I had spent two or three years as a correspondent for the *Canadian Tribune* [the Communist newspaper] in Quebec. My house was raided by the police and my library was confiscated. During the Queen's visit of 1951, my wife and I had gone to Eaton's and had bought some dishes. We lived near Sherbrooke Street, which was along the parade route of the Queen's visit, and we were on our way home. About twenty doors from home we were accosted by members of the Red Squad.

The guy in charge grabbed this cardbroard carton we had and asked, "What's in there?" We told them it was dishes and they opened it up. They opened the box and took pile after pile of excelsior and put them all over the sidewalk. Finally, there were the dishes.

Also, our phones lines were tapped. They heard our conversations. We knew this because it was illegal to have the *Canadian Tribune* at newsstands in Montreal. There were some newsstands which took it and we used to drop off the paper near them. I remember once we had a telephone conversation about the pick-up point and the cops showed up there. They were monitoring us.

In Quebec there were very pronounced elements of a police state for minorities like us. It didn't apply to the mass of the population but it affected us. There wasn't an atmosphere of freedom of inquiry, or of thought. I thought that I could continue my reporting career, which I really enjoyed, so I applied to the daily press for work in Montreal. But I found closed doors, even though I did know some city editors.

I remember seeing the city editor of the *Gazette* and there was no way he could give me work. It's not that they had no confidence in me because they had read my stuff and had known me, but they just said it couldn't be done.

This was at the end of 1956 and one Montreal city editor really greeted me quite warmly. He suggested that I go off to some small town and work as a reporter there and within a year I'd make editor and then I could work my way back to Montreal. In a way, I don't know if they did me a favour by not hiring me because it enabled me to go into different career directions.

At that time, The Mountain Playhouse [atop Mount Royal] in Montreal was a cultural centre and plays were performed there and I thought that I could make a real contribution there. I had always had an interest in and had been involved with the performing arts. Here again, I went to see the people who were running it. They had a feeling of nervousness about my getting involved with them, although there was a grudging acknowledgement on their part that I could make a contribution. So I was left to make a living elsewhere. I had two very young children and I had to go off into a completely different direction, and I entered the business world.

When the RCMP became aware of someone who had been an ex-Communist or someone they would label "subversive," they would visit the people who employed them or were about to employ them. The employers were informed and that would have a chilling effect. There was a cold-war atmosphere and you felt compromised and under suspicion.

I went to work for a major corporation in the city and the RCMP visited them. The corporation decided to launch an investigation.

When I first got the job I had gone in very candidly and told them about my past. In fact, when it was first suggested I apply for the job I said, "Look, I'm not going to see them unless they know who I am and what my background is."

They were informed and I got the job very quickly after the interview because they felt I was very suitable for it. But then the RCMP visited the vice president personally and they engaged a special company to do research on me. As it happened, one of the partners in this research company had, at one point in the past, been a Communist and knew me and liked me. He came and told me about it. That's how I learnt about it.

I guess his report was a favourable one because it didn't affect me and I was not asked to leave the organization I was working for. I may have been lucky. And I went on and did very well there until I felt I wasn't expressing myself sufficiently. The kind of work was organizational planning and I was an assistant to the president.

I had been an organizer and people in business respected the organizational abilities of some Communists. Also, there was a kind of respect for the strong convictions that Communists had. In retrospect, that respect may have been misplaced, just as the convictions may have been profoundly misplaced. There were excesses on both sides because the Communist movement of the period was most comparable to a religious cult. There was a blind adherence to a set of beliefs with an established set of prophets. And it had its credo and commandments with not one bible but several which were linear descendants of the Communist Manifesto through *Das Kapital* down through Lenin's pronouncements and Stalin's revisions of Lenin's pronouncements. All of this was "Holy Writ" and was regarded as such.

People wonder, in retrospect, how we could be so rigid and dogmatic. I remember a friendship I had with a young Jamaican artist who was residing in Montreal at the time. I was close to him and his wife. At that time, one of the responsibilities I had for the Communist Party was chairman of its cultural commission. That function was really to ensure that the artistic production of those artists who were Communists, or around the Communist movement, correctly reflected what was referred to as the "needs of the working class and it's aspirations." In fact, it was an aping of what the Soviet Union considered as being "appropriate" art and this was the time when Socialist Realism, as it was called, was the great thing and Zhdanov was the minister of culture and was telling Shostakovich, Prokofiev, and others how to write music.

As far as the visual arts were concerned, anything which deviated from a postcardish representation of reality was considered bourgeois and meant for an elite. I promoted that line among my colleagues but, of course, I had some discomfort with it because I just couldn't get moved by those pictures. My Jamaican friend, who believed I had judgement and an aesthetic sense about paintings, went into quite a shock one day. We had a discussion about a series of posters that had just come from China. There was one with Stalin and Mao in some great hall. It was really crap, cartoon-like crap. I was talking about this as being art. He never really believed it. Subsequently, I apologized to him about it. I had to call him and say that it was wrong to have promoted this.

On the one hand, I was respected for conviction and courage but there was an incomprehension at the inability to master subtlety in your perception of the reality which surrounded you. You were part of a machine. What blew it up was a realization which happened when the Twentieth Congress of the Communist Party of the Soviet Union was held early in 1956.

Nikita Khrushchev delivered a secret report which detailed the excesses of the Stalinist regime and it was a litany of monstrous oppression in every direction. It listed utter violations of any and every human sensitivity. It got picked up and was published by the *New York Times*. Of course, the view we held at the time was that anything that appeared in what we referred to as the "bourgeois press" was a pack of lies to help isolate the socialist state which held all the hopes and possibilities for the future. But on reading the report it had an eerie sense of truth to it because it echoed so many things which had been said by so many people who had, in years past, been Communists or were associated with the party. People like Arthur Koestler, Ignazio Silone, and many, many others. That report really shook us and revealed the profoundly anti-human and barbarian nature of the regime with which we were suddenly confronted. I felt what, I guess, a defrocked priest must feel.

For many years after, I felt like an impostor in whatever I was doing. No matter that I was doing it well and was paid well for it and got respect for what I was doing, but I just felt it wasn't really me. I was engaged in market research and marketing consulting and I was quite good at it, but I felt it wasn't me. In part, that's because everything you do in life you do for your mother. What my mother wanted was a professional revolutionary. She didn't want a son who was a doctor or a lawyer or a businessman. She had been part of the revolutionary generation in Russia.

The values I had didn't come to me a result of a rational examination of the world as I came to know it as I grew into adulthood but a set of given values which I received, mainly, from my mother. That took a long time to adjust to. There was a sense of fear of the external environment and I was not permitted to enter into the present or future by an environment that was hostile but it was also difficult to penetrate it by the way I had been programmed.

But the imperative of earning a living and having to support a family pushed all these things aside. Both my parents died within a year of each other. This was a couple of years after I left the party. I didn't mourn the loss of my belief and didn't mourn the loss of my parents. Eventually, it caught up with me because a couple of years later I went into a very severe depression which went on for about a year, and traces of it went on a few years longer.

THE TROUBLED DONATION

*The late **Leon Weinstein** was a philanthropist and one of Canada's best-known business people. His father owned a string of grocery stores and he used that base to start the Power Corporation in 1933. He sold out to the giant Loblaw's chain in 1953. He was one of the founders of CITY-TV in Toronto. His office was adorned with photographs of himself and famous personalities: Joan Crawford, Governor General Vincent Massey, Nat King Cole, and Jack Benny. His passion was music and he studied violin* *as a youth ("As a matter of fact, I donated a Strad to the Heritage Foundation"). His family was touched by the blacklist.*

My violin teacher was the conductor of the Toronto Symphony. He had Maurice Solway and all the top violinists as students. One day he asked me, "Your father has a business, no?"

I said yes. And then he advised me, "You go to work with your father." He knew that violinists couldn't get jobs, but I always loved music.

The United Jewish People's Order (UJPO) was Communist tinged and perhaps even stronger than that. Paul Robeson gave concerts there, but Jan Peerce did too, under the auspices of the Jewish Folk Choir and the UJPO. Some of us were involved in the choir and we gave donations to it. But the UJPO was reasonably careful and they didn't talk politics with us. The choir was the choir. They sang the odd song about the working man, but that was it.

When the McCarran Act was passed in the US they stopped people at the border. One day my brother was stopped and we couldn't understand it. He wasn't allowed in. He wasn't alone. My buddy Sam Shopsowitz, "Shopsy," was another example. Once you were stopped you couldn't get in. They didn't tell us what the reason was, only that "you're objectionable and you're a danger to our government." There were no details.

But my brother was never politically active except in the YMHA (Young Men's Hebrew Association). If they would have checked the least bit, the authorities would have found that he should not have been stopped. We managed to get legal representation, first out of Buffalo and then New York City.

It was interesting because the US told you nothing. The lawyers in the States pieced it together. They may have had inside influence. Unless you were semi-affluent and could afford a lawyer, you just couldn't go to the States. It wound up costing us eight thousand dollars.

A lot of innocent people suffered and they had no recourse. My brother Morris was one of them. His wife came from Rochester, New York, and they had relatives in New York City. So he used to visit there, and one day he was stopped completely and there was nothing he could do. But we managed to get the thing straightened out.

My brother had made out a cheque for $300 as a donation to the Jewish Folk Choir. He just made out the cheque that's all! I don't think he ever went to a concert. The RCMP had co-operated with the American authorities and they picked up these cheques.

There were other things, like periodicals which were tainted. The RCMP were watching the UJPO. I'm not defending the UJPO, but I can tell you that there were an awful lot of people there who had nothing at all to do with the Communist Party. But they had given some money to an activity they were interested in.

Within a period of three or four days, we had close to twenty letters of reference for my brother from very prominent people. We had some who turned us down, like the prominent president of a synagogue who told me, "Look, I don't know your brother. If it was you I would send a letter, but I don't know your brother and he may be a Communist."

I don't know how much you know about the McCarran Act, but it was a vicious kind of a thing and a lot of innocent people suffered—people in the entertainment field, in the literary field, in the arts generally. Even to this day, some of the old timers are tinged by the fact that they were investigated, even if they weren't involved with the Communist Party.

CHAPTER SEVENTEEN

THE FBI AND THE RCMP

A "GOLDMINE" OF CANADIAN NAMES IN WASHINGTON

Reg Whitaker is a professor of political science at York University who has accumulated thousands of RCMP files and blacklists. A very careful and meticulous researcher, he enjoys rooting out the truth about the cold war. "I enjoy doing it. It's like being a detective. You have to track down the evidence, and follow leads to find the 'smoking gun.' It's fun to fit the pieces together and figure out what it means. It's kind of a guerrilla war—there's an Access to Information Act and it has certain criteria. I deal with CSIS all the time and have collected thousands of pages from them. Their job is to limit what I receive and my job is to get the most from them. I try to outlast them and keep going back." He is the author of Double Standard: The Secret History of Canadian Immigration *and the co-author of* Cold War Canada: The Making of a National Insecurity State, 1945–1957.

The FBI and the RCMP had been quite close from before the Second World War. The relationship deepened during the war and was very close during the cold war. I was astonished a few years ago when I went down to look at the archives in Washington. I was looking into State Department material such as consular and diplomatic correspondence from American consuls and diplomats in Canada back to Washington. I discovered and pulled out pages and pages of lists of Communists and "fellow travellers."

One list, about twenty pages long, was from St. Catharines, Ontario. There were names, addresses, affiliations, and so on. This had been taken from the RCMP files and passed to an American consul who sent it along to Washington. The interesting thing about this is that Canadian MPs and even cabinet ministers were not allowed to have access to RCMP files.

The RCMP would provide particular advice about a person, but they didn't let people get into their files. Then they were turning around and handing out these files to the American consul. It was incredible! Imagine twenty pages just about St. Catharines. Interestingly, some of the names on the list were people who later became well known.

The RCMP was linked up to American and British and foreign intelligence organizations. Canada had no external intelligence agencies, so they had to divulge information on Canadians in a trade for American information. In effect, Canada was passing on this information, but our politicians professed not to know this was happening. For example, there was a professor named Glen Shortliffe who was offered a position in a US university, but US immigration wouldn't let him in for political reasons. There was a fuss about this in the House of Commons, and Lester Pearson got up and said he was not aware there was any passing of information from Canada to the US. Maybe he actually didn't know because it was going on directly between the RCMP and the FBI.

CHAPTER EIGHTEEN

TRYING TO GET ACROSS II

AFRAID OF TRAVELLING

Peter Hunter *is a former trade union organizer who, after he left the Communist Party, became a successful consultant to transportation and container businesses. His earlier experience as a Communist Party member and left-wing organizer was known to the RCMP and to US officials at border crossings.*

In the 1950s the spillover from the McCarthy hysteria in the States resulted in the fight between the left-wing and the right-wing unions. There were many people who were barred from the United States, not because they were Communists but because they were active trade unionists. I'm sorry to say it but there were people within the trade union movement who utilized the fear of communism to make sure their opponents couldn't get admitted into the United States.

I took it for granted that I wouldn't be admitted into the United States since I had been an organizer with the Anti-Fascist Youth League since 1933. So during the cold war McCarthy hysteria, any active union member with a left-wing union was refused admission to the United States.

How did you get across the border?

I guess I can say it now but I made sure not to go across at any point where one would have to show passports or any other identification. I worked in the Niagara Falls area and I timed crossings very carefully.

As you may know, there are what they call "zero hour" at all of these crossing points when they check on every single individual. So one had to be careful about crossing the bridge.

At Niagara Falls, they were very lax around lunch time. Occasionally during the evening you would go across with one of the local residents and so on. You had to make sure they didn't ask your name at the border. I have a great respect for the border inspectors who, I think, carried in their hats a list of names of people they were looking for.

I left the movement in '55 and then I went to work for a distributor in a trucking operation and was there until 1965. Then I went into the containerization field and did a lot of travel. I was very careful about my trips to the United States, but had to spend a lot of time there.

Once, I went to Miami to do some work with a shipping line and they wanted me to go across to Nassau to complete some work. So I went there. In order to avoid taking a flight to any international point where they checked on passports, I arranged to fly back from Nassau to Toronto. However, the shipping line insisted I return to Miami with them. They booked the flight and I couldn't talk my way out of it.

On the way back to Miami, just as we were putting down, over the loudspeaker came, "Would a Peter Hunter identify himself?" I knew right away that this was it. As I came off the plane, I was "received" and taken in for interrogation. I was held for about two or three hours. They asked for my record. At all border points there was a "library" where they check on all individuals who were banned from entering the United States if they belonged to an organization which was deemed subversive. Thousands of Canadians were on that list. To be taken off the list almost required an act of Congress.

I know some very wealthy Canadians who were on the list only because they donated to a choir or to Soviet aid during the war period when they were supposed to be our ally. These were people who were not Communists or active in any organization.

In my case, they asked the question, "Have you now or have you ever been a member of any organization. . . ." I had to agree that I had been because it wasn't a secret in my case. And so I asked if they could let me proceed back to Canada, but they said if they were to let me out of this room and I was stopped then I could be charged with illegal entry. I was put back on a plane to Nassau and then back to Toronto. Then it took me about six months to get clearance. Strangely, one of the requirements was that I show I had had no connection for fifteen years with the left-wing movement.

I was fortunate that I was in the container business because immigration, at that time, came under the department of transportation. So I was advised to apply for admission to the United States in order to speak at a conference. At that time I was speaking at a lot of container gatherings in the United States. So I went to immigration here and told them I was invited to speak. They said, "Leave it with us."

Weeks later they contacted me, but it was too late for that meeting. Then I was invited to speak at another meeting in Buffalo. I went to the immigration people again and told them I was invited to speak again and that if I was not allowed in this time I would have to state that I had been barred. So they finally arranged that I present myself at Fort Erie border crossing and tell them who I was and they would allow me in for two hours and that I was to come right out again. Later on, I was allowed a visa that allowed me entry any time.

Any regrets about your life on the left?

I am one of the few who has publicly stated my position. Many people throw the baby out with the bath water and dismiss that entire period of their lives, particularly those who were Communists and were active in any section of the left-wing movement. I suppose, partly, they feel that discrimination may result with any exposure of their participation. We underestimate the nature of that.

Even today, there are people who don't want to be associated in any way with any progressive, radical, or left-wing movements of the '30s and '40s. Why? Part of it starts in the family. Some feel that their children, who are now adults and have children of their own, find it difficult to understand why their parents spent so much time and energy in activities in the left-wing movement in the '30s and even the '40s. I know of one case where the son of an active member was refused a job with an insurance company simply on the basis of his parents having been connected with the party.

Some of the people feel it was a complete waste; they spent ten or fifteen years of their lives in a movement which resulted in some terrible crimes throughout the world. When you use the word "Communist" today, you picture a much different thing than you did in the '30s. Then it was full of hope and idealism for the future. Today, you look around the world and you see the results of communism and you wonder what the word even means. For these people, they want to forget that complete period and they simply blot it out. Then you have those who were organizers or full-time activists: these people either look upon it as a complete waste or are able to see the contribution which was made to society in spite all of the faults, weaknesses, and crimes which developed under Stalinism and in the Soviet Union.

When I wrote a book about my experiences I made a joke to someone and said, "Look, I'm charging ten dollars not to put names in the book." Believe it or not, this man reached for his pocket. My wife gave me the dickens and said I shouldn't do things like that. There were many people who didn't want their names mentioned in any way.

NEVER SIGN ANYTHING

"Phillip Solsky" is a pseudonym for a Toronto radio and television program producer. His father, who came out of the left-wing movement in Europe, was prevented from freely entering the United States. These experiences were a source of embarrassment for his mother, who claimed that her husband's involvement in a left-wing Jewish organization ruined his life and career. "Phillip" lived with his parents in Montreal during the '50s and '60s.

What I remember most is that when my father wanted to go to the United States for a wedding or a bar mitzvah he always had to write these letters and ask for permission to be allowed in. He would write to US authorities a couple of months before and say, "I have this wedding to go to on June 29th. Can I have permission to go into the

United States?" He was always waiting to see whether they would let him in. Usually, the response was not a "yes" or a "no"—just nothing. And he would never get there on time. The deadline had come and he wouldn't have heard from them.

He always needed this special permission, but sometimes he would just go and take the chance and hope that they wouldn't check on him that day. He didn't cross the border that often and was always nervous about it. We weren't well-to-do and he couldn't afford to hire a lawyer, and so he wrote the letters himself.

My father was on some kind of a blacklist. He originally came from Lithuania and a lot of his friends were "Bundists." The Bund was made up of a group of left-wingers who weren't Communists because they thought the Communists were anti-Semitic. They weren't Zionists either; in fact they were anti-Zionists. But they believed in a lot of the things the Communists did but they didn't believe in the Communist Party. That's my definition of the Bund.

My father's best friend from those days died recently. She had a Bundist's funeral, which meant there was no rabbi because they're not religious. The eulogy was Yiddish songs because the Bundists were Yiddishists, and the coffin was draped in a red flag. She had been a Bundist all her life. My father may not have actually been a Bundist but he associated with them.

My father's association with another left-wing organization in France got him into trouble here. My father had been living in France before the war. He moved to Paris from Lithuania in about 1920 when he was eighteen years old. The left-wing stigma followed him. When he tried to go to the States he wasn't allowed in. His brother and sister moved to the United States, but he couldn't. He had this stigma as an undesirable, a left-winger, that kept him out of the US. He came to Canada through Portugal on a refugee boat and became an electrician here.

In Canada, he wasn't a member of any radical left-wing Jewish organization. I remember there was this guy named "Fishel" who would visit our house and arrive by bicycle. He wore a cloth hat, was middle-aged, and had bicycle clips around his pants. He was always carrying newspapers in his sack. I liked him because he always patted me on the head and would talk to me. My father enjoyed talking with him in Yiddish, and the newspapers were in the Yiddish language. My father read the papers not because of politics but because they were written in Yiddish.

He read the *Freiheit*, this left-wing Yiddish newspaper brought him by Fishel who also brought him books in Yiddish from the Soviet Union. You know, short stories in Yiddish and that sort of thing. My mother didn't like Fishel very much because she was always concerned about what my father had done to his life. She said that he ruined his life because of these left-wing associations. And was Fishel yet another manifestation of his previous political life? She didn't like having Fishel around and used to throw him out. She was also a bit of a snob and this guy was working class.

Fishel didn't even care about being paid for the papers. It didn't matter whether he was paid or not. If my father wasn't around he'd say, "I have some books for him" and she'd say, "I don't want them." He would just answer, "Never mind the money. I'll come get it another time." My mother was quite worried and would scold my father, "Look, what you've done! Look what you've done to your life."

They didn't have the greatest life, still don't, and weren't rich. And my mother blamed the fact they weren't rich on the fact that my father had these involvements. They could've lived in the States and could've been in California with his sister. His sister was relatively rich and they could've had a better life if he hadn't made a mess of it.

How did it affect my father? He was always cautious and always warned me, "Be careful of what you say, be careful of what you do, never put anything down on paper."

He always wanted me not to take any chances and to make sure I protected myself. It was always cautious and it was only much later that he started to express what was inside him. He voted NDP, probably the only one in his neighbourhood to do so, but he cared more about Jews than he did about politics. You know the old joke . . . "If he would get an assignment to write about elephants, my father would write about 'the elephant and the Jewish problem'." He would approach it that way.

Interestingly, my mother has turned more and more left-wing

over the years, and now, in her dotage, has a quite radical position on most issues.

EDUCATING THE RCMP

Joe Levitt is a retired professor who taught history at the University of Ottawa. A one-time active trade unionist and Communist member, Levitt became disillusioned with the CP and left party ranks along with numerous others in what he calls "the class of '57."

Because of the McCarran Act I was barred from entering the United States for twenty years. My name had popped up in their computer files, so that whenever I had to go to the States I had to get advance permission. I wrote away and got a whole form to fill out and had to get my fingerprints taken. That went on for a number of years. As I understand it, the Act was lifted June 1st and I'm going down there. I took the trouble of getting a copy of the Act and underlining parts and if I come across an official who doesn't know about it, I'll show it to him.

Every time I came to the border there was always a new wrinkle. Somebody would give me one form and someone else would give me another form. There was no standard procedure really. It was a pain and I'm glad it's over. I'm cautious so I always got advance permission. It was quite important because my sister was living in New York and, in case she got sick, I wanted to be able to go there. So I got myself organized and once a year I would ask for permission and then I was all right for a year. Some people got a lawyer. I didn't do that. What I did was to get advance permission every year, which meant a small cost of thirty or forty dollars and getting yourself fingerprinted and sending on the form.

Was it humiliating?

The first time was terrible. This was the most humiliating. I had to get three people to swear that they knew me and that I wasn't a crook and this kind of thing. I had to ask people to sign an affidavit that they knew me and that my character was good and so on. I would go down to the police station here and get myself fingerprinted and they'd send down a form that this was mine and that material belonged to the entry station which was in Buffalo, New York. At one time, it took four or five months to get permission back. But a couple of years ago they began to change the Act, then the border people found themselves in genuine difficulty. They didn't know whether they were stopping me legally or not. The Act was unclear. They still wanted me to send the documents, and I did, but I started to get them back more quickly because they didn't want to be in a position where they might be keeping me out illegally. Now it's all cleared up and I'll be able to go in without problems.

In the '70s you were invited to give lectures to the RCMP on trade unionism and to educate them about the left-wing movement. How was that experience?

I got this call from someone who said, "I'm Corporal so-and-so from the RCMP and I'd like you to come down to teach."

I said, "I'm a socialist, you know."

He said, "I know that and that's why we want you to come down." This was for the security branch, which put on a number of courses. This was just before CSIS was formed. I found myself teaching people in the RCMP about socialism and trade unionism. The person who organized it realized that their people were totally unsophisticated and badly educated. From their point of view, they thought they should get some real information in there so they wouldn't be making stupid mistakes all the time. The kind of people they had in security were high school graduates. They were typically working-class people who had gone into the RCMP to get a career. The reason I was there was because the man who organized this was a corporal who was rather left-wing, and had once tried to start a union in the RCMP. He had sort of realized that these young people didn't know anything about anything. So he got one or two left-wing professors to go down and talk with them. I was one of them.

Imagine how ignorant they were about the left-wing movement—they didn't even know what a trade union was, let alone the difference between a Maoist and an NDPer or a Trotskyite. That was far beyond them. After a while I enjoyed going down there because I found out something about the RCMP and got to like some of them because these were working-class fellows and quite likable. I was asked to be provocative to stimulate them and get them thinking.

The organizer was unhappy about the training they had and in the end I could see why. We gave them a little test and they would write one little paragraph and it was terrible. They may have been prepared to follow left-wingers but they certainly didn't know what was going on. They didn't have a clue. I can't describe the abysmal ignorance they had of the labour movement and the trade unions. They were just badly educated.

This corporal from the Security Service said, "If you think we're bad, you should see the way the RCMP used to be twenty years ago."

SHE'S JUST A CHILD

Phyllis E. Bailey *teaches sociology, psychology, and humanities at a junior college in Montreal and has a private psychotherapy practice. "I'm also very active in promoting the concept of the 'Ombudsperson,' a whistle blower in the political scene." Her father, Max Bailey, was a member of the Labor Progressive Party and was elected to Montreal's city council, where he served from 1947 to 1950.*

My experience may be different than others. I regarded it all as a great adventure. As far as I was concerned, we were saving the world and making it "safe for democracy" and so on. I don't regard myself and my family as martyrs, but we accepted discrimination because it was part of the movement. My parents were not proletariat Marxists; they were very middle class. Many of the people I knew were also middle class and they had also gone into the party because it was, in those days, the only vehicle for social change. It was the only game in town.

My father was very charismatic. He was a city councillor for

District 5. In those days, there were nine councillors from each district. There was an "A" category for the three councillors who were elected by property owners. "B" category councillors were elected by everybody and "C" councillors were appointed. My father fell in the "B" category. He was a very good politician and I've often said that if he were in the Liberal Party, he would have become a cabinet minister. Very astute politically, he made friends with the other councillors in the district and worked with them. He did play a unique role because he was the only one of his political complexion, although, at the time, Montreal city councillors were not identified by political party.

I was very active in working in elections, practically from my birth. My mother was campaign manager for one of the party candidates in 1945. I used to go every day to lick stamps and envelopes and I was so proud. On election nights, I was always around. That was my fun as a kid.

When I grew up people asked, "Did you have fun as a kid?"

I'd say, "Yes, I had a lot of fun working in political campaigns and going to peace rallies."

If they said, "Yes, but what about toys and dolls?" I'd answer, "Toys and dolls? We were too busy saving the world."

When Harry Binder of the party ran for the city council in Montreal, his campaign poster was plastered on every wall and everything that didn't move. It was a very effective poster because his name was coloured with day-glow, iridescent red print. At night, the posters just glowed in the dark. People renamed St. Joseph Boulevard "Binder Boulevard" because of the posters which were everywhere. Right after that campaign I think the city passed a law that you couldn't post political campaign posters, except in very limited areas.

In 1950, when I was fourteen, my parents were refused admission into the United States. My father was a city councillor in Montreal and it was pretty clear that he was somewhat left of centre. He had supported Fred Rose during elections and he was the president of a national Jewish organization, the United Jewish People's Order (UJPO), which was a leftist organization. On this occasion, we were flying down to Miami with my cousin and we were going to be joining her parents who were already there. At that time, you flew to

Miami via New York. When we stopped at La Guardia airport we waited to be called to clear immigration and customs. Since our name began with "B" we should have been among the first to be called, but everyone else but us was called. We knew this was it! Finally, we were summoned and the immigration officer questioned my parents. I had a big mouth and mixed in. I remember my mother pushing me aside and telling the immigration officer, "She's just a child, she's just a child."

When it was all over, my parents were turned back and they let my cousin and me fly on to Miami. If my mother hadn't pushed me aside, I would have said something else and they would have turned me back too. But my mother was also trying to indicate that it was very important that I go to Miami to take my smaller cousin there— she was five years younger than me and she couldn't have gone on to meet her parents alone.

We had relations living in the US and sometimes family celebrations there. My parents couldn't go to any of them and it was very disappointing to them and to me. My father was very adamant that I not get involved directly with the party. He never allowed me to join any organizations because he realized that at some point it might backfire on me. Of course, I was very disappointed because I was very committed to the cause, even long after he lost his commitment. I was an only child and my parents took me everywhere including party meetings. The highlight for me was when we went to these public meetings, there was always an RCMP officer posted at the door. We clearly felt we were superior and if anybody did anything to us it was their problem, not ours.

In Quebec, we had the Padlock Laws to contend with. UJPO had a cultural centre in Montreal and it was open for about ten minutes when it got padlocked. Then it was re-opened. There was a funny story about the Padlock Law, I remember. My father had a friend who was in the party. They both had a lot of so-called subversive books which could give them big trouble if the police ever wanted to walk in to their homes and padlock them. So they took all these books and they buried them, only they didn't remember where and they never found them.

When I was thirteen years old and in high school, I had two friends—Eva and Janet. Eva had a country house and invited Janet and me one summer. We went, and I invited both to my country house in the Laurentians, but Janet said she couldn't come. I reported this to my mother who immediately reacted by saying, "Oh, she probably can't come because we're Jewish and her parents are anti-Semitic." So I went to Janet and asked if that was the reason. She said, "Absolutely not. My parents heard that your father was a Communist."

I didn't see Janet for a long time, and about five years later she rang my doorbell one day. I invited her in and as we talked I learned that she had become a Communist! I thought it was ironic that the girl who wasn't allowed to come to my house because I was a Communist became a Communist.

I believe people who were involved with communism then were a superior group of people intellectually and ethically. They went into it because, as I said, it was the only game in town. They may have been naïve and wrong about the things that were going on in the Soviet Union but they still had a tremendous impact on social change.

Today, workers in this hemisphere are much better off because of the movement. I don't think the unions would have evolved without it. Reforms that came in were introduced because there was a fear that if they weren't, communism would take over.

PARENTS IN TROUBLE

Ann Schabas is the former dean of Library Science and Information at the University of Toronto. Her mother was the late Margaret Fairley, who was the dedicated editor of New Frontiers, *a literary and cultural journal, published by the Communist Party from 1952 to 1957. Among the contributors to* New Frontiers *were the poet Milton Acorn and playwright-writer George Ryga. Ann Schabas' father was the late Barker Fairley, a respected scholar and Goethe expert who taught at the University of Toronto.*

Ezra Schabas is a well-known administrator, writer, and musician.

Born in New York City, he studied at Columbia and Juilliard. He came to Canada in August 1952 and joined the Royal Conservatory of Music at the University of Toronto. They are husband and wife.

Ann: I was studying at Smith College in the States for one year in 1948-49. This was the year that Mom and Dad were arrested at a peace dinner in New York. It was held at the Waldorf Astoria in February or March. The Russian composer Dimitri Shostakovich was there. Dad was working as a visiting professor at Columbia, and Mom had come to visit and they were together at this dinner in New York. The president of Smith College was a friend of my father's and heard on the radio that my parents had been apprehended and escorted from the banquet by officials. This made the news and was on the front page of the *New York Times*. Do you remember that, Ezra?

Ezra: Oh sure. I remember reading about it.

Ann: He got interested in me when he heard I was the daughter of these famous Canadians. [laughs]

Why would your parents be arrested at a dinner for peace?

Ezra: Her mother was a Communist and he was guilty by association. As the editor of *New Frontiers*, which was a cultural magazine which the party sponsored, she was, more or less, the cultural aficionado of the party and was involved in its academic and intellectual matters.

Ann: She was Canadian. They couldn't do anything to the others. Anyway, the two of them were taken out of this banquet and taken somewhere for questioning. Mother was escorted to the border the next day, I believe, by guards. She was taken to the Canadian border and told, "Get out of here." Dad was allowed to stay. He was a distinguished visiting professor at Columbia. I don't think they were prepared to make Dad a public issue.

Ezra: The dinner was sponsored by a US–USSR friendship association.

Ann: The president of Smith College phoned me and asked, "Have you heard the radio?" I said no. "Something's happened in New York to your Mom and Dad. Come on over."

I went over and spent the evening there. He tried to find out what was going on and made phone calls but couldn't get any information until the next morning. I was very upset and had no idea what had become of my parents. I had visions of them in prison and, in fact, they *were* detained. Mom was detained overnight under security before she was taken to the train to Canada. It was about two days before I knew exactly what happened and could speak to her by phone. Dad stayed in the States, where he was halfway through a four-month visit.

Dad went to Aspen for a week-long conference and was one of their distinguished visitors, along with Albert Schweitzer and Thornton Wilder. He was also to go to Bryn Mawr in the fall to give the distinguished Flexner lectures. But he received a letter before that which informed him that his presence wasn't welcome in the States and he could be subject to five years' imprisonment if he was found there. Bryn Mawr honoured him anyway by publishing the Flexner lectures he couldn't give.

My father never went back to the States until shortly before he died. In Canada, Mom encountered rudeness only when she went into her bank and the manager was extremely rude to her. Mom and Dad simply pulled their account. Of course, she was an established member of the community here.

Ezra: Her father kept complaining about not being allowed into the States. Her mother never mentioned it again. I knew her from 1949 and she never mentioned it. He kept talking about why they didn't let him in.

The next time he went across he was his nineties and he was with his second wife. And they just went across for a few hours. I remember Barker was invited to Brandeis University in the 1960s. Brandeis was prepared to fight the whole thing for him. Brandeis went to the State

Department and they wanted a letter from him verifying that he had not been a member of the party. To my knowledge, he just dropped the whole matter and said forget it. He didn't want the bother.

Ann: There's an interesting follow-up to my father's 1949 incident. During the '50s, he was invited to Germany as a distinguished scholar. He went and was in the US zone of Germany, where he was treated like a VIP. All the while, he was excluded from the US. But it was OK for him to be in American-occupied Germany. I'm sure the right hand didn't know what the left hand was doing. I remember we laughed about that.

Were there other incidents?

Ann: In the early '50s, not that long after the New York incident, Mom went to a famous peace conference in Stockholm. She received a very rude reception from immigration authorities here. She was detained in Montreal for a number of hours, and body searched. She had to totally disrobe and it was very upsetting to her. She felt a terrible indignity had been done to her by immigration. We were to meet her and she missed the connecting flight.

Ezra: We don't have to tell you that the record of Canada from the end of the war for about ten to fifteen years was pretty awful. All you had to do was "smell left" and you couldn't get into the country. If you said you were an anti-Communist and had fought the Russians, they let you right into Canada. If you had a good right-wing record in Europe you were admitted to Canada.

In my view, Canada was just as bad as the US. Around 1957 the director of the faculty of music at the University of Toronto wanted to engage an American music professor. He was a very distinguished musician. I knew he had a very left-wing record. He was practically engaged until the last minute. I heard from the director of the faculty of music that the president of the university called him and told him the professor couldn't come because he was a left-winger. That was it and he just couldn't get hired.

What was the difference between the United States and Canada then? It was more obvious there and there were a lot more cases in the US than here but, as far as I am concerned, it took place here too.

MARRIAGE MCCARRAN STYLE

Larry Zolf is a writer, political analyst, and CBC Television producer. Remembered for his investigative work on the program "This Hour Has Seven Days," Zolf was in search of a story in 1963 when attacked by a cane-wielding Pierre Sévigny, associate minister of national defence, who was embroiled in the famous Gerda Munsinger case, which involved fear of espionage and security leaks. Zolf also located the reclusive Hal C. Banks in Brooklyn, New York, for the same program. He is the author of Dance of the Dialectic, Survival of the Fattest: An Irreverent View of the Senate, *and* Scorpions for Sale, *which is partially based on the experiences of his family in Winnipeg.*

At one point, my father wanted to go to the United States as an immigrant. His oldest brother, Nathan, had become a very wealthy developer in Washington. Another brother, Arieh Leib, served in the United States Merchant Marine during the First World War and became head of the American Legion in Miami Beach. He also became a "meshuggeneh" Freemason.

Another brother, Lazer, was very active in the Ladies' Garment Workers Union in New York. His two sons both became major Communists. One was a radio writer who used to script "Ma Perkins" and wrote under the pseudonym of Jack Douglas and was eventually blacklisted since he wrote the official American Communist Party account of the veterans' march on Washington in the summer of 1932 when Generals Patton, Eisenhower, and MacArthur dispersed all these veterans who demanded bonus payments for their service in the First World War. The US army drove the veterans out with tanks and tear gas and fired on their tents. This was an important event and played up by the Communists. The foreword to this account or book by my cousin Izzy was written by John Dos Passos, then a Communist.

So cousin Izzy ended up blacklisted because he was a Communist. He went into the rug business and became a multi-millionaire, but he still remained a Communist. Izzy's brother, Jerry, was a good friend of Paul Robeson and his son was Paul Robeson Jr.'s best friend. Jerry was the chief proofreader at the *New York Times* and his wife was the chief proofreader at the *New York Herald Tribune*. Both were named and denounced by Joe McCarthy. The headlines quoted McCarthy saying, "Communists dominate New York dailies!"

How did all this cause problems for my family in Canada? Because my American relatives were all such big Communists, it caused my sister to get married quickly. She wanted to marry an American and had to rush her marriage before the McCarran-Walter Act came into existence. She was afraid she would be linked to my cousins, particularly Jerry the proofreader who was also the treasurer of the New York State Communist Party.

My sister had a boyfriend from Sioux City, Iowa, and they got married in a senator's office in Washington in 1949 to avoid restriction by the McCarran Act which would have prevented her from marrying an American. My sister couldn't wait for the McCarran Act because she was born in Poland. As a landed immigrant she was worried that she'd be put on the Polish quota and that she'd live as an "alien" year by year in the States and might never become a citizen.

I wrote a fictionalized version of some of this in my book *Scorpions for Sale*. My cousin Jerry once pleaded twenty-two amendments of the constitution during a McCarthy case against him. To him, the witch-hunts and blacklists were just nuisances and didn't in any way diminish his life. He would pick up the phone and speak to the guy who was tapping his phone. Jerry would tell him, "I'm going out for the evening, don't worry about it, just have a sandwich. I'll be back. Relax."

DIS-UNITED COLLEGE

Around 1957 a story took place in United College, a school for members of the United Church of Canada. United College was affiliated with the University of Manitoba but not on the campus of that university, which was way out in Fort Garry. United College was downtown and very convenient for kids like myself from North Winnipeg. It became, maybe against its wishes, a downtown school made up of ethnics—a large influx of Jewish, Ukrainian, and Polish students.

When you signed up for the school you had to go to the morning prayers. I didn't participate in the prayers at all. During the Christian prayers, I would just watch and eat the sandwiches my mother had prepared for me for lunch.

The faculty contained a large number of socialists [CCF supporters] including a legendary character—Harry Crowe. He had been a captain in the Second World War, won a Military Cross for bravery, and fought with the Dutch underground. Politics got Crowe and his group in trouble at United College.

Harry wrote a letter to a fellow professor in which he disparaged the existence of God. He didn't do this in a serious existential way, just in a mocking manner as if to say that it was a silly thing to believe in God. A person who was a snitch read it and thought it was terrible and this person (whom we still don't know) gave it to Mr. Lockhart, the college principal. He had come to United College from a United Church ministry in Toronto, Kingsway Lambton United Church, which catered to, in Marxist terms, the "haute bourgeoisie" in the west end of Toronto. Dr. Lockhart, a Doctor of Divinity, had pretty set ideas about things. When this letter was presented to him, he regarded it as atheistic and Bolshevistic. He fired Harry Crowe. In the process, around thirty professors quit and went to other schools. They sympathized with Harry. It was a raging furore, a cause célèbre. The official excuse was that he was an atheist and had no business in a church college. Harry didn't see it that way and felt he was entitled to his point of view. It was his business if he didn't want to believe in God. Crowe later became research director of the Canadian Brotherhood of Railway Employees and got his hands dirty fighting Hal Banks. Eventually, he became the dean of Atkinson College, York University.

In Canada the idea of a red menace always existed. Canada sent troops to knock off the first Bolshevik government and Canadian troops landed in Archangel. There was always a distrust of unionists here. George Brown, the owner and editor of the *Globe* and a father of Confederation, had been shot and killed by an angry union printer.

PART SIX

CANUCKS IN TROUBLE

CHAPTER NINETEEN

CANADIANS WHO SURVIVED McCARTHY IN THE STATES

SINGING THE BLACKLIST BLUES

Oscar Brand *is originally from Winnipeg. He went to New York in the '40s and was a victim of McCarthyism. He was blacklisted. He later returned to Canada as host of a CTV series called "Let's Sing Out." He lives in New York. He brought along his guitar for the interview.*

Let me first say that the blacklist predates what most of the public calls "McCarthyism." When I first got to New York, just before the Second World War, the establishment in the States had this feeling that folk-singers and balladeers were "neder-persons," people who had to be watched. They felt that folk-singers, by the nature of their work, were anti-establishment. The songs are made by people who have very little respect for bankers and governments.

Today, the things we said or sang about would be looked upon as ordinary, but in those days we were "rattlin' mean, Commie-sympathizers," and very, very dangerous. But the real problem came right after the Second World War. We had the atom bomb and we were very proud and happy about it, although it was a fearsome thing to have. The frightening thing was that other countries, especially Russia, were beginning to get it too, and that was blamed upon the Communist sympathizers of the world. Out of pure hatred and revenge, the blacklisters went after people who believed the atom bomb should not be used.

I remember there was a song called "Old Man Atom," written by Vern Partlow. I wasn't allowed to sing it on the air. Once, I sang it on a series, and when the song was over I was fired. I will give you an example of how it went:

[Strums on guitar and sings]

I'm gonna preach you a sermon about old man atom,
And I don't mean the Adam in the Bible, drat'm,
I don't mean the Adam Mother Eve mated,
But I do mean the ATOM science liberated.
Einstein says he's scared.
Einstein says he's scared, I'M SCARED.

Scared of the atom bomb?
Then all ya gotta do,
Is get the people of the world together with you,
Because if you don't get together and do it, well,
Then one of these days,
You're going to get shot to hell,
And that's no future for a growing boy.

Now, the moral of the sermon I'm trying to say,
Is that the atom bomb is here to stay.
It's gonna stay fixed that's plain to see,
But, oh, my dearly beloveds, are we?
We hold these truths to be self-evident:
ALL men can be cremated equal.

And it goes on to say:

The jingoes took their battle stations,
To turn the clock back on the United Nations,
To get a corner on atoms,
And maybe extinguish every doggone atom,
That wouldn't speak English,
It was "Down with foreign-born atoms,
America for American atoms."

But the atom's international,
In spite of hysteria,

It flourishes in Utah and even Siberia,
And whether you're black, white, red, or brown,
The question's the same when you boil it down,
To be or not to be,
That's the question.

Yes, it's up to the people 'cause the atom don't care,
He just flits around as free as the air,
He don't give a darn about politics,
Or who gets what into whatever fix,
All he wants to do is sit around,
And have his nucleus bombarded by neutrons.

Well, I come to the end, and I hope I made it clear,
About what ya gotta do, and what ya gotta fear.
I'm finished now and here's the thesis,
Peace in the world, or the world in pieces.

[Puts down guitar]

Now, to talk about peace in the world at a time when people were getting frightened about Korea was considered "pinko." It was considered pro-Communist because in those days we were gearing for a new iron curtain confrontation. The excesses it provoked were frightening. It was kind of tough for people like me because I wasn't getting any input from the Communist Party either. I never knew what the line was going to be from one day to another, and since I decided to sing my own songs the way I wanted to I was up against a glass wall, being shot at by both sides. But none of that blacklisting was palatable, not for me.

Then, the House on Un-American Activities Committee came in and started looking around. The McCarran Committee also started looking around and people like Howard Rushmore, or quasi-official groups like Counterattack and Red Channels, began to get power—power given them by frightened people.

They started saying "Were you a Communist in 1929? And if you were for three days, you shouldn't be receiving money which you will now be giving to the party." Or, "Were you a Communist in 1939? No? Then did you go to a party run by Communists?" And these questions frightened a lot of people who wanted to work. I know Burl Ives, who was a pretty strong individual, *asked* to come in front of a committee and gave them a list of about a hundred and ten names: people he had seen at these parties.

When they said to him, "Well, are these people Communists?" he said, "If they are not, they have the same right to come up here and testify as I did." But the damage was done by just raising a name. And, of course, it was even worse at the end when they asked him, "Well, what were you doing at these parties?" and he said, "I was taken there by my good friend Richard Dyer-Bennet." Well, that ended Richard Dyer-Bennet's career as a major performer. Just being mentioned ended your career because even if you proved they were wrong, you were still "controversial."

Television was new in those days. All people wanted was to keep out of trouble. So anybody who was mentioned, or whose name was brought up as questionable, was kicked out. You can't blame the sponsor because what he's saying is, "I put my life into my product. If it doesn't sell then my business goes down. Therefore, it must sell. If consumers won't buy it because of the people I'm hiring, then I better get rid of those people." He entrusted that mission to the advertising agencies and to the so-called continuity acceptance people. Well, I met a few of those poor bast. . . . They had lists in their desk drawers from the McCarran Committee hearings and HUAC hearings.

They had a book called *Red Channels* with a hundred and ten names of people who were considered "pipelines for communism." The names included Zero Mostel, Leonard Bernstein, Jack Gilford, and me. There were men like J. Edward Bromberg who went off and committed suicide. Lots of them just couldn't get work. One day I was making four thousand dollars a day and the next day I was making absolutely nothing. Zero.

JOHN HENRY FAULK

John Henry Faulk, who was a friend of mine, had been blacklisted and kicked off the air because they said he had appeared at a Communist program. Now, I had never seen John Henry Faulk at a Communist program, and I had done a few. Well, he started suing a man named Vincent Hartnett and an upstate New York emporium owner named Johnson. Hartnett was kind of a semi-official investigator who would blacklist you and then clear your name for a few dollars.

Hartnett called me one day and said, "Mr. Brand, we'd like you to help us."

I said, "What is this about?"

He said, "It's about John Henry Faulk. One of the problems we have is proving that John Henry was at a number of parties that we placed him at."

"What do you want from me?"

He said, "One of them was a program in which you had performed a children's show on May Day."

I said, "Now wait a minute, John Henry couldn't have been there because when I perform for children I'm the emcee."

Then he said, "But he was advertised."

"Then it must have been an enticement because he wasn't there."

"Well, try to remember if he was there or not."

I said, "I don't remember his being there."

Then he said, "Well, it would help a lot if you could remember."

For three weeks, Hartnett called me every day to ask if I remembered. He was telling me how it would help him, how it wouldn't do me any harm, and so on. Finally, he stopped calling me. And Johnny won the case.

UPHEAVAL IN HOLLYWOOD

Ben Barzman *was born in Toronto, raised in Vancouver. In the early '40s, shortly after college, he went to Hollywood to write. His thirty-seven films include* Town Without Pity, He Who Must Die, The Blue Max, Christ in Concrete, *and* The Boy with Green Hair. *In the post-McCarthy period he scripted* El Cid *and* Z. *The French honoured him with the Order of Arts and Letters.* **Norma Barzman**, *who started out* *as a Hearst reporter, wrote for television and collaborated with her husband on filmscripts and a novel. Named as Communists, unable to work in the United States, they chose to spend their exile and bring up their seven children in France, where they remained long after the blacklist was over. Ben Barzman died December 15, 1989. Norma Barzman, who tells their story, has been writing a column on aging for the past five years,* The Best Years, *which has appeared in the* Los Angeles Herald *and the* Los Angeles Times. *They were married for forty-seven years.*

Ben and I left Hollywood in February 1949. The Hollywood Ten had already been cited for contempt of Congress, but had not yet been sentenced. At that time, no one believed they would be sent to jail. We didn't flee. We left everything in our house, our bureaus full, packed for what we thought would be no more than six weeks—and turned out to be thirty years!

It happened this way: Eddie Dmytrk, one of the ten who had been cited for contempt for refusing to answer whether he was a Communist, found himself unable to work anymore in Hollywood. He was a director, had been a cutter, a technician. He couldn't write under the table, couldn't do anything but work in movies where he'd started out when he was eighteen. Eddie came to Ben with a project. It was natural, they were friends. Dmytryk was also Canadian and they'd just done *Back to Bataan* together. He said if Ben would adapt Pietro di Donato's book *Christ in Concrete* for the screen, he, Eddie, would take Ben's screenplay to London and try to set up the film with [British movie mogul J. Arthur] Rank.

Eddie couldn't direct in Hollywood but there was nothing that said he couldn't in England. All that was fine, said Ben, except he was working on a film at MGM and had no time for anything else. "Write it at night and weekends," said Eddie. "It's your duty to break the blacklist."

So Ben wrote the screenplay nights and weekends. When it was finished, Eddie took it with him to England and we thought no more about it until the phone rang in the middle of the night. Eddie from London. Rank loved the screenplay and wanted to produce the film. There was only one question that he wanted answered. Eddie had flinched. Surely the question was going to be, "Are you now or have you ever been. . . ?" But no. Mr. Rank—later Sir Arthur—asked very simply, "Mr. Dmytryk, do you believe in God?" Eddie thought a moment, then answered. "If I didn't, I do now," and they shook hands.

But there *was* a condition. Ben would have to come to England to make whatever changes were necessary to shoot in London. After all, *Christ in Concrete* was about an Italo-American bricklayer on New York's East Side. It should have been shot in New York and would have been if McCarthyism had not made it impossible for Eddie to work in America. Ben asked Dore Schary, then head of MGM, to let him go though he was only half-way through his Lana Turner assignment. Dore disapproved of the whole English venture but, when he saw how strongly Ben felt about helping Eddie, finally gave his blessing.

Much later, after Dmytryk returned to the United States and served a jail sentence for refusing to testify, he recanted and named a long list of his friends as Communists. We were among them. In his testimony, Eddie said, "Who but the fanatics would give up a high-priced job in Hollywood, leave home, travel with two little kids and a pregnant wife"—that was me—"in order to break the blacklist?"

It was a particularly bad time for me to leave America. Not only did I have a three-year-old, a two-year-old, and one in my tummy, but I was in the middle of my analysis. My own screenwriting career had just begun. I already had two credits when we left Hollywood but, if it would be hard for Ben to get work in Europe, it would be well nigh impossible for me. I eventually did write a film, *Finishing School*, that was shot in Italy, but the American embassy in Paris had taken away my passport and I couldn't get from France to Italy, where I was needed for rewrites. I was without a passport from July 1951 to July 1958 when the US Supreme Court ruled that the State Department had had no right to take it away. Ben, born in Toronto, had become a naturalized American. When the Americans deprived him of his US nationality, he did not automatically become Canadian again. He was considered stateless and, as such, was given a stateless passport by the French. It was a very long, pleated document like an accordion on which he had to have a visa stamped each time he went to a different country. What irony! I, born a US citizen, was a prisoner in France (even if it was one of the greatest places in the world to be) and here was Ben able to go anywhere on the accordion. And he did: Italy, Spain, France, England. However, when his mother was dying in Los Angeles, the US State Department refused to give him permission to visit her. He had to sneak across the Canadian border into the States for one last visit. "I understand," his mother said. "The Cossacks are riding again."

In the summer of 1954 several American producers we didn't know turned up where we were in the south of France. They tried to make it seem informal, but it actually felt official.

"Listen," one of them said, "we'd like people like you to come back."

The other one said, "How about coming back? You're not all that crazy about it here, are you?"

Ben replied, "We *are* crazy about it here. But you know, we'd like to be back home, we'd both like to be back working where we should be."

"Fine," said the first one, "No problem. We can work it out for you. That's one of the reasons we came."

Now Ben and I knew there was some sort of set-up by which people on the blacklist could clear themselves. It was led by Ward Bond, John Wayne, and Adolphe Menjou. You'd have to go to them and the only way you could really prove you were clean was by saying so-and-so belonged to such-and-such an organization.

"Well, what do I have to do?" Ben asked. "Because I'm not going to. . . ."

"No, no," they said in chorus. "You're not going to have to name anybody. Nothing like that. You just sign this letter."

We looked at the letter. It said that the political organizations we had belonged to or given money to were on the attorney general's subversive list, even groups like the Yugoslav fishermen in San Diego who were always on strike and always needing help. And the Salinas Valley lettuce pickers. The Spanish Loyalists. The Joint Anti-Fascist Refugee Committee. The Anti-Nazi League. The letter said, in effect, "I'm sorry I was born. I didn't know what I was doing when I belonged to these organizations. Everything was all a great mistake."

Ben said, "I was bad, but now I'm good."

"I don't think it was a mistake," I said, looking straight at the two producers. "I'd probably help the Yugoslav fishermen all over again."

"We can't sign that," Ben said quietly.

"Why not?" they asked.

"Because it's not true," said Ben.

One of the two made a guttural sound. "Who cares whether it's true or not? Just sign it."

The other said, "Believe whatever you want. We don't care. Just sign it."

"We can't do that," Ben said. The two of them argued with us for a while, then just looked at us as though we were crazy.

It *was* very difficult to be in a foreign land without papers. For a long period we felt hunted. There was no way of knowing if one bright day we wouldn't be bounced out of the country. But the truth was that both the French and the British, the authorities, were very friendly to us and we never heard of anyone exiled from Hollywood who was obliged to leave France or England. Still, we were never very sure what the official policy was.

So, years later, when we were introduced to the then minister of culture at the Cannes Film Festival, and he said how glad he was to meet us, we asked him what the policy had been towards Hollywood expatriots.

He replied with a series of questions: "Have you been happy here?"

"Oh yes," we replied.

"Has anyone ever bothered you?"

"Oh no," we said.

"Do you and your family feel at home here?"

"Oh yes." I beamed.

"Then I think you know the answer to your question." And he said a very, very flattering thing. "After all the talent Hollywood has taken away from us"—he was talking about the French directors and stars and so forth—"the least they could do, even if they did it in this backhanded way, was to give us some back. Welcome to France."

People were wonderful to us everywhere. All over Europe we were treated like heroes. They seemed to think we were the best of America. I'll never forget the film festival in Karlovy Vary,

Czechoslovakia. After two weeks, the whole festival went for another two weeks on tour to the mines and factories. It was July and hot. The outdoor audiences for the films were always at least 10,000 people. When we presented *Christ in Concrete*, we were introduced with some words that sounded like "persecuty in Hollywoodsky." We bowed to the audience, and over 10,000 people got up and bowed back.

In France we realized we were not alone, that there were people from all over the world who, for the moment, were living there because it wasn't good at home: South Africans, Chileans, Spanish, etc.

When we were introduced to Picasso, he put his arms around us, embraced us, and whispered, "We are the same." It took me a moment to know what he meant, that, like him, we were exiles. Kazantakis too, whose book *The Greek Passion* had been adapted for the screen, had a special feeling for us because we, like him, were exiles. Everywhere we went, we were received well and came to know wonderful people, artists, scientists, writers—Bracque, Monsieur and Madame Joliot-Curie, Paul Eluard—as well as those in the movie business—Truffaut, Costa Gavras, Simone Signoret, Anna Magnani, Sophia Loren, Vittorio De Sica.

We were also happy that our seven children were growing up in France in an atmosphere where education, culture, and openness flourished. We couldn't help but be aware of what was happening at home to the blacklisted families who'd been left behind. We had letters all the time. There were cases of some of our friends' children being blackmailed when they were ten years old.

One kid was paying twenty-five cents a week to one of the other kids. He kept saying, "Unless you pay me, I am going to tell everybody in this school that it was your daddy that was on the TV being questioned by the Un-American Activities Committee, and he was accused of being a Communist, and he wouldn't answer. I'm going to tell everybody." So this child paid, on the dot, right on the nose every week, twenty-five cents.

We were glad we were missing that terrible climate of fear at home, not just the fear of punishment, of having everything taken away, but the fear of our creative friends that they wouldn't be able to do their thing ever again. I think this was enormous.

A friend of ours, a director, who really was a staunch and marvellous man for years, all through the '50s, couldn't direct anymore because he refused to name anyone. He lived in Hollywood and saw himself getting older and other talents coming up—and that he wasn't doing the one thing he could do. Very, very late, just almost at the end of McCarthyism, he named thirty people so he could work again. The crazy thing was he had held out for ten years. If he'd just lasted a little longer, he would have worked anyway.

Instead of Ben's talent lying fallow, as it would have have had we not gone into exile, he actually flourished. He was pushed into writing films that could never have been made at home, films with a universal human content such as *He Who Must Die*, which won an award at Cannes. It was no accident that the first screenwriter to receive a retrospective of his work at the Paris Cinemathèque was Ben and that he was decorated with the Order of Arts and Letters.

Many of the blacklisted people mind when I point out that, without McCarthyism, Ben and I would have been two provincial screenwriters on a Hollywood hill. I don't minimize the destruction that McCarthyism did—the broken careers, the lost talent, the broken marriages, the destroyed health, the children hurt, the human suffering it caused. But for us, well, we were lucky. It opened up the whole world for us. We discovered the United States was not the be-all and end-all and that there was a very exciting world out there.

—